THE TREATMENT OF THE REMAINS AT THE EUCHARIST AFTER HOLY COMMUNION AND THE TIME OF THE ABLUTIONS

THE TREATMENT OF THE REMAINS AT THE EUCHARIST AFTER HOLY COMMUNION AND THE TIME OF THE ABLUTIONS

BY

W. LOCKTON
VICE-PRINCIPAL OF
WINCHESTER DIOCESAN TRAINING COLLEGE

WIPF & STOCK · Eugene, Oregon

Wipf and Stock Publishers
199 W 8th Ave, Suite 3
Eugene, OR 97401

The Treatment of the Remains at the Eucharist
After Holy Communion and the Time of the Ablutions
By Lockton, W.
Softcover ISBN-13: 978-1-6667-3416-4
Hardcover ISBN-13: 978-1-6667-2972-6
eBook ISBN-13: 978-1-6667-2973-3
Publication date 8/18/2021
Previously published by Cambridge University Press, 1920

This edition is a scanned facsimile of the original edition published in 1920.

PREFACE

THE suggestion that it might be useful if he were to compile such a work as this came to the writer from a friend, and, it may be well to explain, his own inclinations would have led him rather to other fields of research. Whatever its value the book is the result of an attempt to carry out two requests. The first was that the question of the proper time for the consumption of the remains at the eucharist, and any ablutions in connection with the English rite, should be investigated from a historical point of view. The original essay dealing with the matter appeared in the *Church Quarterly Review* for April, 1917. On its publication there was a further request from various quarters that the material collected with any suitable additions should be preserved in a more permanent and accessible form The present book in which the earlier essay is very much enlarged and modified is the response to this second request. In the course of the investigation it was found impossible to treat the original question at all adequately by itself, and a number of kindred subjects had almost of necessity to be examined and discussed at the same time; but still the work is not intended to be a treatise on reservation, and so there is no discussion of many questions, such as the incident of Gorgonia. It is not claimed that the subject has been treated as exhaustively as might be possible by one who had unlimited time at his disposal, and it is probable that very much other evidence exists, and might be brought to light by lengthy research in the great libraries, but it is hoped that sufficient examples have been given from the more accessible sources to show the correct development of practice with regard to the different matters treated, and in all probability further research would make really but very little difference to the final conclusions. The writer has laboured under the disadvantage of doing his work amid the stress of other quite different tasks, and for the most part away from any important library, and even, as a consequence of the war, away from the majority of his own books.

It is interesting to note how the examination of even such small liturgical points as the disposal of the remains of the consecrated elements after the communion and the ablutions serves to bring out the connection and dependence of the various documents considered, and so may be not without value for the more general history of liturgical development. The writer has endeavoured to let the authorities give their evidence in their own words, and for this reason, although for the purposes of the book translations were inevitable, they have been made as literal as possible. Anyone wishing to study the original documents will find in every case an adequate reference. An apology may perhaps seem to be needed for what may appear to be unnecessary repetition of the same or similar texts, but any attempt at tracing the growth and elaboration of a ceremony would have been impossible otherwise. Experience also has proved to the writer that few people will ever take the trouble to look up the references given, even when only to other parts of the same work, and that if an argument depends upon a document quoted only on another page the evidence is too often entirely overlooked, and even declared to be non-existent.

The author wishes to thank a great number of friends, so many that it would be impossible to draw up a complete list, for kind assistance on special points, without which he would have been unable to write the essay at all, and particularly to the editor of *The Church Quarterly Review* for his courtesy in allowing portions of the original article to be reprinted.

W. L.

WINCHESTER,
  7 *March*, 1920.

CONTENTS

CHAP.		PAGE
I.	EARLY EVIDENCE	1
II.	IN THE EAST	19
III.	IN THE WEST	35
IV.	THE SANCTA	45
V.	THE PORTION OF THE HOST LEFT ON THE ALTAR	63
VI.	ON MAUNDY THURSDAY	75
VII.	IN LATER DAYS IN THE WEST	98
VIII.	THE DEVELOPMENT OF THE ABLUTIONS	118
IX.	THE ABLUTIONS IN BRITAIN	149
X.	THE ORDER OF COMMUNION AND THE FIRST PRAYER BOOK	171
XI.	THE SECOND PRAYER BOOK AND THE ELIZABETHAN SETTLEMENT	183
XII.	THE SCOTTISH PRAYER BOOK AND THE PRAYER BOOK OF 1661	203
XIII.	THE WORSHIP OF THE LAMB	217
XIV.	CONCLUSIONS	238
	APPENDIX. RESERVATION AND THE BOOK OF COMMON PRAYER	248
	INDEX	273

CHAPTER I

EARLY EVIDENCE

ANY practice which has for its object increased reverence towards the holy sacrament of our Lord's body and blood is worthy of the careful consideration of all faithful Christians. We remember St Paul's words:

Whosoever shall eat the bread or drink the cup of the Lord unworthily, shall be guilty of the body and the blood of the Lord....For he that eateth and drinketh, eateth and drinketh judgement unto himself, if he discern not the body[1].

Though in a different degree, all unworthy treatment of the consecrated elements and failure to "discern the Lord's body" must likewise be deserving of condemnation. It was to avoid any possibility of such dishonour that in the course of time various rules arose in different parts of the church for the disposal of the remains of the consecrated species when the communion was ended. It may therefore be of value to examine the evidence about the primitive and later customs in the matter, and then to investigate the history of the present rubrics of the Book of Common Prayer dealing with the subject, so that we may the better understand their exact significance.

In his *First Apology*, addressed to the emperor Antoninus Pius, describing the eucharist, as celebrated perhaps at Ephesus, Justin Martyr († *c.* 167) writes:

And after the president has given thanks, and all the people have responded, those called deacons among us distribute to each of those present of the bread and wine and water over which thanks have been given, and carry some away to those who are absent[2].

[1] 1 Cor xi 27, 29.   [2] *Apol.* I. lxv. 5, Migne, *P.G.* VI. col. 428.

Later we read:

And there follows the distribution to each, and the partaking of those things over which thanks have been given; and to those who are not present they are sent by the deacons[1].

Whether the deacons left the church immediately after the communion of the people before such final prayers as there may have been, or waited until the service was completely over, there is nothing to show, and probably the difference would not have been great, for the communion is the natural climax of the service, and Justin thought no further prayers worthy of mention. Nor are we told anything about what happened to the remnants not needed for the communion either in church or at home. That there was at this period a worthy method of disposing of any surplus of the consecrated elements, which would be followed by a reverent washing of the sacred vessels, seems certain in view of the statements of Tertullian and others about the great care with which the sacrament must be handled.

Tertullian says:

We suffer anxiety if anything of the cup, or even of our bread fall to the ground[2].

The so-called Egyptian Church Order, now generally recognised as the work of Hippolytus († 235), requires a person who reserves the eucharist at home to take great precautions, and likewise the priest during the liturgy. We read:

But let everyone take heed that no unbeliever partake of the eucharist, nor any mouse or other animal, and that nothing of it fall, or be lost, for the body of Christ is to be eaten by the faithful and not despised. For blessing it indeed in the name of God thou hast taken the chalice as the antitype of the blood of Christ. Wherefore be careful not to spill it, lest a strange

---

[1] *Apol* I lxvii 5, *PG* VI col 429.
[2] *De Corona*, 3, Migne, *PL*. II. col. 80.

spirit lick it up, as though thou despisest it: thou wilt be guilty of the blood as one who scorns the price by which he was redeemed[1].

This is the order according to the most ancient text, the Latin version of the Verona fragments. There are also ancient translations into Ethiopic, Arabic and Coptic. The Arabic and Coptic texts represent a later recension, which according to the Latin rendering given by Renaudot, taken apparently from the Arabic, runs:

Everyone will take the greatest heed that no unbeliever be admitted to the communion of the mysteries; also that no mouse or other animal approach them, or that nothing fall, and he sin, since it is the body of Christ and His blood. No one of the faithful therefore who communicates in the mysteries ought to be negligent with regard to it, for nothing ought to be spilled from the chalice after it has been blessed in the name of the Lord, and he has taken it, because it is the blood of Christ. Be most careful therefore, whosoever thou mayest be, that nothing of it be spilled, so that no unclean spirits pollute it, and be not thou one who despises the blood of Christ, and is guilty as a scorner of the blood by which he was redeemed[2].

In the so-called Testament of our Lord (c. 350), which is based on the Egyptian Church Order, the reference to the bread has disappeared. We read:

He who spilleth of the cup gathereth up judgment to himself. Similarly also he who seeth and is silent and doth not reprove him, whoever he may be[3].

In the so-called Canons of Hippolytus (fourth to sixth century?) we have in an Arabic translation a still later modification of the same rules, quite changing their

[1] Connolly, *The so-called Egyptian Church Order*, pp. 190–1. Hauler, *Didasc Apos Fragm* pp 117–8 Cf Horner, *The Statutes of the Apostles*, pp. 180–1, 261, 326–7
[2] Renaudot, *Lit Orient Coll* vol. I. pp. 289–90. Cf. Horner, *Statutes of the Apostles*, p 261
[3] Cooper and Maclean, *The Testament of our Lord*, p. 128.

original scope, and a text akin to the Coptic and Arabic recension, and particularly the version given above, is presumably the basis of it. We note that the reference to private reservation has disappeared. We read:

But let the clergy take the greatest heed that they invite no one to partake of the sacred mysteries except believers only. Let a clerk stand in readiness near the altar, and when the chalice is prepared let him stand on guard so that no fly fly about over it, and that nothing fall into it, for from this there may arise for the priests the guilt of mortal sin. Consequently let someone keep guard over the holy place. But let him who distributes the mysteries, and those who receive, take very great heed lest anything fall to the ground so that no evil spirit get possession of it[1].

Similar directions abound in later days in various documents, and considerable evidence to the same effect may be drawn from the fathers early and late. Origen († c. 254) says:

You who are accustomed to take part in the divine mysteries know how when you receive the body of the Lord you keep it with all care and reverence lest even a little of it fall, that nothing of the consecrated gift be lost. For you believe, and rightly believe, yourselves guilty if anything of it fall through negligence. But if you employ, and rightly employ, such great care with respect to that body which is to be reserved, how do you think that it is less awful to have neglected the word of God than His body[2]?

Between these words of Origen and the directions of the Egyptian Church Order there is a close affinity, and there may be even a literary connection, and there is again apparently a reference to private reservation.

St Cyril of Jerusalem (c. 348) adopts a similar attitude with regard to the great care to be exercised in handling the sacrament. In his catechical lectures he says:

[1] Canon XXVIII. §§ 206–9 Connolly, p 78 Achelis, *Die Canones Hippolyti*, pp 119–21
[2] *In Exod* XIII. 3, *P G*. XII. col. 391.

Then after thou hast with carefulness hallowed thine eyes by the touch of the holy body, partake thereof, giving heed lest thou lose any of it. for what thou losest is a loss to thee as it were from one of thine own members. For tell me, if anyone gave thee gold dust, wouldest thou not with all precaution keep it fast? How much more cautiously then wilt thou observe that not a crumb falls from thee of what is more precious than gold and precious stones[1]?

A sermon, formerly attributed to St Augustine, but belonging more probably to St Caesarius of Arles († 542), also bears witness to the great care shown by Christians lest any of the sacrament should fall to the ground. Like Origen the writer argues from it that the word of God ought to be treated with not less respect. We read.

I ask you, brethren and sisters, tell me, what seems to you to be of more value the word of God or the body of Christ? If you wish to answer truly you ought surely to say this, that the word of God is of no less value than the body of Christ. And so however great care we observe when the body of Christ is ministered to us that nothing of it fall from our hands to the ground, let us observe the same care lest the word of God which is administered to us be lost from our hearts while we are thinking or speaking of something else. For a man will be none the less guilty who hears the word of God carelessly than he who has allowed the body of Christ to fall to the ground by his negligence[2].

The same opinion we see about the scrupulous care exercised by the faithful lest even a small portion of the sacrament be lost is expressed in many writings differing very widely in date and place. Yet unless there was some seemly method of disposing of the remains after communion, including a reverent cleansing of the chalice and

---

[1] *Catech.* XXIII. *Mystag.* V. 21, *P.G.* XXXIII. col. 1125 (Church's translation, *Library of the Fathers*, p. 279).

[2] Augustine, *Sermones*, App. *Sermo* ccc., otherwise *L. Homil.* Hom 26, *P.L.* XXXIX. col. 2319.

paten, such acts of profanity must have been of regular occurrence: this in view of the strongly expressed opinions of so many writers about the general attitude we can hardly conceive to be possible.

Origen is witness to a custom, founded apparently on the rules of the Mosaic law, by which what was left over of the eucharist was kept until the morrow, but no portion of the remains reserved until the third day, the Christian practice thus agreeing exactly with that of the Jews with regard to the consumption of certain of the sacrifices. On such precedents, as we shall see, all later rules for the disposal of the remnants of the sacrament after communion are ultimately based. We read:

For the Lord when He gave the bread to His disciples saying, Take and eat, did not defer it, nor command it to be kept until the morrow. The same significance perhaps is to be found also in the fact that it (Leviticus) does not command the bread to be carried on a journey, that you may always bear the bread of the word of God, which you carry within you, fresh....Another figure of the sacraments indeed there is where it commands also what is left over to another day to be eaten, and nothing indeed to be reserved till the third day[1].

Origen is drawing out a mystical lesson from our Lord's words as well as from Leviticus, and he cannot be taken as disapproving of reservation in itself, and the practice must have been quite common in his day and before, as is implied indeed in the other words of his quoted above, and as we see in the works of other writers, as Tertullian and Cyprian. Private reservation is also clearly referred to as the ordinary custom in the extract from the Egyptian Church Order. The words of Cyril of Alexandria († 444) to Calosyrius at a later date undoubtedly represent the traditional view of the church on the permanent effects of consecration. We read:

[1] *Hom. V in Levit.* 8, *P G* XII col 459

EARLY EVIDENCE

And I hear that they say that the mystical benediction avails nothing for sanctification if any of it be left until another day. But they are mad who say such things, for neither is Christ other than Himself, nor His holy body changed, but the power and vivifying grace of the benediction abide perpetually in it[1].

In the so-called liturgy of St Clement, found in the eighth book of the Apostolic Constitutions, we are told for the first time what actually happens to the remains in the service after the communion. We read:

And when all have received, both men and women, let the deacons take what remains over and carry it into the sacristy (pastophorium)[2].

This takes place immediately after the communion and before the last prayers. Unfortunately nothing is said about their final disposal, whether they are reserved in the sacristy till the morrow, or for a longer period as in later days, or consumed there immediately, for which also there is considerable evidence at a later period. Reservation until the next day only would seem to be the more usual custom at this date.

The practice of reserving the sacrament in the sacristy is referred to in what appears to be in origin a marginal note which has been interpolated in some texts of Jerome's Commentary on Ezekiel xl. We read:

Wherefore the sacristy in which lies the body of Christ Who is the true Bridegroom of the church and of our souls is rightly called the bridal chamber or *pastophorium*[3].

In the Sahidic Ecclesiastical Canons (cap. LXIII–LXXIX) we have in a shortened form and somewhat modified in places the directions, but not the prayers, of the eighth book of the Apostolic Constitutions. Here what is left

---

[1] *Adv Anthropomorph.* 1, *P G* LXXVI col 1073–6.
[2] Brightman, *Eastern Liturgies*, p 25.
[3] *In Ezek.* xl. See Freestone, *Sacrament Reserved*, p. 110.

over from the communion remains on the holy table apparently until after the blessing and dismissal, when we find rules for its disposal. We read:

Whatsoever remains over let the presbyters and the deacons gather up, taking careful heed that there be not much over that so there be not exceeding great judgment upon them like the sons of Aaron and the sons of Eli whom the Holy Ghost smote because they refrained not from setting at nought the Lord's sacrifice: how much more them that shall think scorn of the body and blood of the Lord, deeming that it is only bodily food that they receive not spiritual[1].

In an ancient Coptic collection of constitutions of uncertain date we read·

If it happens on the day of some solemn feast that any of the eucharist remains over, it should be treated with honour: and the following day the priests should divide it among themselves and communicate therefrom. If no one is found who can consume it, it should be reverently buried somewhere, but not burnt; for the honour due to the holy bodies does not allow them to burn them. but they bury them[2].

In the nineteenth of a set of Arabic canons ascribed to the council of Nicaea, and widely accepted by about the seventh century, we find directions for the disposal of the remnants of the eucharist. We read:

As often as commemorations are made in churches and monasteries, or at the tombs of the martyrs, and any of the eucharist is left over, let the priests honour it in the morning of the following day before they communicate. But if what is left over is much let them divide it among themselves and each take his portion, but only once by way of a single morsel whether small or great, and let it not be done a second or third time[3].

---

[1] Brightman, p 463.
[2] *Perpétuité de la Foi*, 1841, III. 7, vol. III col. 212.
[3] Hardouin, *Concil. Collectio*, vol. I col 506.

EARLY EVIDENCE

Hesychius († c. 438) in his commentary on Leviticus compares the Jewish and Christian practice with regard to the remains of the sacrifices. He says:

The body of Christ the living Bread which came down from heaven...ought to be baked and eaten within the church in the holy place, that is, at the altar, and never elsewhere. Wherefore Paul commanded the Corinthians, When ye come together...or despise ye the church of God and shame them that have not (1 Cor. xi. 20–22). And this is so because there entirely the mystic supper ought to be celebrated....But that which was left of the flesh and the bread he commanded to be burned in the fire. And this also we now see done before our eyes in the church, and whatever happens to remain unconsumed is committed to the fire: not simply that which has been kept one or two or many days, for as it appears it was not this that the lawgiver commanded, but that which was left he ordered to be burned[1].

Evagrius in his *Ecclesiastical History* (c. 594) gives the usage at Constantinople in his day, and before. We read:

It is considered an ancient custom in the imperial city that whenever a large quantity of the sacred pieces of the spotless body of Christ our God remained over uncorrupted boys of those who attend the school of grammar should be summoned to eat them[2].

The same practice apparently obtained also in Gaul at about the same date. In the sixth canon of the second council of Mâcon in 585 we read:

Whatever remnants of the sacrifices are left over in the sacristy after the completion of mass on Wednesday and Friday, let innocent boys be brought to church by him whose business it is, and a fast having been imposed upon them, let them receive the same remnants sprinkled with wine[3].

---

[1] *In Lev* 11, *P G.* xciii. col. 886–7.
[2] *Hist. Eccles.* iv. 36, *P.G.* lxxxvi. col 2769.
[3] Hardouin, vol. iii. col. 462.

The mention of the fast seems to preclude the possibility that only unconsecrated hosts are intended as in later days. The phraseology also is identical with that used with reference to the disposal of the remnants of the sacrament in the East.

At a synod held at Constantinople under the patriarch Nicholas Grammaticus in the days of the emperor Alexius Comnenus I (c. 1085) one of the questions brought forward for decision by certain monks had to do with the disposal of the remains at the eucharist. Though late it will be convenient to give the answer here. According to Theodore Balsamon the twelfth century canonist, we read:

Question 5. Ought the priest to eat the things which are offered in the church, as the oblations and liquids, indiscriminately and as he wills, and ought he to eat them as common bread? And if many such things have been gathered what ought he to do with them? Answer. The fragments of the exalted (consecrated) oblation they ought not to eat save only in the church, until they have consumed everything, and the remnants of the others not with milk, or cheese, or eggs, or fish, but separately and by themselves[1].

The seventh canon of Theophilus of Alexandria (385–412), sometimes referred to in this connection and misunderstood, may be given for comparison. We read:

Let the clergy divide the things which are offered for the purpose of the sacrifice after those needed for the mysteries are consumed, and let not a catechumen eat or drink of them, but only the clergy and the faithful brethren who are with them. For since they were brought to the altar, and of them parts were taken for the divine gifts, and those were hallowed, how shall any of them be given to the uninitiated to consume[2]?

---

[1] Balsamon, *Interpretationes Canonicae*, P G cxxxviii col 944
[2] Balsamon, *Theoph Alex Quaes*, P G lxv col 41.

EARLY EVIDENCE

The custom prescribed by the decree is similar to that mentioned by the pseudo Jerome, whose words also are frequently misinterpreted. He says:

And after the communion whatever remained over from the sacrifices eating there in church a meal in common they consumed them in like manner[1].

There can be no doubt that the reference in both cases is to the portion of the people's offerings or sacrifices not needed for the mysteries, that is, what was not required for the consecration, not what was left over from the communion, and the practice is well attested otherwise, but both the extracts, and particularly the former, have been interpreted differently, and as we shall see by English divines[2], of the remains of the consecrated elements, a natural misunderstanding perhaps when the offering of the people was obsolete. Balsamon is quite clear about the exact meaning of each of the texts he gives. He says:

The Canon gave no orders at all with regard to the fragments left over of the holy consecrated bread and the rest (i.e. the wine), and did not prescribe how they should be used. The Answer however divided the consumption of the oblations into two; yet about the wine which was offered the holy synod gave no decision; but Theophilus decreed that this also should be consumed in the same way as the loaves, and rightly as I think, for the wine is not consecrated but only hallowed[3].

At this point it will be convenient to consider the apocryphal letter of Clement to James the Lord's brother, and it will be useful for our purpose to quote it at somewhat greater length than is usually done. It belongs apparently to the seventh century, and so what is described represents the practice of that date. We read:

The sacraments of the divine secrets were committed to the three grades of the clergy, to the priest, the deacon and the

---
[1] *In* I *Cor.* xi, *P L.* xxx col 751.
[2] See pp. 197, 207, 211, cf p. 209
[3] *P.G.* cxxxviii col 944.

minister, who with fear and trembling ought to guard the remnants of the fragments of the Lord's body that no corruption be found in the sacristy, lest through acting negligently grave injury be brought to a portion of the Lord's body. But if the communion of the body of our Lord Jesus Christ is carelessly distributed and the priest does not trouble to admonish the minor officials, let him be smitten with a grievous curse, and a meet stroke of humiliation. Let so many hosts indeed be offered on the altar as ought to suffice for the people, but if any remain until the morrow, let them not be reserved[1], but be carefully consumed by the clerks with fear and trembling. But let not those who consume the residue of the Lord's body which has been left in the sacristy come together immediately to receive common food lest they think that the food which is being digested...be mingled with the holy portion. If therefore the Lord's portion be eaten in the morning let the ministers who consumed it fast until the sixth hour, and if they received it at the third or fourth hour, let them fast until the evening....

And the palls and veils which have been soiled in the service of the sanctuary, let the deacon and lower ministers wash near the sacristy, not casting the coverings of the Lord's table out of doors from the sacristy, lest unhappily tiny fragments (pulvis) of the Lord's body fall by chance from the linen washed out of doors, and it be sin to him who does it. Therefore we command that these holy things be kept with care by the ministers within the sacristy. And let a new bowl be provided and except for this purpose let nothing else touch it, but let not this bowl be used for washing any veils except those which pertain to the worship of the Lord's altar. Let the palls of the altar alone be washed in it, and the veils of the doors in another...

We command also that none of the fragments of the Lord's oblation be set before anyone at the table who is excommunicate from the church, or a layman. How dost thou know whether thou art not bestowing the bread of the sacristy on the unworthy? How dost thou know if those on whom thou art bestowing it are clean from women?...Again and again we

---

[1] "Quod si remanserint in crastinum non reserventur."

commend to your charge the fragments of the Lord's body. Let the chalice also be prepared for bearing the blood of the Lord with entire cleanliness of service, and let the minister prepare it lest, if the chalice be not well washed, it become sin to the deacon who offers it....From the beginning of the epistle up to this point I have entrusted the sacraments to your charge to look after them well where no mouse dung may be found among the fragments of the Lord's portion, and that nothing corrupt remain through the negligence of the clergy, lest men come wishing to receive healing for themselves, and, when they see what is corrupt, be seen to receive it rather with ridicule and disgust, and through the negligence of the clergy fall into sin[1].

We notice at once the similarity between the requirements of the first part of this letter with regard to the disposal of the remains of the sacrament, and the directions of the Egyptian Church Order, and Origen and others. It is quite clear that the remains of the sacrament are not consumed during the service immediately after the communion, but are carried into the sacristy. With regard to their subsequent treatment a question of translation makes a considerable difference. The usual translation in later days, when the document was quoted so widely in the West as an authority, was "if any remain let them not be reserved until the morrow," but this is almost certainly incorrect. These directions, like others we have already considered, are plainly based on the rules of the Mosaic law for the disposal of the remains of sacrifices. In the Pentateuch we find two different rules for this according to the occasion. In one case the remains may be kept and eaten the second day, but if left until the third day they must be burned (Lev. vii. 16, 17; xix. 6); in the other the remains may be eaten only on the day of the sacrifice, and if kept until the morrow they must be burned (Ex. xii. 10; xxix. 34). Origen, as we noticed, compared both these

[1] *P.G.* I. col. 483–7.

requirements with usages prevailing with regard to the eucharist, and though for the purpose of his mystical interpretation he argued that it was not by Christ's ordinance that it should be kept until the morning, yet he assumed that frequently it would be so reserved. Those of whom Cyril of Alexandria wrote to Calosyrius, who did not regard the consecration as lasting until the next day, were probably influenced by the second of the rules given above. We note however that both the Levitical regulations assume that the remains will have been kept at least until the morrow before it will be necessary to dispose of them by burning. It seems therefore almost impossible that the letter of the pseudo Clement can mean anything different. Translating in this way "if any remain until the morrow" we note that the phrase is exactly what we find in each case where the subject is mentioned in the Pentateuch (Ex. xii. 10; xxiii. 18; xxix. 34; cf. Lev. vii. 15; xix. 6; xxii. 30). The various times mentioned for consuming the remains of the sacrament, in the morning, or at the third or fourth hour, suggest that it does not take place immediately after the liturgy, but on a separate occasion, and therefore apparently on a different day. What is to be consumed is that "which has been left in the sacristy," again suggesting a time other than immediately after the liturgy, and with this the tense of the verb agrees, for it is literally, "if any have remained." It would seem then that the intention of the letter of the pseudo Clement is that the remains of the sacrament should be kept until the next day, and that then they must be consumed by the clergy and not reserved, though they are still consecrated, and must not be confused with the unconsecrated oblations, being still "the communion of the body of our Lord Jesus Christ." This agrees exactly with the Arabic canons of the council of Nicaea: "As often as...any of the eucharist is left over, let the priests honour it in the morning of the following day before they communicate[1]." It is also just what we find in the ancient Coptic rule quoted above: "If it happens on the day of some solemn feast that any of the eucharist remains over, it should be treated with honour: and the following day the priests should divide it among themselves and communicate therefrom[2]." The practice to which Hesychius is alluding when he speaks of burning the remains of the eucharist which have been kept "one or two or many days," seems also, as he claims, connected with the Levitical rule, though his argument that they should be burned immediately is scarcely correct, for the remains of the sacrifices were not burned until the morrow[3]. The custom of giving what was left to boys also points in the same direction, for certainly at the council of Mâcon, and probably in the East, the boys were only fetched on certain days[4]. That the remains of the consecrated breads should be kept at least until the next morning seems to have been at one time an almost universal custom, and there can be little doubt that the letter of the pseudo Clement should be correctly translated as above—"if any remain until the morrow, let them not be reserved."

We must however notice one piece of evidence which at first sight appears to tell against this interpretation, and it is to be found in one of the Canons of Athanasius. These canons survive only in the Arabic and Coptic, but they appear to belong to the date of Athanasius, and they may be due to the saint himself. We read:

And concerning the holy mysteries, the body of Christ and His blood, they shall not let aught thereof remain over from evening to the morning, but shall do with it whatsoever they will. The holy altar having been prepared, and so long as the holy mysteries are thereon, ere he hath raised it up the readers shall not be silent before it, but shall sing in the word of God or shall repeat the psalms....And because it is His body and

[1] See p 8
[2] See p. 8.
[3] See p. 9.
[4] See p. 9.

blood, so shall they not leave praising Him, until the time when the place is cleansed[1].

Another canon however seems to show that the reference is not to the consecrated elements at all. We read:

An offering that remaineth over from yesterday they shall not offer, neither that which hath been divided in pieces in any church, but bread warm, fresh and whole[2].

From this it seems clear that the former canon has nothing to do with the remnants of the sacrament, but that it refers to the unconsecrated oblations of the people which must not be used in the eucharist except on the day on which they were originally baked and offered; and this explanation fits in exactly with the purpose of the rest of the canon. We have therefore nothing here which testifies to the existence of a custom which would contradict our interpretation of the passage in the pseudo Clement, that the remains of the consecrated hosts were not as a rule disposed of until the next day.

Nothing is said about the consumption of any remains of the chalice in the letter of the pseudo Clement, or whether the residue of the consecrated wine was also reserved. We are only told that it is the duty of the minister to see that the chalice is well washed. In view of the rubric in the liturgy of the Apostolic Constitutions, and later custom in the matter, at any rate on occasions, both in East and West, it seems probable that this too was taken into the sacristy, and reserved in a similar way. Anything in the nature of ablutions, and the necessary cleansing of the vessels, must thus have taken place in the sacristy, and not before the conclusion of the service.

At a superficial view the letter of the pseudo Clement, though requiring reservation of the remains for one day, might seem to forbid it altogether for a longer period, but

[1] Riedel and Crum, *The Canons of Athanasius*, pp. 48-9.
[2] Riedel and Crum, p. 42, cf. p. 129

there appears to be no evidence of the existence of any such custom, or that it was ever so interpreted. Some, such as those mentioned by Cyril of Alexandria in his letter to Calosyrius, appear to have argued against reservation in any form, but the letter was never so understood, and continuous reservation was the common practice both before and after its appearance. In the rule for dealing with "the remnants of the fragments of the Lord's body," or "the residue of the Lord's body," for the necessary disposal of which, as remains of the sacrifices, precedent could be found in the Mosaic law, in view of the reasons put forward for similar customs elsewhere, the writer without any doubt had in mind the requirements of the Pentateuch. With the question of the continuous reservation of that which was wanted for its proper purpose he is not concerned, and the Old Testament certainly failed to supply any rule which was applicable. Yet the existence of such perpetual reservation is evidently supposed, for the words "let them not be reserved," suggest it, as also the fact that some might come to partake of the sacrament as an act of devotion and be scandalized to find it corrupt. The use of the reserved species for purposes of communion is not condemned but rather the reverse, and the argument is that it is not seemly that the faithful should have to receive that which had been negligently kept for an indefinite period and had become foul. To prevent all abuse "the residue" or "the remnants of the fragments of the Lord's body" were not to be used for communion at all, or even given to laymen, but consumed by the clergy. Consequently separate provision would have to be made for continuous reservation, and so in reckoning the people for whom the hosts to be consecrated are to suffice account would have to be taken of those who were expected to communicate with the reserved species and the needs of the sick, so that they might be independent of any accidental surplus. Though misunderstood on one point, some such interpretation as this, which indeed is identical with that given by St Thomas Aquinas[1], has always been put upon the directions of the letter, and it has been rightly regarded as condemning, not the seemly reservation of the sacrament, but the negligent treatment of what was left over from communion.

[1] *Summa*, Pars III Quaes LXXXIII Art. v, *P L.* IV. (Second Series), col. 848. See p 42

CHAPTER II

IN THE EAST

WE have already noticed the practice of burying the remains of the eucharist among the Copts. It seems to have been not unknown elsewhere, and to have continued to a much later period in orthodox circles. Cardinal Humbert in his controversial work against the Greeks, written in 1054, contrasts what he considers their unworthy methods of dealing with the remnants of the sacrament with the better custom said to prevail in the churches at Jerusalem. We read·

If anything of the holy and venerable eucharist remain over in the churches of Jerusalem they neither burn it nor put it into a pit, but store it away in a clean pyx, and the following day communicate the people from it: for they give communion there daily because there assemble thither Christians from various provinces, who because of their faith and exceeding great love towards the Son of God desire to communicate there, for as much as that place is more venerable and sacred than any place in the whole world....But to inter or bury the holy eucharist in the earth, as some are said to do, or to put it in a pot, or to pour it away, is gross negligence and not the fear of God[1].

We have here evidently a reference to the contents of the chalice as well as to the bread.

Nothing is said in any of the texts of the Greek liturgy of St James, which have come down to us, about the disposal of what remains after the communion, or about any ablutions, but we get some information from the Syriac

---

[1] *Adv. Calumn Graec.* 33, *P L.* CXLIII col 952

form of the rite. In an explanation of the liturgy drawn up by Dionysius Barsalibi, Bishop of Amid, at the end of the twelfth century, but sometimes wrongly ascribed to John Maro († 707) the founder of the Maronites, we read after the communion and thanksgiving:

And immediately he commends them to the divine grace saying, *Go in peace*....When the priest is about to say this commendation he should put his right hand on the altar and immediately turn round to the people, and make crosses over them with it, and they should say Psalm xxxiv., *I will always give thanks*...and afterwards (to the tune) *Voices of praise* they sing, *Thy body which I have eaten*...or (to the tune) *Be glad O ye righteous, Not to judgment or condemnation*.... And then he seals[1] the people saying, *The blessing of our Lord Jesus Christ*....And after he has consumed the body and drunk the blood and ministered (i e performed the ablutions), and wiped the vessels he says, *Because I have eaten of thy body*...[2].

In the Syriac liturgy of the Maronites, who were received into communion with the Roman church in 1182, according to the edition printed at Rome in 1592, we read:

The priest says the final seal common to all the anaphoras, *Bless us all*....The priest says, *Go in peace*....He drinks the blood and says, *By thy vivifying and living blood*....The deacon (says Psalm xxxiii), *I will always give thanks*....And afterwards (to the tune) *Voices of praise* they sing, *Praise the Lord, all ye people, Alleluia, Thy body which I have eaten*....Another hymn (to the tune) *Be glad O ye righteous, Not to judgment or condemnation*....At the end the priest seals them, *The blessing of our Lord Jesus Christ* ...After the consumption of the body the priest ministers (i.e. wipes and cleanses the vessels), and says this prayer, *The oblation which we have today offered*....And when he wipes the paten he says, *May the living fire of thy precious body and blood*....And when he wipes his fingers thrice, and

---

[1] I e blesses with the sign of the cross So a "seal" is a blessing
[2] Assemani, *Codex Liturgicus*, vol. v p 396. Cf. Connolly and Codrington *Two Commentaries on the Jacobite Liturgy*, p. 69.

first those of his right hand, he says, *Let my fingers rehearse thy praises*....At his left hand he says, *Guard me, O Lord, from all harm*....And when he drinks the wine which he had mixed for the ablution he says, *They shall be satisfied*...(Ps. xxxvi). When he wipes the chalice he says the prayer of Ephraim, *Wipe away, O Lord with the sponge of thy mercy*....And after the seal he says, *Because I have eaten of thy holy body*...[1].

In the common order of the Syriac liturgy as used by the Syrian Jacobites, and similarly in the liturgy of the Christians of St Thomas on the Malabar coast, we read after the communion and thanksgiving·

The seal, *May God who has granted us*....The priest puts his right hand on the altar, and says this prayer of commendation, signing the people thrice with the sign of the cross, and says, *Go in peace*....The priest bowing before the table of life says within himself this prayer for himself secretly, *By the oblation which we have today offered*....After he has finished all things which pertain to the ministering (i.e. consuming the remains) of the body of Christ he says, *The Lord is my shepherd*, and the rest of the psalm (xxiii). And he wipes the paten and says, *If any member remain, let it remain to thy knowledge which created the world. If any member remain, may the Lord be its keeper, and be merciful to us.* And after he has finished wiping the chalice he says, *What shall I render unto the Lord* ...After he has wiped the chalice with a sponge he says this prayer of Mar Ephraim, *Wipe away, O Lord, with the sponge of thy mercy.* ... And when he washes his hands he says, *May the living fire of thy precious body and blood*....And he washes his fingers thrice, beginning with the right hand, and says, *Let my fingers rehearse thy praises*....At the left hand he says, *Guard me, O Lord, from all harm*....And when he drinks the wine which he has mixed for the ablution[2] he says, *They shall be satisfied*...(Ps xxxvi). He washes his hands in water and says this psalm, *Be thou my*

---

[1] Assemani, vol v pp 215-223
[2] Lit. the "deaconess," that which is employed in the ministry, or service (of cleansing the fingers and chalice)

judge...(Ps. xxvi). He wipes his hands and says, *Bring unto the Lord*... (Ps. xxix)...Verse, *Not to judgment or condemnation*...[1].

The similarity between these rubrics of the Maronite and Jacobite rites suggests that there has been little change in the ceremony of the ablutions since the Maronites submitted to Rome at the end of the twelfth century, and the fact that both sets of rubrics, and particularly the Maronite version, are very similar to the description given by Dionysius Barsalibi, confirms the idea.

In the anaphora of St James at the time of communion we read:

And these verses, as also many others, are diminished or lengthened according to the number of communicants. Immediately the priest wipes the vessels with the help of the deacon, and then is said the prayer of thanksgiving[2].

At first sight this rubric seems to suggest that the ablutions took place immediately after the communion. Yet it would be curious if two anaphoras of the same rite ordered entirely contradictory customs on such a point as this, and we notice that only the wiping of the vessels is mentioned, and nothing is said about any consumption of the remains, or of any washing either of the vessels or of the priest's hands. It seems more probable that we have a practice similar to that ordered in certain texts of the liturgy of St Chrysostom after the priest's communion, where we read:

And he receives thrice from it, and then wipes both his own lips and the holy chalice with the veil which is in his hands[3].

---

[1] Renaudot, vol II pp 25–28 Cf Brightman, pp 106–8 Howard, *The Christians of St Thomas and their Liturgies*, pp 250–263

[2] Renaudot, vol II p 42

[3] Hammond, *Liturgies Eastern and Western*, p 125 Cf Swainson, *The Greek Liturgies*, p 140 Daniel, *Codex Liturgicus*, vol. IV. p. 368.

In the Coptic liturgy of St Basil, according to a manuscript of perhaps the fourteenth century, after the prayer of inclination which follows the communion we read at the very end of the liturgy:

Let the priest say the benediction, *O Lord be merciful unto us*... When he has finished the washing of the vessels, let him drink the water which remains in them, and let him dismiss the people when he has said the benediction[1].

The modern service books make it clear that the ablutions still come at the end of the service between the prayer of inclination and the final blessing, though only the washing of the priest's hands is mentioned. In the 1887 edition we read:

The people shall say, *Kyrie eleison*. Then the priest shall pour water upon his hands, and shall make the sign with a little thereof upon the table and shall say, *Angel of this sacrifice*....Then he shall wipe his face with his hand and his brother priests above and below, and the whole congregation (shall do the like), and he shall bless them and give them the dismissal, and shall end with reading the blessing[2].

In the fourteenth century commentary of Abu'l Bircat on the Coptic liturgy we read with reference to the consumption of the remains:

And when he has completed these things with regard to the distribution of the communion, the priest will take care that if by chance any particle however small of the body be left over he gather it up and give it to those ministering at the altar. Let the deacon also bear away the chalice in which the priest has communicated with the despoticon[3], and likewise the blood if any of it be left over[4].

The remains of the particles intended for the people are evidently consumed immediately after the communion, but the chalice used at the consecration and for the

---

[1] Renaudot, vol 1 p 25
[2] Brightman, p 188
[3] The central portion of the host
[4] Renaudot, vol. 1 p. 293.

priest's communion into which the despoticon was placed, is taken away. According to an ancient canon, however, neither it nor the other sacred vessels are cleansed until after the service is ended, for it is the function of the priests and deacons who performed the liturgy, and so it is unlikely that the despoticon and the remains of the chalice are consumed earlier. We read:

It is forbidden to priests to give any layman the duty of washing the chalice and the other sacred vessels, or to permit them to drink the water of ablution, which ought to be drunk by the priests and deacons who have officiated[1].

Among *Questions and Answers according to the Doctrine of the Fathers* of uncertain date we find a decision prescribing what is to be done when a particle of the consecrated host is discovered after the ablutions, and this makes it still plainer that the cleansing of the vessels takes place after the service. We read:

After the communion, when the liturgy is finished, and the priest has washed the sacred vessels, and has drunk the water of their ablution, if he finds a particle of the holy body on the table of the altar or in the veil what ought he to do? Should he receive it after having taken the ablution? Ought the water which he has drunk to be considered as having caused him to break his fast or not, since it has been poured on the paten and chalice which were imbued with the holy body and the precious blood? When the sacred ministry of the liturgy is finished and the priest has washed the sacred vessels, and has drunk the water of their ablution, if he finds any particle of the body as has been mentioned above he ought not in any wise to take it, but he should enquire if there is any priest among his colleagues or any deacon who has communicated and who has not taken the water of ablution, and if he finds such an one he should give him the particle of the body which he has found. Afterwards he should again wash his hands over the paten and give

---

[1] *Perpétuité de la Foi*, III. 7, vol. III. col. 211.

him who has received the particle the water of ablution to drink. If there is no ecclesiastic or layman fasting and of age to receive the communion the priest should still beware of taking it after he has taken the water of ablution of the sacred vessels and of his hands, the liturgy being finished and the distribution of the body of Jesus Christ ended, because he has broken his fast by the water which he has drunk and therefore cannot receive the communion of the holy body. He should then place this particle which he has found on the paten and light two candles about it and a lamp towards the east: then he should himself stay to guard the body until the following day. And when the liturgy is celebrated he should receive it fasting without performing any function at the altar, and he should wash his hands with water which he should drink. After all this he should do a very severe penance because of the negligence he has shown with regard to the body and blood of the Son of God which was poured out for the salvation of His creatures[1].

In the rite as used by the Coptic Uniats the directions have been considerably Romanized, and both the consumption of the remains and the ablutions take place immediately after the communion. In the text of the liturgy as given by the Marquess of Bute, which is based on the edition (in Coptic and Arabic) of Raphael Tuki, Bishop of Arsinoe, printed at Rome in 1736, though taking note of modern practice, we read:

If there are communicants they approach and he communicates them saying to each, *This is in very truth the body and the blood of Emmanuel our God   Amen*. He then moves the paten crosswise towards the people, turns, and replaces it on the altar. He consumes what remains of the sacred host, saying again, *This is in very truth the body of Emmanuel our God. Amen*; and then after cleansing the paten into the chalice what remains of the blood, saying, *This is in very truth the blood*

---

[1] *Perpétuité de la Foi*, III 7, vol III col. 211-2. Cf. Renaudot, vol I p. 294.

of Emmanuel our God. Amen. He holds out the chalice into which the deacon pours some wine, and the priest says, *Peace be unto all.* The people answer, *And unto thy spirit.* He drinks the wine. Then wine and water are poured over his fingers into the chalice and he drinks it, and wipes and arranges the chalice saying meanwhile inaudibly in Arabic, *Our mouth is filled with gladness...*[1].

The Nestorian custom is very extraordinary, and obviously arose through a corruption of the practice by which the remains of the consecrated elements were consumed after the service. After the blessing which concludes the liturgy proper there is a "Prayer on receiving the Holy Thing," and another "In ordering the Mysteries[2]." This ordering is really the consumption of what remains after the communion of the people, and the previous prayer is explained by the fact that according to modern usage the celebrant himself does not communicate until after the benediction when he consumes what is left. In earlier days certainly the usual custom prevailed by which the priest communicated after the Lord's prayer which marked the end of the eucharistic prayer, and before the communion of the people, and it is this which is described in the Liturgical Homilies of Narsai († *c.* 502)[3]. At some later date the priest's act of communion was postponed and combined with the consumption of the remnants of the sacrament left from the people's communion, at the close of the service.

At Constantinople the practice of giving the remains of the eucharist to children survived until quite a late period, for Nicephorus Callistus (*c.* 1333) in his *Ecclesiastical History*, taking up the words of Evagrius, says the custom was still in vogue in his youth:

---

[1] Marquess of Bute, *Coptic Morning Service*, p 113
[2] *The Liturgy of the Holy Apostles Adai and Mari*, S P C K, p 38. Cf Brightman, p 304
[3] Connolly, *The Liturgical Homilies of Narsai*, p 27

A custom has prevailed for a long time in the queen of cities that whenever there was a large quantity of pieces of the spotless and divine body of our Lord and God and Saviour Jesus Christ left over the priests should fetch uncorrupted boys of those who attend the school of grammar, and that they should eat the remnants fasting. And this indeed frequently happened to me also when I was quite a boy, and particularly when at a tender age I was engaged in study in the sacred courts[1].

In the Paschal Chronicle for the year 624 we get some information about the arrangements at the conclusion of the liturgy among the Greeks, but nothing is said definitely about the consumption of the remains, or the ablutions of the vessels. We read:

It was arranged that there should be singing after all have partaken of the holy mysteries, as the clergy are about to put away the precious fans, patens, and chalices, and other holy vessels in the sacristy, after the removal of all things from the credence after the distribution and the singing of the last verse of the Communion[2].

A canon of the Typicon of Nicephorus, patriarch of Constantinople (806–815), gives some particulars with regard to the ablutions:

Let the priest look at the people first and sacrifice the holy gifts so that there may not be a superabundance, and let no one dare to touch them alone but for thyself do thou distribute them to the people, and after they have partaken of them wash the chalice round with wine twice and with water once in the fear of God[3].

We have reference to several points in the service in these directions, before the consecration, the communion,

[1] *Hist Eccles* XVII 25, *P G* CXLVII col 280
[2] *Chronicon Paschale*, *P G* XCII col 1001
[3] Pitra, *Juris Eccles. Graec Hist et Mon* vol II p 341.

and the ablutions, and there is nothing to show when the last takes place.

In the texts of the liturgies of St Basil and St Chrysostom as given in the ninth century Barberini manuscript nothing is said about the consumption of the remains or of the ablutions, but at the end of the latter we find "a prayer at the gathering up of the holy gifts, *The fulness of the law...*" corresponding to "a prayer in the sacristy" in the former[1], so that both must have taken place in the sacristy after the service.

In an eleventh century codex of the liturgy of St Chrysostom we have an expansion of the short rubrics of the earlier text. The liturgy of St Basil agrees almost identically. We read

> Then the communion being finished and the holy remnants taken up from the divine table, the priest prays on, *We give thee thanks*....And when he is about to return the holy gifts where they were set forth, on taking them from the holy table the deacon censes them thrice. The priest says to himself, *Be thou exalted*...and taking them up he says aloud, *At all times, now and always and for ever and ever*. And on returning from the prothesis[2] both deacon and priest, the deacon says, *Stand up. Having received the divine, holy, spotless, immortal, heavenly and lifegiving, awful mysteries of Christ, let us give thanks to the Lord*....A prayer at the gathering up of the holy things, *The fulness of the law*...[3].

We note that the remains of the consecrated elements are taken away to the prothesis by the priest and deacon together after "Be thou exalted," and before the deacon's call to thanksgiving. The consumption of them evidently takes place in the sacristy, or at the prothesis, after the

[1] Brightman, p 344.
[2] The place where the oblation is set forth, properly the act of setting it forth
[3] Swainson, *The Greek Liturgies*, pp. 141-3 Cf. pp. 169-71.

service. The title of the prayer said meanwhile now speaks of "holy things," not of "holy gifts."

In an order for the liturgy published by Philotheus, Patriarch of Constantinople in the fourteenth century, the directions of the canon of Nicephorus are elaborated, and we read that the deacon washes the chalice thrice with wine and water, and wipes it with the sponge, and washes his hands and lips, saying *Nunc dimittis*, etc. With regard to the priest it says "He washes (his hands) thoroughly[1]."

In a sixteenth century manuscript of the liturgy of St Chrysostom we have still further development, and again we find practically the same directions in the liturgy of St Basil. We read:

Then the deacon taking the holy paten sponges it over the holy chalice quite thoroughly, and with care and reverence covers the holy chalice with the veil. Likewise also he puts the star and the veils over the holy paten. And they open the door of the sanctuary, and the deacon, bowing once, takes the holy chalice with reverence and goes to the door, and elevating the holy chalice shows it to the people, saying, *In the fear of God and love draw near*....And both the deacon and priest return to the holy table and the priest censes it thrice, saying to himself, *Be thou exalted*....Then taking the holy paten he puts it upon the head of the deacon, and the deacon takes it with reverence, looks outside towards the door, and saying nothing departs to the prothesis and puts it down. And the priest bows and takes the holy chalice, and turns towards the door, and looks at the people saying, *Blessed be our God*. Then he says aloud, *At all times, now and always and for ever and ever*... And immediately he says secretly the prayer, *We give thee thanks*....The deacon standing in the accustomed place says, *Having received the divine*....A prayer at the gathering up of

[1] Sirkov, *Histoire de la correction des livres en Bulgarie au XIVe siècle* (in Russian), vol. I p 172 See Gabrol and Leclercq, *Dictionnaire d'Archéologie Chrétienne et de Liturgie*, vol. I. Pt. I. col. 110.

the holy things, secretly, *The fulness of the law*....After the prayer the priest departs and standing in the accustomed place distributes the antidoron[1]. Then he makes the dismissal.... And having blessed the people he goes in again. And after the dismissal, if there is no deacon the priest enters the prothesis and receives what is left in the holy chalice, carefully and reverently. And he washes the holy chalice thrice and looks if anything, what is called a pearl, remain. Then he says, *Lord now lettest thou*....And he gathers together the holy things, the chalice and the paten with the veils according to custom; but if there is a deacon he does it. And the priest departs into the sacristy and unvests[2].

We notice that the "holy things" are no longer the consecrated elements, but the sacred vessels.

The modern rubrics are almost identical with those of the sixteenth century. The prayer "We give thee thanks" said secretly by the priest is no longer said after the communion of the people, but after the priest's own communion and before the opening of the door of the sanctuary. The latter part reads:

And when this (the dismissal) is finished the priest enters through the holy doors and departing to the prothesis says the following prayer secretly, *The fulness of the law*....And the deacon enters, but he through the north part, and gathers up the holy things with fear and safety so that nothing at all even the least portion of the holy things fall away or be left behind, and he washes his hands in the accustomed place. And the priest goes outside and distributes the antidoron to the people. Then entering the sanctuary he puts off the priestly vestments, saying, *Lord now lettest thou*...[3].

The authorities of the Greek Church in Bayswater have very kindly supplied some further particulars with regard to modern practice:

[1] The blessed bread, the remains of the unconsecrated oblations left over from the prothesis
[2] Swainson, pp. 140–4.   [3] Brightman, pp 398–9.

After loud utterance of the priest, *At all times, now and always and for ever*, the priest himself, and not the deacon, removes the consecrated elements to the table of the prothesis. When more than one priest is officiating from that moment onwards, and especially after the dismissal, one of the other officiating priests, or the officiating deacon, could consume the consecrated elements. But if the officiating priest has no assistant (priest or deacon) he has no time to consume them other than after the distribution of the antidoron[1].

Further details are as follows.

At the close of the liturgy the officiating priest carries the consecrated elements to the table of the prothesis, where the officiating deacon, and if not the officiating priest, consumes the remainder. He then pours a little warm water and wine into the chalice to cleanse it, and consumes these also. He repeats this action several times, until he is certain that no "particle" or "pearl" remains, and consumes them each time. Then in order to remove any dampness from the interior of the chalice, he uses a special cloth with which he wipes it, and then he places a round sponge in it, leaving it there till the next liturgy[2].

The late Mr W. J. Birkbeck has given a description based on his own observation of what happens at the consumption of the remains of the consecrated elements and the ablutions in the Russian Church. He shows the full liturgical setting. We read:

After the communion of the people the priest places the chalice, now containing the whole of what is left of both species of the holy sacrament, on the altar, and the deacon after removing with the sponge the *merides* (or unconsecrated particles of bread placed on the paten at the beginning of the service in memory of the mother of God, and the various saints and members of the church living and departed on behalf of whom the liturgy is offered) from the paten into the chalice,

---

[1] Letter dated Sept. 17th, 1916
[2] Letter dated Jan 11th, 1916

covers it with the veil.... The priest then says the post-communion prayer of thanksgiving at the altar. He then goes to the royal doors and blesses the people saying, *O God, save thy people and bless thine inheritance,* and the choir sing the anthem, *We have seen the true light,* etc. during which the priest returns to the altar, and after censing the altar with three swings of the censer gives the paten to the deacon to take to the prothesis table, and after adoring takes the chalice in his hands and showing it to the people says, *Blessed is our God, always now and ever, world without end,* and then while the choir sing another troparion[1] he takes the chalice to the prothesis table and puts it down. Then follow some more prayers, occupying three whole pages of the Russian service book, consisting chiefly of a short litany said by the deacon, the *Let us go forth in peace,* which corresponds with the Western *Ite missa est,* and the long prayer behind the ambo[2], which the priest comes out into the nave to read. It is only after this that the deacon, if he has already communicated, returns to the prothesis and consumes what remains of the holy sacrament, and takes the ablutions, the priest meanwhile distributing the antidoron, or bringing the cross into the nave for the people to kiss. But supposing as is most frequently the case on ordinary days, that the deacon has not made his communion, then the priest himself returns to the prothesis and takes the ablutions, but not until after the whole service is over and the people gone[3].

Mr Birkbeck has also given the usage of other Eastern churches with respect to the consumption of the remains of the eucharist and the ablutions, the observed practice agreeing generally with the rubrics of the liturgies:

With regard to the practice of other Eastern rites besides that of the Orthodox Eastern Church in this matter I can only

[1] A short hymn
[2] The pulpit, originally in the middle of the church.
[3] Letter dated Aug 15th in *Church Times* for Aug. 19th, 1910, vol LXIV. p 216

speak positively with regard to the Syrian Jacobite and the East Syrian Nestorian rites. Both of these agree with the Orthodox Eastern Church in deferring the consumption of what remains of the blessed sacrament and of the ablutions to the end of the service and not taking them as in the Roman rite immediately after the communion[1].

With regard to the Uniat rites when I saw the Syrian Jacobite and the Chaldaean Uniat rites the ablutions were taken after the blessing. The Ruthenian books retain the Byzantine rubrics, and in the vast majority of instances in which I have seen their rite used, whether in Rome or in Austria, they have been strictly followed so far as the ablutions are concerned. Only on two occasions, once in Galicia and once in Vienna, have I seen the rubric disregarded and the Latin custom followed. But this was before Leo XIII in the early nineties took measures against the tinkering of the Uniat rites in a Latin direction, and I am informed that this disregard of plain directions would not be possible now[2].

In the Armenian liturgy which is Romanized at various points the remains are consumed immediately after the communion before the thanksgiving and blessing. We read:

During the communion the choir sing the hymns proper for the day, and also, *We have been filled*....Whilst the choir is singing the priest consumes what remains of the sacred elements, and then repeats in secret these prayers of thanksgiving, *We give thanks unto thee*...[3].

In all these different extracts illustrating the practice of the churches of the East at so many different places and times we find great variety of usage, but whether the remains of the consecrated species remained on the altar until the end of the service or not the primitive practice

---

[1] *Church Times*, Sept. 2nd, 1910, vol LXIV p. 272.
[2] *Church Times*, Sept. 16th, 1910, vol LXIV p. 352
[3] Fortescue, *The Armenian Church*, pp 107-8. Cf Daniel, *Codex Liturgicus*, vol. IV p. 478

still persisted in the majority of instances where Roman influence is absent, and they were not disposed of until the liturgy was ended, and in any case the cleansing of the sacred vessels did not usually take place until the service was finished; and clearly while the custom of consuming the remains of the eucharist after the conclusion of the service continued nothing in the way of ablutions of the sacred vessels could possibly take place at an earlier point. There can thus be little doubt but that this was the primitive usage in the matter, and that in the earliest days all cleansing of the vessels must have been performed afterwards in the sacristy.

CHAPTER III

IN THE WEST

THE practice of giving what remained over of the consecrated elements after communion at mass to boys continued in the West, as well as in the East, for some centuries. At the third council of Tours under Charles the Great in 813 a word of caution on the subject was still found necessary:

> Priests must be expressly admonished that when they have performed the sacred solemnities of the mass, and have communicated the people, they give not the body of the Lord carelessly to boys, or any other persons who are standing by, without distinction[1].

Traces of this custom, and of child communion, are found much later. About the year 1198 in a synod held under Odo of Paris it was decreed:

> Priests are straitly charged that they in no wise give hosts, even though not consecrated, to boys[2].

The synod of Clermont in 1268 modified this prescription and evidently has unconsecrated hosts chiefly in view.

> We forbid priests to give hosts, though not consecrated, to boys except on Easter Day, in the place of blessed bread, and then let them eat them immediately, and not carry them out of the church[3].

Another modification of the Parisian canon was issued at Bayeux (c. 1300):

---

[1] Hardouin, vol IV col 1025
[2] Hardouin, vol VI 2, col 1945   [3] Hardouin, vol. VII col 593

We forbid priests in any wise to give sacred hosts to boys under the age of seven years[1].

Here apparently it is consecrated hosts which are prohibited, as in 1255 at Bordeaux, where a canon, known evidently at Clermont, forbade anything but blessed bread to be given to boys even for communion at Easter[2].

On Maundy Thursday there was a similar custom of giving unconsecrated hosts to the poor, presumably those whose feet were washed in the ceremony of the Mandatum, and it persisted for some centuries, for we find it in the Statutes of Lanfranc, the Constitutions of Ulrich of Cluny, the ancient Ordinary of Corbie, and the Customs of St Benignus of Dijon, representing the practice of the eleventh and twelfth centuries[3].

The sixteenth council of Toledo in 693 required the eucharistic loaves to be made of only moderate size, because of the difficulty otherwise of consuming the remains. We read:

The assembly has unanimously decided that no bread be set forth on the altar of the Lord to be hallowed by the benediction of the priest save that which is whole and fair, which has been prepared with care. And let not anything big but only those of moderate size be offered, as the custom of the church maintains, so that the remnants of it, if they are to be reserved, may be more easily reserved without any injury in a moderate compass, or if it is necessary to consume them, it may not oppress and overload the stomach of him who takes them[4].

A canon of uncertain date, perhaps belonging to the synod of Rodomum about the year 878, reads:

We have been told that certain priests when they have celebrated mass, refusing themselves to consume the divine

---

[1] Hardouin, vol. VII col 1228   [2] Hardouin, vol VII col 471.
[3] Martene, *De Ant Eccles. Ritibus*, 1783, vol. IV. lib III cap XIII. § xxxiii p. 126
[4] Hardouin, vol FII. col. 1797

mysteries which they have consecrated, give the Lord's cup to poor women who offer at mass, or to certain laymen who know not how to discern the Lord's body, that is to distinguish between spiritual food and carnal. How contrary this is to the whole religion of the church the piety of the faithful knows. Wherefore we forbid it to all priests, so that no one for the future may presume to do this; but let him either consume it himself with reverence, or entrust it to either the deacon or subdeacon who are ministers of the altar to gather up[1].

The pseudo Alcuin (eleventh century?) likewise tells us that this duty was entrusted to the deacon and subdeacon. He says:

The subdeacon is the under-minister, because he is under the deacon, that is, under the minister....The sacrifice being finished he takes up the mysteries of the body and blood of the Lord which were left over, to be gathered up or carried away by the deacon[2].

A passage in the life of St Adalbert, Bishop of Prague († c 997), in language almost identical with that of the pseudo Alcuin, speaks of a similar custom at the end of mass:

Whatever was left over of that from which he and the newly baptized had communicated he commanded to be gathered up, and he kept it for himself, wrapped in a most clean cloth, to carry it away for viaticum[3].

The document most frequently quoted as the authority for the traditional practice of the West with regard to the disposal of the remnants of the eucharist after the communion is the apocryphal letter of Clement the First of Rome to James the Lord's brother, which we have already discussed[4]. We find it quoted by most of the early

[1] Hardouin, vol. VI. 1, p. 205.
[2] *De Div. Off.* in Hittorp, *De Div. Cath. Eccl. Off. et Myst.* 1610, col. 269.
[3] *P.L.* CXXXVII. col. 884.   [4] See pp. 11–18

canonists. Remigius, Bishop of Coire (*c.* 830), entitles his extract "What is allowed with regard to the Lord's body[1]." In the forged decretals of the pseudo Isidore (*c.* 850) according to some manuscripts the summary of the passage is "that the sacraments of the divine secrets are committed to three orders, and that priests, deacons and ministers perform the sacraments of the church carefully and without negligence[2]." Regino of Prüm († 915) heads his quotation "Carefulness with regard to the Lord's body[3]." Burchard, Bishop of Worms († 1025), summarises the rule as follows, "So many oblations as will suffice for the people are to be offered, and what are left are not to be kept till the morrow[4]." Ivo of Chartres († 1115) quotes the letter in each of his two collections, heading it in one case "By whom the Lord's sacraments are to be handled," and in the other "So many hosts are to be offered on the altar as will be able to suffice the people, and what is left is to be consumed by the clergy with fear and trembling, and with great carefulness[5]." Cardinal Gregory includes the passage in his collection called *Polycarpus* (*c.* 1124)[6] and Gratian in his *Decretum* (*c.* 1151)[7]. Gratian repeats the title of Ivo of Chartres, "By whom the Lord's sacraments are to be handled." In Gratian it is included in the official *Corpus Juris Canonici* of 1572–85, and all later editions. From the different summaries it is plain that the canonists considered the document authoritative as a whole and not simply on one or two points, and clearly it was regarded as something more than a relic of bygone times of no force for the present. Though when properly interpreted it has really nothing to do with the question, being concerned with the

---

[1] *P L* cii col. 1093–4.
[2] Hinschius, *Decretales pseudo Isidorianae*, p 46
[3] *P L* cxxxii col 225–6.   [4] *P L.* cxl. col. 754.
[5] *P L* clxi col. 1079, 165.
[6] *P L* clxxxvii. col. 1740, n. 136
[7] Pars iii. *De Cons.* Dist. ii c 23, *P L.* clxxxvii. col. 1740

disposal of an accidental surplus and not directly with the reservation of the sacrament at all, as a matter of fact it is historically the ultimate source of the modern rules for the reservation of the consecrated host and its renewal.

Not only was what was left over from the communion consumed in the sacristy, but this was also, as in the East, the place of reservation. In the Gelasian Sacramentary (*c.* 700, and later) in the mass of Maundy Thursday we read:

They communicate and reserve of this sacrifice until the morrow; and thence let them communicate[1].

On Good Friday we are told:

The prayers above written being finished, the deacons go into the sacristy. They proceed with the body and blood of the Lord which remained the day before, and place it on the altar[2].

There would appear to have been reservation in both kinds, or at any rate this was probably the original meaning of the rubric.

The *Missale Francorum* (*c.* 700) mentions the reservation of the hosts in the sacristy and quotes the letter of the pseudo Clement. In the allocation to the subdeacon we read·

The oblations which come to the altar are called the shew-bread. Of these oblations only so much as is able to suffice for the people ought to be placed on the altar, that there be no decay in the sacristy[3].

These instructions are repeated a number of times in various forms for use at ordination at Rome and elsewhere, and are to be found in the Pontificals of Egbert († 766) and Dunstan († 988), and other English books[4]. In the early days it was obviously the custom in England as in other

---

[1] Wilson, *Gelasian Sacramentary*, p. 72.   [2] Wilson, p. 77.
[3] Thomasius, *Opera*, vol VI p 343.
[4] Martene, vol. II lib. I. cap. VIII. Art XI. Ord. II. III. IV xiv. xvii. pp. 34, 38, 42, 70, 84

countries, to reserve the sacrament in the sacristy. King Alfred in his translation of Bede's *Ecclesiastical History* says of Gregory the Great:

His body was buried before the housel porch.

The housel porch is clearly the place where the sacrament is reserved, but in the original Latin it is "secretarium," or sacristy[1].

The Leofric Missal (c. 1070) prescribing the ceremonies of Good Friday gives a version of the directions of the Gelasian Sacramentary, and the same are found in numerous other books. We read:

The deacons go into the sacristy and proceed with the body of the Lord, which has remained from the previous day, but without the consecrated wine, and place it upon the altar[2].

Evidently the reservation in both kinds is no longer allowed, but the custom is clearly known, and was perhaps still the practice in some places.

Giraldus Cambrensis († 1223) in his celebrated *Gemma Ecclesiastica* gives the instructions of the pseudo Clement, adding an exception of the hosts for the dying. We note the generally acknowledged authority of the letter in Britain as elsewhere. He says:

Let not the priest presume to prepare or consecrate more hosts than ought to suffice for the people: but if they remain let them not be reserved until the morrow, except a few for viaticum, but be received with fear by the clergy[3].

The various rules for the renewal of the reserved sacrament are to be traced back ultimately to the letter of the pseudo Clement. This is stated very plainly in an eleventh century codex of the Abbey of St Martial at Limoges. We read:

[1] Bede, *Hist. Eccl.* II. 1, Ed Ang. Sax. and Latin, Cambridge, 1644, p. 107.
[2] Warren, *Leofric Missal*, p 96
[3] Girald. Camb *Gemma Eccles.* I 8, Ed Brewer, vol. II p. 27

IN THE WEST

It is the custom at Limoges because of the precept of Pope Clement with reference to caring for the Lord's body, that not only in the monasteries, but also in all the churches of the primate of Limoges, lest through lapse of time any decay should be discovered in the fragments of the Lord's body, that the body of the Lord should be renewed twelve times in the year, and that the old which is changed should not be consumed except by the clergy[1].

In the thirteenth century statutes of the abbey of St Victor at Paris we find a special direction with regard to the disposal of the remains of the eucharist after the general communion at Easter. We read·

The priors and claustrales ought to observe that at Easter in communicating the people they use caution that what is left over of the sacrament be not reserved more than eight days[2].

It is interesting to see the comment of the canonist Lyndwood in his *Provinciale* (c. 1422) on the directions of the letter of the pseudo Clement, *Tribus enim gradibus*, which he quotes from Gratian, and its bearing on the practice of reservation, universal in his day. He says:

The priest will always have the eucharist ready for the sick (*De consec.* Dist. II. cap. *Presbyter*). Nor does cap. *Tribus* of the same distinction, where it is forbidden to reserve surplus hosts placed on the altar, prevent it: for it is true that they ought not to be reserved for the need of those consecrating, but for the need of the dying[3].

St Thomas Aquinas († 1274) had written to much the same effect, and quoted the same two authorities from Gratian, the letter of the pseudo Clement, and a canon of the council of Worms (Aix-la-Chapelle, in 809[4]?). He explains the epistle not as forbidding all reservation but the

---

[1] Martene, vol. I lib. I. cap v. Art. III. § IX p. 252.
[2] Martene, vol. III. lib IV. App. *Ant. Stat S. Vict.* XII. p. 292
[3] Lib III Tit 25 *De custodia eucharistiae*, cap. *Dignissimum*, verb. *Die dominica*, Ed Oxford, 1679, p 248
[4] *Capit. Reg. Franc.* I p 161, in *Monumenta Germaniae Historica*.

reservation of any chance surplus left over by accident from the communion, an interpretation which we decided was the only one possible in view both of the wording of the letter and contemporary practice. We read:

11. Further truth ought to correspond to the figure. But with regard to the paschal lamb, which was a figure of this sacrament, it is commanded that nothing of it should remain until the morning. It is unfitting therefore that consecrated hosts should be reserved, and not immediately consumed.... To the eleventh objection we reply that the truth ought to correspond to the figure so far as this, namely that no part of a consecrated host from which the priest and ministers, or even the people communicate, ought to be reserved until the morrow. Wherefore we find (*De consec.* Dist. II. cap. *Tribus gradibus*) Pope Clement I at the beginning of his second epistle decreed that "so many hosts be offered on the altar as ought to suffice for the people, but if any remain let them not be reserved until the morrow." Yet because this sacrament has to be consumed daily, but the paschal lamb was not consumed daily, so it is necessary to reserve other consecrated hosts for the sick. Wherefore in the same distinction cap. 93 we read, "Let the priest have the eucharist always ready so that when anyone is sick he may communicate him immediately, lest he die without communion[1]."

The old practice of burning or burying the remains of the eucharist survived, according to the Penitentials, whenever the sacramental species was marred by neglect of any kind, or decayed. In the Rule of St Columban (*c.* 600) we read:

Let him who has shown negligence towards the sacrifice so that a worm is found in it, even though it be whole, burn it in fire near the altar and put away the ashes underneath the altar, and himself do penance forty days[2].

[1] *Summa*, Pars III. Quaes LXXXIII. *De ritu eucharistiae*, Art. v. *P L* IV (Second Series), col 844, 848
[2] *P L* LXXX col 222.

In the Penitential of Theodore (668–690) we read:

Every sacrifice which has become corrupt through the foulness of age must be burned in fire[1].

In the Penitential of Egbert (735–766) we read.

Let him who has neglected the sacrifice so that there are worms in it, and it has lost its colour and taste, do penance for twenty, thirty or forty days, and let it be burned in fire, and its ashes put away under the altar[2].

We might quote likewise from many other penitentials containing similar rules for dealing with the sacrament in various contingencies. Like provision is made, we may note, in the penitentials ascribed to Gregory III (731–741), the Venerable Bede († 735), Halitgar, Bishop of Cambrai (817–831), Robert of St Victor, in the Canons under Edgar († 975), and in codices belonging to the monasteries of Bobbio and Rheinau, the Colbertine Collection at Paris and the library of St Vito of Verdun[3]. Such directions for burning the remains of the eucharistic species in certain cases appear in the mediaeval missals, as those of Salisbury and York, and they are still found in the modern Roman missal in the preliminary rubrics.

Our examination of the evidence has shown that throughout the West, and also in England, in the early days, and apparently up to the eleventh century in some places, in accordance with the directions contained in the letter of the pseudo Clement the remains of the consecrated elements, whether for reservation or not, were taken to the sacristy to be disposed of, and on ordinary days were consumed there, usually by the priests or other ministers, but sometimes by boys. The consumption so

---

[1] Haddan and Stubbs, *Councils and Ecclesiastical Documents*, vol. III. p. 187.

[2] Haddan and Stubbs, vol III. p. 427.

[3] Martene, vol. I. lib. I cap v. Art. v. pp 255–7. Thorpe, *Ancient Laws and Institutes of England*, II. p 252 Gerbert, *Mon. Vet. Lit. Alemann.* vol. II. p. 23.

long as it took place in the sacristy could hardly be otherwise than after the conclusion of mass, and according to the original meaning of the letter of the pseudo Clement not till the next day. The decrees of the councils of Tours and Rodomum seem to suggest that in the ninth century the consumption of the remains took place in the church, but this may not be intended: and the ordination address to the subdeacon appears to assume the continuance of the ancient custom. The probability is that, contrary to the common custom of the East, the hosts were not taken away to the sacristy until the service was completely over, and this must have been the case when a priest celebrated without assistant ministers, but at present we have had no direct evidence. We shall consider the point later in connection with the portion of the priest's host put down on the altar till the end of mass.

CHAPTER IV

THE SANCTA

IT will be of value for our enquiry into the early method of dealing with the remains of the consecrated elements after communion in the West to consider the exact significance of the term "Sancta," and the ceremonies connected with it, and then what we can learn on a kindred subject, the portion of the priest's host which, according to the custom of the Roman church and elsewhere, was put down on the altar after the fraction to remain there till the end of mass.

In the First Roman *Ordo* (c. 770) of Mabillon, according to the Colbertine manuscript, we read:

But before they come to the altar the deacons put off their planets[1] in the presbytery, and the district subdeacon receives them, and gives them to the acolytes of the district to which the deacons belong, and then two acolytes holding the pyxes with the Sancta uncovered, and a subdeacon following after them, holding his hand on the mouth of a pyx, shows the Sancta to the pontiff or the deacon who precedes him. Then the pontiff or deacon with bowed head salutes the Sancta, and looks to see if there be more than is necessary, that he may order it to be placed in the conditorium[2,3].

Later on we read

When he says, *Pax Domini sit semper vobiscum*, let him drop of the Sancta into the chalice[4].

And again we read:

And when he (the pontiff) has communicated let him put of that Sancta which he has bitten into the chalice in the hands

[1] I e chasubles
[2] Perhaps an aumbry, or cupboard
[3] Mabillon, *Mus. Ital.* vol. II p. 8.
[4] Mabillon, vol. II. p 13.

of the archdeacon, saying *Fiat commixtio*; and he is confirmed by the archdeacon[1,2].

From these extracts we gather that the word "Sancta" is a name for the consecrated elements in general, and its use is by no means limited to the particle which is employed for what is sometimes called "the ceremony of the Sancta"; and it is the same in the slightly differing texts of other *Ordines*. The term is used for the whole of the reserved sacramental species which is brought in by the acolytes, and this must have been a considerable quantity, as more than one pyx is mentioned, for that put aside in the conditorium as well as for that placed on the altar, and also for the newly consecrated host from which the pope makes his communion.

We may illustrate this general use of the word for the sacramental elements. The singular form, "Sanctum," is used by Tertullian[3] and also by Cyprian[4], while the Greek form $\tau\grave{o}$ $\ddot{a}\gamma\iota o\nu$ is suggested by the use of Matt. vii. 6, of the eucharist in the *Didache*[5]. In an ancient missal of the church of Angers we find the words "Sanctum cum sanctis" used at the commixture, and in another "Sancta cum sanctis," the latter being found also in a Rheims missal of 1491[6]. These are presumably in imitation of the Mozarabic "Sancta sanctis" at the same point, which is a Western equivalent of $\tau\grave{a}$ $\ddot{a}\gamma\iota a$ $\tau o\hat{\iota}\varsigma$ $\dot{a}\gamma\acute{\iota}o\iota\varsigma$ in the Eastern liturgies. Whatever may have been the original intention of this formula it is clear that the first of the times the adjective is used it refers to the Holy Sacrament. As the word "Sancta" appears in the Roman *Ordines* the grammatical construction is uncertain, for we find "cum Sanctis," "mittit Sancta," "de ipsa Sancta" in the First

---

[1] Communicated with the sacrament of the blood
[2] Mabillon, vol II. p 14.
[3] *De Spect.* 25, P L I col 657
[4] *De Lapsis*, 26, P.L. IV. col 486   [5] *Didache*, IX 5
[6] Martene, vol I. lib I cap IV. Art. IX § II p 151.

Ordo according to some texts; but in the Colbertine manuscript the first two run "cum Sancta," "mittit de Sancta[1]."

We must now return to a consideration of the precise significance of what was done with the Sancta during mass. That the sacrament consecrated on a previous occasion was brought to the altar at the celebration of mass appears also from other authorities, and it was in no sense merely a Roman custom. Presumably it was the whole of what was reserved. Gregory of Tours († 594) says:

The passion being read with the other lessons which the priestly rule required, the time for offering the sacrifice drew nigh, and the deacon, having taken the tower in which the mystery of the Lord's body was kept, began to carry it to the door, but when he had entered the temple that he might place it upon the altar it slipped from his hand and was carried into the air and so came to the altar, the hand of the deacon being quite unable to overtake it[2].

A similar account is found in the description of the Gallican mass attributed to Germanus of Paris († 576):

But now the church in sweet tones hymns the body of Christ as it comes to the altar, no longer with trumpets unrestrained but with spiritual voices singing the greatness of Christ. And the body of the Lord is thus brought in towers because the sepulchre of the Lord was hewn in the rock in the form of a tower, and within it was the couch on which the Lord's body rested, and from which He rose in triumph, the King of glory[3].

The word "tower" appears to be the common name for the receptacle for the reserved sacrament, not merely for the vessel in which it was brought to the altar for use at a particular ceremony. We find numerous allusions to it, and there is a form for blessing one in the Gallican Sacrament-

---

[1] Mabillon, vol II pp 8, 13, 14.
[2] *Mirac Lib I de Gloria Martyr.* 86, *P L.* LXXI col. 781.
[3] *De Sono, P.L.* LXXII. col. 92–3.

48 THE SANCTA [CH.

ary[1]. St Remigius of Rheims († 533) in his will required a tower and chalice to be made[2], and St Aridius in the same century four towers and four chalices[3]. Fortunatus sings of a tower as bearing the sacred body of the Lamb[4]. Bishop Lando of Rheims († c. 645) left a golden tower to his cathedral[5]. The life of St Didier of Cahors († 659) joins chalices and towers together in the description of church ornaments[6]. The use of the term persisted into the seventeenth century, or at any rate the vessel for the reservation of the sacrament was sometimes made in this shape at that date, as at the monastery of Marmoutier at Tours, the churches of St Lawrence, Rouen, St Benet, Paris, at Laon, and in Bourges cathedral[7].

According to Roman custom the Sancta brought to the altar before the beginning of mass would seem to have been reserved from a previous papal mass. To grasp the full meaning of the observance it will be necessary to enquire also into the kindred customs in connection with the Fermentum or Leaven, the use of which appears to have been a substitute for the earlier practice of concelebration, and a sign of unity. The earliest clear mention of the Fermentum is to be found in the life of Pope Miltiades (311–314) as given in the *Liber Pontificalis*, and also in similar words in certain ancient catalogues of the Roman bishops, which for the earlier lives are the basis of it:

He caused that the consecrated oblations from that day (Sunday) should be sent throughout the churches from the consecration of the bishop,—which betokens the Fermentum[8].

[1] Neale and Forbes, *Ancient Liturgies of the Gallican Church*, p. 362.
[2] *P.L* LXV. col 971.   [3] *P.L* LXXI col. 1147
[4] *Miscell.* III. Carmen 25, *P.L.* LXXXVIII col 144
[5] *P.L* LXV. col 971.
[6] Krusch, *Mon. Germ. Hist* , *Vitae* IV. *Vita* 15, p. 576.
[7] Martene, vol I. lib. I. cap. v Art III § VI p. 252 Thiers, *Traité de l'Exposition du St. Sacrement de l'Autel*, 1677, pp 39–42 Cf Freestone, *Sacrament Reserved*, p 218, also for references above
[8] Duchesne, *Lib Pont* vol I p 168 Cf p 74, and *Acta Sanctorum*, April, vol I p xxix.

THE SANCTA

Later in the same century Siricius (384–399), so the same authorities assert, made it a necessary condition to receive the Fermentum before a priest could celebrate at all. We read:

Siricius...ordered that no presbyter should celebrate mass throughout the whole week unless he should receive the element consecrated by the bishop of the appointed place, a token which is called the Fermentum[1].

The well-known letter to Decentius, Bishop of Gubbio, attributed to Innocent I (401–417) likewise speaks of a weekly distribution of the Fermentum. He says:

But about the Fermentum, which on the Lord's day we send to all the titular churches, you wished to consult us unnecessarily, since all your churches are situated within the city, and the presbyters of these, because on that day on account of the people entrusted to them, they cannot assemble with us, for that reason receive the Fermentum consecrated by us at the hands of acolytes, that especially on that day they may not judge themselves separated from our communion: but I do not think it ought to be done in the country districts, because the sacraments must not be carried far, nor do we intend it for the presbyters appointed to the different cemeteries, for they have the right and licence to consecrate them[2].

The use of the Fermentum was not limited to the station masses, for no mass could be said without it throughout the week, and it was the sign of the Pope's permission to celebrate. In the ancient gloss on the letter to Decentius found in a codex in the library of St Emmeram at Ratisbon, the Fermentum was only distributed five times in the year, but no mass might be said by a priest in the station churches without it. It runs:

With regard to what is called the Fermentum it is the custom among the Romans that from the mass which is sung on

[1] Duchesne, I. p. 216 Cf p. 86 and *Acta Sanct.* April, vol. I. p. xxxii.
[2] *P L.* xx col 556–7

Maundy Thursday, Holy Saturday, Easter Day, Pentecost and the Nativity of our Lord there should be reserved (of the Sancta) throughout the whole year, and wherever in the stations the pope himself is not present at the mass, it is put into the chalice from that mass when he says *Pax Domini*. And this is called the Fermentum. And on Holy Saturday no priest in the baptismal churches communicates anybody until he has put into the chalice of that Sancta which the pope has offered[1].

We note that the Fermentum is taken from the Sancta, the common name for the eucharistic elements, consecrated by the pope on the five occasions. A description of the ceremony is to be found in the First *Ordo*, though it is not stated that the Fermentum is taken from the Sancta:

When *Pax Domini* ought to be said a particle of the Fermentum which was consecrated by the Apostolicus is brought by the subdeacon oblationer and given to the archdeacon, and he offers it to the bishop, and he makes the sign of the cross with it thrice, and saying *Pax Domini* puts it into the chalice.... The like is done also by a presbyter when he says mass in a station....Bishops who preside over cities do all things exactly as the chief pontiff[2].

In the Gallicanized *Ordo* of St Amand the word Fermentum is not used, but simply the more general term Sancta. There is a full description of the observance on Easter Eve:

On that night none of the presbyter cardinals stand there, but each says mass at his own title, and has leave to sit on the throne and say *Gloria in excelsis*. And each presbyter sends a mansionary[3] from his title to the church of the Saviour, and they wait there until the Sancta is broken, having corporals with them. And the subdeacon oblationer comes and gives to

---

[1] Mabillon, *Iter German. Descript.* pp. 65–66. Cf. Mabillon, vol. II pp. xxxviii, xxxix.
[2] Mabillon, vol. II. pp. 16–7.
[3] Sacristan or sexton, a minor church official

them of the Sancta which the pontiff has consecrated, and they receive it in the corporals and each returns to his title, and gives the Sancta to the priest. And with it he makes a cross over the chalice, and puts it in it, and says, *Dominus vobiscum*, and all communicate[1].

In the description of mass as said by a bishop or priest on an ordinary day the *Ordo* of St Amand tells us how the Fermentum, which here too is called simply the Sancta, was used. We read·

And when he says *Pax Domini* the subdeacon holds in a corporal at the corner of the altar some of the Sancta which the pontiff has consecrated, and the deacon takes it and gives it to the bishop or priest, and then making a cross over the chalice he says *Pax Domini*[2].

The Fermentum was reserved from the mass of Maundy Thursday, but as there was no celebration of the eucharist from that time until Easter Eve, when it was again distributed, the majority of it would be used to add to the stock of the Sancta, from which communion was given on Good Friday, only part of what was distributed on Maundy Thursday being used on that day, the rest being reserved as on other occasions. According to the Einsiedeln *Ordo* the communion on Good Friday is the reason for the distribution of the Sancta on Maundy Thursday:

And when the whole oblation has been broken the Apostolicus communicates alone. And he likewise blesses the chrism and commands that there be a distribution of it to the titular and other churches, either by the oblationer of the year, or his assistant. Similarly also of the holy sacrifice, which they reserve for the Friday[3].

In the description of the Good Friday ceremonies we read:

[1] Duchesne, *Christian Worship* (Eng. trans), 1904, pp. 470–1
[2] Duchesne, *C.W* p. 464
[3] Duchesne, *C W*. pp. 481–2.

And they go again to the Lateran singing *Beati immaculati*. But the Apostolicus does not communicate there, nor the deacons. And whoever wishes to communicate communicates from the pyxes of the sacrifice which was reserved from Thursday: and anyone who does not wish to communicate there goes to the other churches of Rome, or to the titles, and communicates[1].

Once again, as in the First *Ordo*, we hear of the pyxes (capsae) for the reservation of the sacrament, which presumably was distributed in considerable quantities on Maundy Thursday to the various churches.

The practice described in the Einsiedeln *Ordo* seems to be identical with that with which the ritualist Amalarius of Metz became familiar on his visit to Rome in 832, when he learned that the *Ordo* with which he was acquainted, akin to *Ordines I* and *II* it would seem, was no longer a description of current practice. In *Ordo I* we read at the end of the description of the Maundy Thursday ceremonies:

Having washed his hands the pontiff comes to the altar and all the people communicate in their order, and he reserves of the Sancta for the morrow[2].

Misled by some such order as this Amalarius had written:

The heavenly bread, that is, the body of the Lord, is reserved from the Thursday until Good Friday....On Good Friday the body of the Lord is not consecrated. It is necessary that those who have a wish to communicate should have the sacrifice from the previous day[3].

When Amalarius arrived in Rome he learned that this was no longer the custom, but that the actual practice was in agreement, not with *Ordo I*, but with what we found in the Einsiedeln *Ordo*. He says:

[1] Duchesne, *C W* p 483 [2] Mabillon, vol II p 21
[3] *De Eccles. Officiis*, lib. I. 12 Hittorp, col 330

THE SANCTA

In the above-mentioned book I found it written that after the salutation of the cross two priests should bring the body of the Lord which was reserved the previous day, and a chalice with wine not consecrated that it may be consecrated then, and the people communicate from it. Concerning which statement I asked the Roman archdeacon and he replied, "In that station where the Apostolicus salutes the cross nobody communicates[1]."

We may note that the pseudo Alcuin in his comments on the matter, evidently based on the words of Amalarius, plainly identifies the Sancta with "the body of the Lord." He says:

With reference to the same day (Maundy Thursday) we read in the *Ordines* that there should be reserved of the body of the Lord for communion on the morrow....And because on Good Friday the body of the Lord is not consecrated it is necessary that those who have a wish to communicate should have the sacrifice from the previous day; yet the Romans do not do this[2].

The *Ordo* of St Amand describes a practice similar to that of the Einsiedeln *Ordo* except that the Sancta remains on the altar until the end of the service. We read in the account of Maundy Thursday:

Mass being finished, the deacon says, *Ite missa est*. And the Sancta are reserved until the morrow[3].

Yet there is no communion at the station, but only at the titular churches. After the solemn prayers we read:

Then the presbyters return to their titles, and at the ninth hour they repeat the lessons and responsories, the gospel and also the solemn prayers, and adore the cross, and all communicate[4].

It seems plain from the evidence that the term Sancta was used of the Holy Sacrament generally, though at

---
[1] *De Eccles Officiis*, lib 1 15 Hittorp, col 340
[2] *De Divinis Officiis* Hittorp, col. 249.
[3] Duchesne, *C W* p 467. [4] Duchesne, *C W*. p. 468.

Rome the word is not found apparently except for what is consecrated by the pope, and the Sancta of which we hear is the sacrament which had been distributed to the titular churches from a papal mass. The Sancta brought to the pope on his approach to the altar at the stational church, part being put into the chalice at *Pax Domini*, does not really differ from what on other occasions was called the Fermentum, which was used in exactly the same manner when another celebrated, both alike being part of the sacred elements which had been consecrated by the pope, and were reserved in the different churches of Rome for use at the various masses held there throughout the year, whether the pope or another was celebrant, and on Good Friday for the communion of the faithful.

In the later Gallican Appendix to the First *Ordo* (ninth century?), as in the *Ordo* itself, the word Sancta is used of the consecrated hosts generally, and quite apart from any particular ceremony of putting it into the chalice. In the description of the Maundy Thursday service, much as in the *Ordo* itself, we read:

> Mass being finished, they communicate in the appointed order, and they reserve of the Sancta for the morrow according to custom[1].

The order for Good Friday is an elaboration of what we noticed in the Gelasian Sacramentary, and is the same both in *Ordo I* and in the Appendix to it; the Sancta is evidently the whole of the reserved sacrament. We read:

> The two former priests as soon as they have saluted (the pontiff) enter the sacristy, or wherever the body of the Lord which remained from the previous day had been placed, and put it on a paten; and let one subdeacon hold before them a chalice with wine not consecrated and another a paten with the body of the Lord; and one priest takes the paten and another the chalice which they are holding, and they put them

---

[1] Mabillon, vol II. p 32.

down on the bare altar....The pontiff descends to the altar and says, *Oremus. Praeceptis salutaribus*....When they have said *Amen* he takes of the Sancta and puts it into the chalice, saying nothing, and all communicate in silence[1].

We may note other passages from the *Ordo* of St Amand illustrating the use of the word Sancta:

And when they have made the fraction the archdeacon takes the holy chalice from the subdeacon, and another deacon the paten from the acolyte, and they come before the pontiff. The pontiff takes the Sancta from the paten, bites a piece from the particle, and with it makes a cross over the chalice, saying secretly *Fiat commixtio* and the rest. Then the pontiff is confirmed, the chalice being held by the archdeacon. Then the bishops or priests, take the Sancta from the hand of the pontiff, and go to the left part of the altar, and place their hands with the Sancta on the altar, and so communicate.... Then he (the archdeacon) gives the chalice to the bishop who communicated first, and goes to the pontiff, and receives the Sancta from his hand, and likewise the other deacons. And they go to the right part of the altar and communicate....Then the archdeacon takes the chalice from the bishop, and the subdeacon comes holding the smaller strainer in his hand, and takes out the Sancta from the chalice, and puts it into the former cup from which the archdeacon will communicate the people[2].

And a presbyter receives it from his hand, and makes a cross with the Sancta over the cup and puts it within[3].

On Maundy Thursday we are told:

And he (the pontiff) goes to his throne, and the priests, and deacons also, break the Sancta, and meanwhile *Agnus Dei* is sung. Then the pontiff communicates alone, and the deacon covers both the Sancta and the chalice on the altar with a corporal....And the Sancta are reserved until the morrow[4].

[1] Mabillon, vol II pp 23, 35
[2] Duchesne, *C W* pp 461-2.
[3] Duchesne, *C W* p 463
[4] Duchesne, *C W* pp 466-7.

In *Ordo II*, a Carolingian version of *Ordo I*, we note a change in practice from what is described in the original text, and the Sancta is already on the altar when the pope appears:

And the pontiff passes to the top of the choir, and on the higher step, bowing his head to the altar, first adores the Sancta[1].

The explanation is apparently that the direction has been modified so as to suit the Gallican method of reservation over the altar. Of reservation on or over the altar we have a number of examples in Gallican circles at this period. The Synodical Admonition attributed to Leo IV (847–55), and incorporated in many tenth century documents makes an order to this effect:

Let nothing be placed upon the altar except the chests and relics, or perhaps the four gospels and a pyx, with the body of the Lord for the viaticum of the sick[2].

Regino of Prüm († 915) in visitation articles based on this Admonition mentions it twice:

Enquiry should be made if the pyx is always over the altar with the sacred oblation for the viaticum of the sick[3].

Every priest should have a pyx or vessel meet for so great a sacrament, where the Lord's body may be carefully stored for the viaticum of those who depart from this world...and it should always be over the altar well fastened on account of mice and evil men[4].

The reference seems to be to a vessel standing on the altar, rather than a receptacle over it and separate from it, as an aumbry.

In the *Ecloga* ascribed to Amalarius, really a Gallican *Ordo*, we likewise note the Sancta on or over the altar:

The bishop coming to the altar first adores the Sancta, and afterwards gives the Pax to the priests and deacons....After

---

[1] Mabillon, vol. II. p. 43.   [1] *P.L* cxxxii. col. 456.
[3] *Notitiae*, I. 9, *P L* cxxxii. col. 187.
[4] *Notitiae*, I 70, *P.L.* cxxxii. col. 205–6.

THE SANCTA

the bishop has adored the Sancta he goes to the right of the altar[1].

In *Ordo II* the Sancta is used in a similar manner to what we noticed in *Ordo I* as a link between mass and mass:

(After the pontifical benedictions are finished, as is the custom in these parts) when he says *Pax Domini* he puts some of the Sancta, which had been offered, into the chalice[2].

The words in brackets are found only in certain manuscripts. Their Gallican origin is evident, but they afford valuable testimony to the widespread use of the *Ordo*.

In Mabillon's *Ordo IV*, which is the conclusion of the *Ecloga* of Amalarius[3], we find the Sancta no longer used to link together consecutive masses, but apparently only to join the priest's mass with the pope's, as was the purpose of the Fermentum. We read:

Then he (the pope) says *Pax Domini*. He does not put any of the Sancta into the chalice as is the custom with other priests. When he breaks the host he says *Agnus Dei*, and the fraction being performed, when the Apostolic Lord communicates he bites off a piece for himself and puts the rest into the chalice, making a cross with it thrice over the chalice, saying nothing. And he is confirmed from the chalice which the archdeacon holds[4].

Amalarius comments on the difference of custom with regard to the commixture

I notice that by different people the dropping of the bread into the wine is variously performed, for some first drop of the Sancta into the chalice, and afterwards say *Pax Domini*, while others postpone the putting of it until the Pax is finished and the fraction as well[5].

This difference of practice at an episcopal mass survived in many places even when the custom of using the

[1] Mabillon, vol II. pp. 550-1.
[2] Mabillon, vol II. p 49
[3] Mabillon, vol. II p 560.
[4] Mabillon, vol II p 62
[5] *De Eccles. Officiis*, lib III. 31. Hittorp, col 432

Sancta from a previous mass had died out. We read in the eleventh century mass of Flacius Illyricus, and similarly in various other Gallican documents, as, for example, codices belonging to the church of Verdun, and the monastery of St Gregory at Basle:

> Let not the bishop put part of the obley into the chalice as priests are wont to do, but wait until, the benediction being finished, he ought to communicate, and then taking a piece which he had broken off before, and holding it over the chalice let him drop it in saying *Sacri sanguinis commixtio*[1].

Durandus, Bishop of Mende († 1296), bears witness to the divergence of custom at the pope's mass. He writes in his well-known *Rationale*:

> The chief pontiff does not let the particle of the host drop into the chalice immediately, but after making the sign of the cross thrice puts it down on the paten, and after the kiss of peace goes up to his throne and sits down there. In the sight of all he takes the larger portion of the obley from the paten which the subdeacon had brought from the altar, and dividing it with his teeth, consumes one particle of it, and puts the other into the chalice, and drinks of the blood with a reed[2].

The two different practices clearly arose from the fact that at Rome a portion of the consecrated host was put into the chalice at two points of the service, as we noticed in the directions given in *Ordo I*, the first being a particle of the Sancta reserved from a previous day, and the second a piece of the host from which the pope communicated. Similar directions are repeated in *Ordines II* and *III*. Amalarius noted the double immission prescribed in the Roman *Ordo* he knew, though apparently without realising that on the first occasion the presanctified species was used. Commenting on the place where it

---

[1] Martene, vol I lib I cap iv Art xii Ordo IV. p. 185. Cf. Ordo XV p 213, Ordo XVI p 216, etc

[2] Durandus, *Rationale Div Off* lib iv *De Communione Sacerdotis*, f lxxvii.

says that the pope puts the remainder of the host which he has bitten into the chalice, he wrote:

If this is so done in the Roman church it is possible to learn from them what the putting of bread twice into the chalice may mean, for nothing which is done in this service according to the order of the fathers is void of significance[1].

The use of the word Sancta as a general name for the consecrated elements, and particularly for the reserved sacrament, continued for centuries.

In the Common Roman *Ordo* of Hittorp, belonging perhaps to the eleventh century, after the account of the blessing of the oils on Maundy Thursday we read:

Then let the pontiff wash his hands and the deacon go to the altar and uncover the Sancta. And let the pontiff coming to the altar divide the obleys for the fraction, and let all the people communicate in order[2].

In the description of the Good Friday ceremonies we are told after the embolismus at the conclusion of the Lord's prayer:

And when they have said *Amen* he takes some of the Sancta, and puts it into the chalice, saying nothing[3].

In the pontificals of Egbert of York († 766), and Tirpinus, Archbishop of Rheims, which survive in early tenth century manuscripts, we have a reference to a use of the Sancta similar to that at Rome. We read·

On Maundy Thursday mass is celebrated at the Lateran at the sixth hour. The pontiff begins by saying *Oremus* and *Deus a quo*. Then the Sancta are placed on the altar[4].

In St Gall MS. No. 1394, which is an Irish fragment of the eighth or ninth century, we read:

Holding the Sancta in his hands he signs the chalice with

---

[1] *De Eccles Officiis*, lib III. 31 Hittorp, col. 433
[2] Hittorp, col 67   [3] Hittorp, col. 75
[4] Martene, vol III. lib IV cap. xxii p 101.

the cross and then the Pax is given. And the priest says *Pax et caritas Domini*, and drops the Sancta into the chalice, and the people give the Pax one to another and communicate[1].

The Sancta is here evidently the newly consecrated host, not part of the sacrament reserved from a previous occasion.

The directions given in a tenth century *Ordo* of the monastery of Corbie about what is to be done on Maundy Thursday are particularly noticeable, and we shall have to refer to them again. We read:

But when the priest has broken the Sancta let him put one portion into the chalice, and communicate from another, but the third let him put down on the altar. And let him be confirmed by the deacon from the chalice, but only on this day. After he has confirmed the priest let the deacon place the chalice on the altar, and let him take the larger paten and put on it whole hosts of the Sancta and place it on the left side near the chalice[2].

On Good Friday the directions are almost the same as those of Hittorp's Common Roman *Ordo*, the fact that the two *Ordines* have a common source coming out more clearly here than in the account of the Maundy Thursday service. We read:

When they have said *Amen*, let him take of the Sancta and put it into the chalice saying nothing, and all communicate in silence[3].

In the twelfth century customs of the abbey of St Benignus at Dijon we read similarly on Good Friday:

The priest follows and says with a loud voice *Praeceptis salutaribus* with the Lord's Prayer, and the collect following, *Libera nos*. And when he has said, *Per omnia saecula saeculorum*, he takes of the Sancta and puts it into the chalice....Then the

---

[1] Warren, *The Liturgy and Ritual of the Celtic Church*, p 177.
[2] Martene, vol IV. lib III cap xiii § xliii p 128
[3] Martene, vol. IV. lib. III. cap. XIV § xlii. p. 139.

priest communicates first from the Sancta and afterwards distributes to all in order[1].

A tenth or eleventh century *Ordo* from the Imperial Library of Vienna after the blessing of the oils reads as in the Common Roman *Ordo*:

Then let the pontiff wash his hands, and the deacons go to the altar and uncover the Sancta.

At the end of the service there is the usual direction:

And they reserve of the Sancta until the morrow[2].

In a twelfth century missal of the bishop of Riva, and in a fourteenth century pontifical of Arles, we get almost identical directions:

Then let the priest or bishop communicate alone, and the deacon covers the Sancta on the altar with a linen cloth.... Afterwards let the priest wash his hands and the deacon go to the altar and uncover the Sancta: and let the priest come to the altar and divide the obleys for the fraction, and let all the people communicate in order[3].

Similar words are found in many descriptions of the Maundy Thursday service. At Beauvais in the eleventh century, at Besançon, and the monastery of St Germanus in the twelfth, and in the *Ordo* of Bishop Fulco of Angers in the fourteenth, we find "Let the deacons go to the altar and uncover the Sancta[4]."

The order of the Roman *Ordines*, "Let the Sancta be reserved until the morrow," appears in a tenth century pontifical of Sens[5], and a twelfth century *Ordo* from the Imperial Library of Vienna[6], and elsewhere.

---

[1] Martene, vol. IV pp. 139-40.
[2] Gerbert, *Monumenta Vet. Lit. Alem.* vol. II. pp. 78, 80.
[3] Mabillon, vol. II. p. lxx. Cf. Martene, vol. III. lib. IV. cap. xxii. p. 117.
[4] Martene, vol. III. lib. IV cap xxii. pp. 112, 110, 115, 92
[5] Martene, vol. III lib. IV. cap xxii p 88
[6] Gerbert, vol. II. pp. 200-1.

The use of the term "Sancta" as the common designation of the consecrated elements, whether reserved or not, is thus very widespread and persistent; and other examples might be quoted. It is by no means limited to Rome. In particular the common explanation, which limits it to the portion of a host consecrated on a previous occasion and put into the chalice at the words *Pax Domini* when the pope celebrated at a station mass, appears to be entirely without foundation.

CHAPTER V

THE PORTION OF THE HOST LEFT ON THE ALTAR

THE portion of the host broken by the celebrant and laid down on the altar till the end of mass appears to have been closely connected with the Sancta. In *Ordo I* according to the St Gall manuscript we read:

Then the pontiff breaks the obley on the right side, and the particle which he breaks off he leaves upon the altar; but the rest of his own oblations he puts on the paten which the deacon holds, and returns to his throne....And the altar being emptied of the oblations, save for the particle which the pontiff left upon the altar from his own oblation which he broke (because they so keep the rule that while the solemnities of mass are being performed the altar should not be without the sacrifice), the archdeacon looks to the choir and nods to them to say *Agnus Dei*[1].

In the Colbertine manuscript the whole section "save for the particle...the sacrifice" is omitted. The note is thus probably a Gallican addition, but the practice described, being found in all the recensions of the *Ordo*, is certainly Roman.

There is no definite statement on the subject, but it would seem that the portion of the host which remained on the altar till the end of mass was reserved until another day, and was added to the stock of the Sancta, taking the place apparently of what was used at the commixture by the pope.

In *Ordo II* the directions are much cut down:

Then the pontiff breaks the obley on the right side, and the particle which he breaks off, he leaves upon the altar, but the

[1] Mabillon, II. pp. 13, 14.

rest of his oblations he puts on the paten which the deacon holds, and returns to his throne....And the altar being emptied of the oblations, the archdeacon looks to the choir and nods to them to say *Agnus Dei*[1].

In *Ordo III* the directions are practically the same and the host is called the Sancta. We read:

Then the pontiff breaks the obley on the right side, and the particle of that Sancta which he has broken he leaves on the altar[2].

In *Ordo IV* there is no need to leave a particle on the altar till the end of mass, for in accordance with Gallican custom the Sancta is reserved on or over the altar, and the host is broken into two pieces instead of three, one being consumed by the celebrant and the other put into the chalice. As the reserved host is not used for the commixture there is no need to replenish the stock of the Sancta.

In *Ordo V* likewise the host is broken into two pieces only, but the celebrant consumes neither. The part laid upon the altar is distinctly separated from what is to be used for the communion, and presumably it is left untouched until the end of the mass. We read:

Let the bishop divide between them (two patens brought by the deacon) the sacred body which has been consecrated, and let him break one of the obleys, and from it put one particle on the corporal, and the other into the chalice when he says *Pax Domini*[3].

The usual custom was for the host to be divided into three portions, as it still is, and a mystical reason for it, ascribed to Pope Sergius († 701) by Ivo of Chartres († 1115) and Gratian († 1151) is frequently quoted. We read:

Threefold is the body of the Lord. The portion of the obley which is put into the chalice shows the body of Christ which

---
[1] Mabillon, vol II pp 49, 50   [2] Mabillon, vol II. p. 59
[3] Mabillon, vol II. p. 68

has already risen, the portion eaten Christ walking still upon the earth, the portion remaining on the altar until the end of mass His body lying in the grave, because the bodies of the saints will be in their graves until the end of the world[1].

Amalarius in describing the fraction uses an *Ordo* akin, as we have seen, to the First Roman *Ordo* for the basis of his exposition, and gives a lengthy explanation of its meaning, also quoting Sergius. We read:

There follows in the aforementioned little book....Then the pontiff breaks the obley on the right side, and the particle which he breaks off he leaves upon the altar, but the rest of the oblations he puts on the paten which the deacon holds[2].

Concerning the portion of the obley which remains on the altar. Threefold is the body of Christ....By the particle of the obley dropped into the chalice is shown the body of Christ which has already risen from the dead, by that eaten by the priest or people, that walking still upon the earth, by that left on the altar, that lying in the graves. The same body brings the obley with it to the grave, and holy church calls it the viaticum of the dying...and that particle remains on the altar until the end of mass because the bodies of the saints will rest in their graves until the end of the world[3].

That the portion of the host left on the altar is reserved is clear, but presumably only for the sick. As we noticed in discussing the Sancta Amalarius appears to know nothing of the ceremony of putting the presanctified host as such into the chalice.

At the synod of Quiercy, held in 838 under Louis the Pious, various opinions of Amalarius were condemned, and in particular the ideas expressed in the exposition of the three parts of the priest's host, which he had borrowed from Sergius. We read·

[1] Ivo Carn *Panormia*, I 140, *P L.* CLXI col 1076. Gratian, *Decretum*, Pars III. *De Consec.* Dist II. c 22, *P L.* CLXXXVII col 1740
[2] *De Eccles Off* lib III. 31 Hittorp, col. 433
[3] Lib III 35. Hittorp, col. 435

And so the aforesaid teacher asserts among other things that the body of Christ is threefold and tripartite, that indeed there are three bodies of Christ...asserting that the one is Christ, another the faithful who are alive, another those who are departed, and that Christ indeed is contained in the particle of the chalice, the living in the fragments on the paten, but the departed in a certain particle on the altar[1].

It is plain from their manner of referring to it that the fathers assembled at Quiercy were not familiar with the practice of leaving a host on the altar until the end of mass, and that it was a Roman custom at that time not yet adopted at any rate in parts of Gaul. The fact that Amalarius was condemned for employing the explanation of Sergius does not appear to have affected its subsequent popularity in Gaul as elsewhere.

Rhabanus Maurus († 856), who claims to describe Roman custom, and quotes a Roman *Ordo*, uses very similar words to Amalarius. We read·

Let the priest break the obley on the right side, one particle being left upon the altar, and the rest of the oblations let him put on a paten which the deacon holds. By the particle of the obley dropped into the chalice he shows the body of Christ which has already risen from the dead, by that eaten by the priest and people, that which still walks with the disciples on the earth after the resurrection, and shows Him alive, by that left on the altar he suggests Him lying in the grave and deserted by His disciples in His passion[2].

The pseudo Alcuin (eleventh century?), quoting Remigius of Auxerre († 908), gives a similar explanation, and evidently the custom of reserving the third portion of the host on the altar till the end of mass still obtains·

Pope Sergius ordered that at the time of the fraction of the Lord's body *Agnus Dei* should be sung by clergy and people. Threefold is the body of Christ....By the particle of the obley

---

[1] Mansi, *Concilia*, vol XIV col 742, 745
[2] Rhabanus Maurus, *De Inst Cler* lib I 33 Hittorp, col 586

put into the chalice is shown the body of Christ which has already risen from the dead, by that eaten by the priest or people that walking still upon the earth, by that left on the altar until the end of mass that lying in the tomb until the end of the world[1].

In his explanation of the duties of the subdeacon, already quoted, the pseudo Alcuin suggests that the disposal of the entire remains of the sacrament, as well as of the third part of the host placed on the altar, was postponed until the end of mass:

The sacrifice being finished he takes up the mysteries of the body and blood of the Lord which were left over, to be gathered up or carried away by the deacon[2].

Though the words used, "peracto sacrificio," might refer to the consecration that explanation is impossible here; they are hardly used of the communion, but might refer to the end of the service, an explanation which agrees well with his interpretation (taken from Remigius of Auxerre) of *Ite missa est*—"Mass is complete, both the oblation on our behalf and the prayer[3]."

A description of the practice of St Adalbert, Bishop of Prague († c. 997), the phraseology of which, as we have seen, is very similar to that of the pseudo Alcuin's explanation of the duties of the subdeacon, can hardly refer to anything before the end of the service. We read:

Whatever was left over of that from which he and the newly baptized had communicated he commanded to be gathered up and he kept it for himself wrapped in a most clean cloth, to carry it away for viaticum[4].

In the tenth century Corbie *Ordo* for Maundy Thursday, which, we noted, was a modification of a Roman *Ordo*, it is quite plain that the sacrament to be reserved for the

---

[1] *De Divinis Officiis* Hittorp, col 277
[2] Hittorp, col 269   See p 37 above
[3] Hittorp, col 295
[4] *P L* cxxxvii col 884   See p 37

morrow remains on the altar until the end of mass. We have already quoted part of the description, but it may be given in full:

When the priest has broken the Sancta let him put one portion into the chalice and communicate from another, but the third let him put down on the altar...and let the deacon take the larger paten and put on it whole hosts of the Sancta, and place it on the left side near the chalice...and let the deacon take from the larger paten as many of the obleys as will suffice to communicate the people....And immediately let that which remains on the altar be covered by the two deacons, each with a clean linen cloth...and after the Post Communion prayer let not the deacon say, *Ite missa est*, but let all things be finished with that prayer. And let those obleys which had remained covered upon the altar be preserved until the morrow according to custom[1].

Though it is not definitely stated, it would seem as if the third part of the host which remained on the altar, as well as the whole hosts, was reserved until the morrow; at any rate nothing is said about its consumption.

In the *Ordo* of St Amand, contrary to the usual rule in the matter, it is plainly stated that some of the hosts are to be reserved. We read at the offertory.

He (the deacon) gives them (the obleys) to the archdeacon and with them he makes three or five rows upon the altar, so much as will suffice for the people, and then some remain until the morrow according to the requirement of the canon[2].

After the consecration we are told.

When the pontiff has said *Pax Domini* the subdeacon takes the paten from the acolyte, and gives it to the archdeacon, and he holds it at the right hand of the pontiff, and he breaks one of the obleys which he offers for himself, and puts down the chief part of it upon the altar, and places the whole obley

---

[1] Martene, vol IV lib III cap XIII §§ xliii, xlv p. 128.
[2] Duchesne, *C W.* p 460

v]   THE PORTION LEFT ON THE ALTAR   69

and part of the other on the paten, and the archdeacon returns the paten to the acolyte, and the pontiff goes back to his throne[1].

Nothing is said about what happens to the portion of the obley placed on the altar, but presumably it becomes part of the Sancta reserved until the next day.

When the pope himself celebrates there is no mention of the putting of a piece of the host consecrated on a previous occasion into the chalice, a point we noticed in various Gallicanized *Ordines* of later date, but when a bishop or priest celebrates in his stead a particle of the Sancta consecrated by the pope is put into the chalice at *Pax Domini*. The conclusion that the portion of the host placed on the altar is reserved and added to the Sancta when the pope celebrates seems to receive confirmation from the direction, given below, that when another celebrates it is to be used for the communion of two of the bishops, for then of course it would be impossible to use it to replenish the stock of the Sancta, since this is limited to what is consecrated by the pope himself. After the division of the rest of the obleys for the fraction, we read

Then the bishop returns to the altar to break the portion of the obley which remained, and when they have performed the fraction the deacon announces the station, as is the custom. And both bishops and priests come to communicate before the altar, and the bishop gives two of the particles to the first of the bishops into his hand, and he who receives them returns one of them to him, and he holds the particle in his right hand until they communicate, as above, and then he places his hands upon the altar, and communicates himself, who has said the mass[2].

In the explanation of the order of the mass given by Bernold of Constance († 1100) in the *Micrologus*, and based on Roman and Gallican *Ordines*, the reasons given for the

[1] Duchesne, *C W*. p 461   [2] Duchesne, *C.W.* pp. 464-5.

threefold division of the host have been modified, and the third portion is used for the communion when not required for the sick, and only in that case does it remain on the altar till the end of mass. There is no putting of a particle of a presanctified host into the chalice, and there is not necessarily anything reserved. We read:

But when he says *Per Dominum nostrum* he breaks the host on the right side according to the *Ordo* to show the piercing of the Lord's side. Then he breaks the greater portion into two that he may be able to deal with three parts of the Lord's body, for one he ought to put into the chalice, making a cross, when he says *Pax Domini*, to show the union of body and soul in the resurrection of Christ; the second indeed the priest himself of necessity consumes before partaking of the chalice according to the Lord's institution, but the third he of necessity puts down for those about to communicate, or for the sick. Nor is this in any way without real symbolical significance. For in a threefold manner is the Lord's body understood.... The third, that which now rests in Christ, is also aptly figured by the third particle reserved on the altar, which we are accustomed to call the viaticum of the dying[1].

John of Avranches (*c.* 1065) describes a similar practice, and again it is the third portion of the broken host, not a whole host, which is reserved on the altar, when required, for the sick. We read

Let the deacon offer the paten to the priest, and on it let the priest divide the body of the Lord into three parts. Putting one of the parts into the chalice let the priest say with a loud voice *Pax Domini*, and immediately add in secret *Fiat commixtio*. With another let him communicate himself, the deacon and subdeacon. The third, the viaticum, if there be need, let him reserve on the paten until the end of mass...The third, which remains on the altar, holy church calls the viaticum of the dying, that it may be shown that they ought not to be considered dying who die in Christ, but sleeping until they

[1] *De Eccles. Observ.* 17. Hittorp, col. 741.

are brought by such and so mighty a Leader to eternal life; but if there be no need, let the priest or one of the ministers receive the third part[1].

According to the *Gemma Animae*, ascribed to Honorius of Autun (*c.* 1123), the third part is usually given to the subdeacon, and it is only reserved for the sick on occasion. The reservation has now become quite formal in a pyx, not merely the leaving of the particle on the altar till the end of mass. We read:

The bishop breaks the obley because the Lord broke the bread for the disciples at Emmaus. He divides the obley into three parts, and retaining one for himself gives two to the deacon and subdeacon, because the Lord after breaking the bread apportioned one part to Himself, and two to Cleopas and Luke[2].

Concerning the three parts of the obley. The obley is not consumed whole, but is divided into three; one is put into the chalice, another is consumed by the priest, the third is placed in a pyx as the viaticum for the dying, because the body of Christ is threefold....The piece left on the altar is the body of the Lord resting in the tomb, that is, the church dead in Christ, but about to rise again through union with the body of Christ[3].

Peter Lombard († 1164) and Innocent III († 1180) both quote the words of Sergius with regard to the three parts of the obley[4], but say nothing which gives any information whether the practice of leaving the third part on the altar until the end of mass was still in use.

Hugh of St Victor († 1141) likewise gives the exposition of Sergius, as an alternative explanation of the three portions of the broken host, and his words imply that the

[1] *De Offic Eccles.*, *P L* CXLVIII col 36–7
[2] *De Ant Ritu Miss.* lib I. 63. Hittorp, col 1197–8.
[3] Lib I 64, col 1198.
[4] *Sententiae*, Lib IV Dist XII 6, *P L.* I. (Second Series) col. 356. *De Sacro Altaris Mysterio*, lib VI. c. 3, *P L* CCXVII. col 907.

practice with regard to the third was not yet obsolete. We read.

Yet Pope Sergius speaks otherwise on these points, for he wishes the union of the body and soul of Christ made in the resurrection to be signified by the commixture of the body and blood, for he says, The piece of the obley put into the chalice shows the body of Christ which has already risen, the piece eaten that walking on the earth, the piece put back on the altar until the end of mass, the members of Christ, that is, the bodies of the saints, resting in their graves until the end of the world[1].

By the time of St Thomas Aquinas († 1274) the practice of leaving the third part of the priest's host on the altar until the end of mass has become a thing of the past, though he thinks the interpretation ascribed to Sergius as still of value. We read.

To the eighth objection we reply that, as Pope Sergius says, (and it is found *De Consec.* Dist. II. cap. 22), Threefold is the body of the Lord...the portion remaining on the altar until the end of mass is the body lying in the grave, because the bodies of the saints will be in their graves until the end of the world—though their souls are in either purgatory or heaven. Though this rite is not now observed, namely that one portion should be reserved until the end of mass, because of the danger, yet the significance of the portions remains the same, which indeed they have expressed in metre saying, "The host is divided into parts; that which is soaked denotes the fully blessed, that which is dry the living, that which is reserved those who are buried[2]."

Evidently Aquinas does not realise the connection, which comes out quite clearly in the *Gemma Animae* of Honorius of Autun[3], between the third part of the broken

---

[1] *De Offic Eccles* lib II 39 Hittorp, col. 1409

[2] *Summa Theologica*, Pars III Quaes LXXXIII *De ritu eucharistiae*, Art v, *P L* IV (Second Series), col 847

[3] See p. 71.

host which was put down on the altar till the end of mass and then reserved, and the hosts for reservation which still remain on the altar until the conclusion of the service, or he would not have regarded the custom as entirely obsolete

According to Durandus († 1296) the portion of the host put down on the altar remained there until the end of mass even when, not being required for the sick, it was consumed by the ministers of the altar, and presumably this was the original custom when it was not to be reserved longer, which does not appear to have been always the case, and it agrees exactly with our conclusion about the time of the consumption of the remains of the consecrated elements, that it did not take place until the service was over. Like St Thomas Aquinas he fails to realise that the treatment of the hosts to be reserved is historically a continuation of the practice by which the third part of the priest's host remained on the altar until the end of the liturgy. We read:

According to Pope Sergius...the portion reserved until the end of mass according to the ancient custom of the Roman church for the ministers or the sick signifies all the dead...Pope Sergius says, Threefold is the body of the Lord...the portion remaining on the altar till the end of mass the body of Christ, or according to others, the body of the faithful hidden in the grave. This part remains on the altar till the end of mass because the bodies of the saints will be in their graves until the end of the world. The part however which is reserved until the end of mass is no longer in use[1].

Though at first sight all these accounts seem very similar we can trace out the gradual modification of practice due to the change of ideas. We gather that in the earliest days the remains of the consecrated hosts were not dealt with until the conclusion of the service, and that the presence of the sacrifice on the altar until the end of

[1] *Rationale Div Off* lib IV cap li *De Fractione Hostiae*, f. lxxv

mass was considered so important that one of the pieces of the host broken at the fraction was retained on the altar even during the communion to ensure that some should remain, and it was for this purpose originally that the host was broken into three parts. Afterwards the third portion of the host was reserved and added to the supply of the Sancta, which was thus undiminished by the papal mass, and if necessary could be used for the commixture on another day. Even after the custom of putting a particle of the presanctified host into the chalice was limited to a priest's mass, the host continued to be broken into three, and the third part was reserved on the altar till the end of mass, being apparently consumed by the ministers when not required for the sick. At length, however, the practice lapsed, except when there was special need for reservation, and the third part was used with the rest of the consecrated elements for the communion.

CHAPTER VI

ON MAUNDY THURSDAY

THE earliest clear reference to the reservation of the sacrament on Maundy Thursday in the West is to be found, as we have already noticed, in the Gelasian Sacramentary (c. 700, and later). We read:

They communicate and reserve of this sacrifice until the morrow; and thence let them communicate[1].

On Good Friday the direction runs:

The above written prayers being finished the deacons go into the sacristy. They proceed with the body and blood of the Lord which remained the day before, and place it upon the altar[2].

We are told nothing how or when the consecrated elements were taken into the sacristy for reservation, but as what was reserved was that which had been specially consecrated in excess of the needs of the communion on Maundy Thursday the custom was presumably much the same as on other days. Practically the same words are repeated in various later service books, as the Leofric missal, but the point is still left undecided. In Roman *Ordo I* we read:

All the people communicate in their order, and he reserves of the Sancta until the morrow[3].

In the Gallican Appendix to *Ordo I* we find similar directions, and though no precise moment is mentioned, save that it is after the communion, we learn that a traditional custom is followed:

Mass being finished they communicate in the appointed

---
[1] Wilson, *Gelasian Sacramentary*, p 72
[2] Wilson, p. 77.   [3] Mabillon, vol II p 21

order, and reserve of the Sancta until the morrow according to custom[1].

In the *Ordo* of St Amand we get more definite information about the time, which agrees with what appears to have been the practice on ordinary days. We read·

Mass being finished the deacon says, *Ite missa est*, and the Sancta are reserved until the morrow[2].

The rules of the monastery of Corbie of the tenth century, though more elaborate, are to the same effect as regards the time of reservation. We read:

Let them (the deacons) return to the priest that they may communicate, and the rest in order. And after the Post Communion prayer let not the deacon say, *Ite missa est*, but let all things be finished with that prayer. And let those obleys which had remained covered upon the altar, be preserved until the morrow according to custom[3].

It is interesting to note the development in the manner of reserving the sacrament on Maundy Thursday at Cluny. In the earlier versions of the Constitutions, dating from the first half of the eleventh century, according to different manuscripts we read·

All ought to communicate, even the children, and the levite ought to send so many hosts to mass that some may be reserved for the morrow[4].

All ought to communicate, even the children, and so many hosts ought to be sent to mass that when the brethren are communicated there may remain enough for all to communicate from them on the morrow[5].

The Constitutions of Sigibert give more-details. We read·

So many hosts ought to be offered as will suffice also for communion another day. Let all the brethren communicate,

---

[1] Mabillon, vol II. p 32.   [2] Duchesne, *C W*. p 467
[3] Martene, vol IV lib III cap xiii §§ xliii, xlv. p. 128
[4] Albers, *Consuet Clun Ant* p 18   [5] Albers, p 48

even the children. Let nothing of the blood of the Lord remain in the chalice, but let all be consumed. After mass let the deacon and the secretary and the lay brethren come with candles and thurible, and take the chalice and the paten which has the Lord's body, putting another paten upon it, and wrap it in most clean linen, and put it away upon some altar, or in a most clean coffer, and let there be a light before it all day and all night until matins[1].

Ulrich's version of the Constitutions of Cluny (late eleventh century) gives an identical practice. We read:

Mass being finished, the tablet is struck as a sign for vespers... Meanwhile the Lord's body is put away by the priest behind the altar on a golden paten, and the paten between golden plates, and the plates again between silver tablets which were made for the text of the gospel. And thus it is carried from the altar with candles and very much incense[2].

The Customs of the monastery of St Benignus at Dijon (twelfth century) are based on those of Cluny, and the sacrament is carried away likewise during vespers, but they need not be quoted[3]. Similar directions are to be found in various places at this period. The Carthusian rule (c. 1130) disapproved of such elaborate ceremonial on the occasion, and preferred the simplicity of an ordinary day, the host being reserved as usual at the high altar. We read:

One host of the larger size ought to be consecrated in this mass for Good Friday, and this we wish put back in the usual place at the high altar, and forbid sepulchres to be made for the reserving of it after the manner of the seculars, or other preparations not fitting for our solitude[4].

English custom about the time of putting the sacrament away varied much as in other places. In the Constitutions

---

[1] Albers, *Consuet Sigib Abb* xxx. p 93
[2] Martene, vol IV lib III cap xiii § xlvi p 128
[3] Martene, vol IV lib III. cap xiii § xlvi p 128
[4] *Ordin Cart* c xlix. 6 Cf Martene, vol IV lib III cap. xiii. § xlvii. p. 129

of Lanfranc (c. 1077), akin to those of Cluny and Bec, the sacrament is put away after mass during vespers. We read·

Mass being finished let evening prayer be said on the forms[1]. Meanwhile let the priest go in procession, and when he has come to the altar proceed to the appointed place most fittingly prepared, and there repose the body of the Lord[2].

The directions contained in a pontifical of the latter half of the twelfth century at Magdalen College, Oxford, are obviously based on those of Lanfranc. We read:

And the brethren and those who wished of the people being communicated, and the ampulla of the sacred chrism being adored and kissed, the three deacons already mentioned carry back the same ampullae into the sacristy with devotion, and put them by in a fit place for safety. And let the blood on the same day be entirely consumed. Of the obleys let so many be reserved until the morrow as will be able to suffice for all to communicate. Mass being celebrated, let the bishop, the same procession going before him with which he came to the altar, proceed to the appointed place, and there repose the body of the Lord, the place being censed both before and after the reposing of it[3].

In the pontifical of Bishop Lacy of Exeter († 1455) the description of the procession of the oils is much the same as in that at Magdalen College, and there is clearly a literary connection between the two. With respect to the reposing of the hosts we read:

And let the bishop take for reservation as many whole hosts in the sacrifice of the Lord's body as will suffice for Good Friday. But on this day let the blood be entirely consumed.... The prayers being finished with the antiphon, let the bishop immediately begin the antiphon, *Coenantibus*. The canticle,

---

[1] This is explained more fully in the Customs of St Benignus of Dijon, "The forms being turned over and the brethren stretched out prostrate upon them" Martene, vol IV. lib III. cap. xiii § xlvi p 128
[2] Martene, vol IV lib III cap xiii § xlvi. p 128.
[3] Wilson, *The Pontifical of Magdalen College* (H B S), p 168.

Magnificat. Meanwhile let the altar be censed. And so when these things are done let the bishop turn to the altar, and say to the people, *Dominus vobiscum.* The Post Communion prayer, *Refecti.* And so let the office be finished, the deacon saying, *Ite missa est.* And so let mass and vespers finish together. And let the hosts be put away reverently in a seemly place by the bishop and ministers of the altar clad in their sacred vestments[1].

In the *Ordinale* of Augustinian use, belonging to Holyrood and dating from the middle of the fifteenth century, the text of the description of the Maundy Thursday procession of the sacrament is an elaborated form of that in the Magdalen College pontifical, being akin also to that in the pontifical of Bishop Lacy, though now the hosts are carried away during vespers and before the end of mass. We read·

Let the deacon put so many hosts for consecration as will suffice today and tomorrow for himself and for those of the clergy and faithful people who wish to communicate....And the brethren being communicated and the Communion sung let the prelate begin the antiphon, *Calicem salutaris,* at the altar. And while the vesper psalms are sung in choir let him, saying these psalms with his ministers, place the hosts to be reserved for the morrow on the corporals on which they were consecrated, folding the same corporals over, and placing the corporals folded upon one of the chalices let him give it to the deacon to carry, and let him carry it with great care and let the prelate follow, the same procession going before him with which he came to the altar, and let them proceed to the place properly prepared for this purpose, and there let the same prelate, taking it again from the deacon, carefully and fittingly repose the Lord's body, the place being censed both before and after, and as long as the Lord's body remains there let a light burn continuously. This being completed let him return to the altar. And the psalms being said let him begin the antiphon, *Coenanti-*

---

[1] Barnes, *Liber Pontificalis of Edmund Lacy,* pp 74-5

bus, immediately, and this being finished after *Magnificat* let the priest turn to the people and say, *Dominus vobiscum*, and the prayer *Ad complendum*, and the deacon, *Benedicamus Domino*; and let mass and vespers finish together[1].

In the three earliest known missals of Sarum use, dating from the latter half of the thirteenth century and the beginning of the fourteenth, now in the John Rylands Library at Manchester, the Library of the Arsenal at Paris, and the Library of the University of Bologna, there is no description of the procession or information about the time at which it took place. We read at the offertory only:

Let three hosts be put for consecration by the subdeacon, and of these let two be reserved for the morrow, one to be received by the priest, the other that it may be reposed with the cross in the sepulchre[2].

The same rubric was repeated in the printed Sarum missal[3]. It is found also with but verbal alterations in the rules of the various churches which imitated Sarum use, as in the Exeter *Ordinale* issued by Bishop Grandisson in 1337[4]. It appears likewise in the printed Hereford missal[5]. In the Hereford missal there is also another rubric directing the sacrament to be taken to the place where it is to be reserved during *Magnificat* before the end of mass. We read:

This fifth antiphon being finished, let the antiphon, *Coenantibus*, be begun immediately. The psalm, *Magnificat*. Meanwhile let the bishop put away the hosts to be reserved for the morrow with lights and incense in a proper place set apart for the purpose. The antiphon, *Coenantibus*. The antiphon being repeated after *Magnificat*, let the priest say the prayer with

---

[1] Eeles, *The Holyrood Ordinale*, pp. 105–6.
[2] Legg, *The Sarum Missal*, p 104
[3] Dickinson, *Missale Sarum*, col 303
[4] Dalton, *Ordinale Exon* vol. 1 (H B S.), p 318.
[5] Henderson, *Missale Herford*. p. 87.

ON MAUNDY THURSDAY

Dominus vobiscum and *Oremus* in the accustomed manner. The prayer, *Refecti*. And so let mass and vespers finish together[1].

The Hereford rubrics at this point are almost verbally identical with those of the Sarum missal at various dates, and must be derived from them, but the Sarum books have nothing corresponding to the section, "Meanwhile let the bishop...for the purpose," and so it is evidently a later addition and derived from a different source.

The offertory rubric "Let three hosts...sepulchre" is found also in a York missal of the fifteenth century now at Sidney Sussex College, Cambridge, but this manuscript copies Sarum rules on many points, and the direction is absent from other manuscript York missals, and from the printed editions[2]. There is, however, in all extant York missals, both manuscript and printed from the fourteenth to the sixteenth century, a rubric dealing with the reservation of the sacrament on Maundy Thursday. We read:

And let the adults of the church communicate. Let the blood be entirely consumed. Let there be reserved of the body of the Lord until the morrow, and let it be reverently reposed by the prelate where it is to be reserved. The Communion, *Dominus Jesus*[3].

This rubric, though ordering the sacrament to be removed from the altar before the end of mass, like the corresponding rubric at Hereford, is easily recognised by the phraseology as belonging to an earlier date. On Good Friday the York missal says the bishop takes the chalice containing the sacrament from the armariolum[4], and this name though ultimately Gallican seems to suggest possible Roman influence, being found in this connection in *Ordines XIV* and *XV*. On several other points such as the number and endings of the collects the York missal, both in the printed editions and in some of the manuscripts,

[1] Henderson, pp 89–90 [2] Henderson, *York Missal*, vol I p 97
[3] Henderson, vol I p 98 [4] Henderson, vol I p 107. See pp 84–5.

has since the fourteenth century appealed to a Roman *Ordo* and the custom of the Roman church, quoting the *Micrologus*[1]. Similarly perhaps Roman influence, direct or indirect, may have affected the time for the removal of the sacrament from the altar on Maundy Thursday.

The evolution of this custom at Rome is particularly interesting, and it rose apparently in connection with the distribution of the Fermentum. We noticed in the *Ordo* of St Amand, and similarly in the gloss on the letter of Innocent I to Decentius that the Fermentum was sent away from the pope's mass to the titular and other churches before the end of the service. In the Einsiedeln *Ordo* we found two processions, or at any rate two goings from the altar, on Maundy Thursday during the mass, first that of the oils, and secondly that of the consecrated hosts. It will be useful to repeat the description:

And when the whole oblation has been broken the Apostolicus communicates alone. And he likewise blesses the chrism, and commands that there be a distribution of it to the titular and other churches, either by the oblationer of the year, or his assistant. Similarly also of the holy sacrifice, which they reserve for the Friday[2].

In the Roman *Ordo X* (eleventh century) which deals with the Holy Week ceremonies, and textually is an elaboration of the rules of *Ordo I*, we have a further development. We read·

Afterwards, let the ampullae be carried back in procession, as they were brought in, to the sacristy, or place where they ought to be put, and thence let it (the oil) be distributed to anyone as is fitting and it shall be required. And the pope communicates on his throne those who wish to communicate. Yet let whole obleys of the body of the Lord be reserved for Good Friday, but the blood of the Lord be entirely consumed. The kiss of peace is not given, *Agnus Dei* is said, and the

[1] Henderson, vol I. pp 168–9. Cf. Hittorp, col 735–6
[2] Duchesne, *C.W* pp. 481–2.

Communion, *Dominus Jesus Christus*. But before the pope returns to the altar to finish mass let the junior of the cardinal presbyters carry the body of the Lord, placed in a pyx, to the place prepared, preceded by cross and lights, and with a canopy over. Then the pope returns to the altar and says the prayer, *Refecti vitalibus*, and this being finished the deacon says, *Ite missa est*[1].

The direction about the oils is clearly only another version of that found in the Einsiedeln *Ordo*, while that with regard to the sacrament appears to be evolved from the instructions about the Fermentum, and instead of the departure of the ministers to the titular churches with the Sancta, we have a procession to the place of repose.

In *Ordo XIV*, which is ascribed to James Cajetan, though not entirely his compilation, we find as regards the Holy Week ceremonies an expansion of *Ordo X*, and much of it is incorporated with little alteration. There is, however, no mention of the procession of the sacrament, and the whole section, "But before the pope...and with a canopy over," is omitted[2]. The explanation does not seem to be very difficult. The *Ordo* belongs to the earlier part of the fourteenth century, to the beginning of the period of the exile of the papacy. In the papal chapel or local church there were naturally and of necessity many modifications of customs which were adapted only to the basilicas of Rome, and the method of reservation was also changed. The usual place for the reserved sacrament in the pope's church was now no longer in the sacristy according to the ancient traditional usage of Rome, but at or over the altar in accordance with Gallican custom. The description of the ceremonies on the feast of the Annunciation makes this point quite plain. We read:

The cardinal bishop who served the pope at mass does not put off his vestments since he has to carry the boat with the incense to the pope at the proper time, and to cense the altar

---

[1] Mabillon, vol. II. p. 101. [2] Mabillon, vol. II. p. 357.

and the coffer in which is reserved the body of the Lord, and likewise the pope[1].

The special reservation on Maundy Thursday seems to have been no exception to the rule, and there would thus be less scope for a procession of the sacrament, so that we are simply told that the hosts are to be "reverently reserved."

In *Ordo XV* we find the procession of the sacrament re-introduced. This document is founded on both *Ordines X* and *XIV* for the Holy Week ceremonial, and incorporates large extracts from both, including elements of *Ordo X* which were omitted in *Ordo XIV*. It represents a later development of the ceremonies at Avignon in its earliest draft, but the text which has survived has been modified because of the return of the pope to Rome. Yet the account of the procession of the holy sacrament on Maundy Thursday, as the phraseology shows, is a description of Gallican practice. We read:

And before he washes his hands in the great papal bowls, let the pope himself, or the cardinal bishop who serves him at mass, carry to the armariolum[2] in which it will be reserved till the morrow, the aforementioned chalice with the body of Christ covered with the veil, and the other end of it hanging from his left shoulder, holding the chalice with both hands in the midst, lights, the cross and incense going before in procession with devotion. And when it is put away he genuflects, and censes the body of Christ, and then returns to the altar, and washes his hands according to custom[3].

This account is evidently based on that of *Ordo X*, but the next section gives a modification of the shorter text of *Ordo XIV*. One important change in ceremonial had evidently grown up at Avignon. In *Ordo X* it is the

---

[1] Mabillon, vol II p 352. Cf *Ordo XV*, pp 473–522
[2] The chest, near the high altar in Gallican churches, in which are kept the vessels, etc, for mass
[3] Mabillon, vol II p 483

junior cardinal priest who carries the holy sacrament to the place of repose on Maundy Thursday, and who likewise brings it back on Good Friday. In *Ordo XIV*, though nothing is said about the carrying of the sacrament to the place of repose, it is the same person who brings it back on Good Friday. In *Ordo XV*, however, we find it is the pope himself, or the celebrant, who performs both functions, and there is a note on the date of the change·

Then he (the pope) goes with cross, lights and incense to the armariolum or chest, in which the chalice with the body of Christ was reserved from the previous day. And the same custom has existed from the days of John XXII, Benedict XII, Clement VI, Innocent VI, Urban V, Gregory XI and Urban VI, bishops of Rome, to the present time. And the pope himself goes to the armariolum, or chest, and brings the body of Christ to the altar,...although according to James Cajetan the junior cardinal priest was accustomed to carry the body of Christ to the altar in the olden days[1].

If from motives of reverence the pope himself must bear the sacrament to and from the place of repose on Maundy Thursday and Good Friday with all due honour, we see a reason why after the return to Rome there was a reversion to the more primitive custom which still obtained generally elsewhere, and the hosts to be reserved were retained on the altar until the end of the service, for it would not be considered seemly for the celebrant to leave the altar in procession with a long train of attendants in the middle of mass. We shall consider the documents bearing on this matter later.

The description of the Holy Week ceremonies in the Carmelite *Ordinale* of 1312 is in some points similar to that of *Ordo X*, and on examination there seems to be a literary connection, though it is obscured by modifications and additions of later date. We read.

Thence let the ministers of the altar and the rest of the

[1] Mabillon, vol II. p 493

brethren communicate according to the manner prescribed in rubric xlv. Yet let consecrated hosts be reserved, one for the office to be performed on the morrow, another if there be need for the sick. The Communion, *Dominus Jesus*. The communion being finished let them begin vespers at once....The psalms finished let the deacon take the chalice with the consecrated hosts in it, covered with the paten and a corporal.... *Magnificat* being said, when the deacon begins the antiphon again as before, let him immediately bear away the chalice with the sacrament to the place prepared by the sacrist, candlebearers preceding him, and there with due reverence and a light let it be reserved. But let the deacon immediately return to the altar. The antiphon after *Magnificat* being finished let the prelate turn to the congregation and say, *Dominus vobiscum*, then *Oremus* and the final collect, *Refecti. Dominus vobiscum*. The deacon, *Benedicamus Domino*, or, *Ite missa est*, where the chrism is consecrated[1].

The Customs of Bec (1290–1310) likewise order the procession of the sacrament immediately after the communion and before the end of mass. We read:

When all have communicated the priest and the deacon, the cantor also assisting, wrap up the consecrated hosts in corporals. Then let the priest offer incense, and the deacon, all genuflecting, carry them away with the greatest care to the appointed place, lay brethren going before with candles and a censer. Meanwhile after the communion let the cantor of the week say *Dominus Jesus*. And when the levite has put away the hosts let him offer incense, and so return to the altar. Then let the priest say, *Dominus vobiscum*, and the Post Communion of the mass, and the deacon, *Benedicamus Domino*, as on a festival[2].

The custom of removing the sacrament from the altar before the end of mass immediately after the communion is by no means so prominent a feature in documents

---

[1] Zimmerman, *Ordinaire de l'ordre de Notre Dame du Mont Carmel* (1312), *Bibliothèque Liturgique*, vol XIII pp 164–5

[2] Martene, vol IV lib III. cap XIII § xlvi p 129

describing the ceremonies of Maundy Thursday as the procession of the consecrated oils at this point, and the commoner custom was that by which the sacrament remained on the altar till the end of mass, when the procession to the place of repose followed immediately, or during vespers. The solemn removal of the consecrated hosts after the communion for use on the morrow seems to have been limited chiefly to monastic churches, where as a rule in the absence of the bishop a procession of the oils was impossible. In the various Roman *Ordines* the chrism is an object of great reverence, and Amalarius in explaining it says:

The ampulla with the chrism signifies in a manner the body of the Lord which He took of the Virgin Mary[1].

It was not therefore unnatural, particularly as a procession of the oils was in so many churches impossible, that the procession of the sacrament, which was the true body of the Lord, should take the place of that of the chrism which could only symbolise it, though in origin as we have seen the two were in no sense alternatives. There was also, we may note, a similar substitution in the Palm Sunday procession, where the sacrament came to take the place of the book of the gospels[2], but it cannot be discussed here.

It will be interesting to note the development of the Maundy Thursday procession of the host in the later Roman books. In the first printed missal of 1474 we read:

Today the priest reserves in a proper and convenient place one host consecrated for the following day on which there is no consecration, or also more if it shall be necessary for the sick. But the whole of the blood he consumes. Then the brethren communicate at once, and afterwards mass is finished[3].

[1] *De Eccles Offic* lib 1 12 Hittorp, col 329
[2] Compare Hittorp, col 46 ff, col 246, and Martene, vol. IV. lib. III. cap XII §§ XIII–XV, pp 119–20, for the development of this procession.
[3] Lippe, *Missale Romanum* (H B S), vol 1 p 158.

Nothing is said how or when the host is put away. In the pontifical of 1497, and also in that of 1503, it takes place after the service. We read.

He proceeds in the mass up to the communion of the body and blood inclusively, which the bishop alone receives. And this being done, the deacon puts the consecrated hosts to be reserved for the morrow into a chalice or vessel prepared for the purpose, and reverently places it in the middle of the altar.. The bishop signs the altar when he says the gospel of St John.... And the deacon who has ministered to the bishop at the altar puts away the sacrament consecrated for the morrow in a place arranged suitably for the purpose[1].

The various directions in the book of ceremonies of Patricius and Marcellus, published in 1516, about which we shall have occasion to speak further later on, show great elaboration. When the pope is present but not celebrating we read:

A little before the communion the master of ceremonies brings the chalice before mentioned from the credence to the altar to put away in it the body of the Lord to be reserved. Having made his communion in both kinds the celebrant before he purifies himself reverently puts away the body of the Lord to be reserved in the chalice last prepared, and the deacon covers it with a pall, a paten being placed over it, and a silk veil, and reverently places it in the middle of the altar. Then the celebrant purifies himself in the same place, and reverence being made to the sacrament without mitre, as it were sideways at the epistle corner, standing there with face turned to the people, out of reverence for the sacrament he washes his hands and finishes mass....At the end of mass *Ite missa est* is said. Mass being finished the pope gives the benediction but not the indulgences, and the celebrant signs the altar saying *Initium sancti evangelii*, and goes to the faldstool.... Then the pope descends to the altar, where kneeling down he reverently censes the body of the Lord put away in the chalice

---

[1] ff. clxxi –clxxviii

for the morrow, swinging the thurible thrice. Then having made his reverence he devoutly takes the chalice with the sacrament, and bareheaded carries it under the canopy, which the senior bishops who assist the pope and are waiting outside the screen of the chapel in their copes, carry holding their mitres in their hands. And the procession is in this order.— First the esquires of the pope, the proctors of the orders, the advocates with their secretaries, the chamberlains, the nobles and the orators, the singers of the pope chanting the hymn, *Pange lingua*, the clerks of the closet, the auditors, two acolytes with candlesticks, the subdeacons, one of them in a tunicle while the other, prepared as above, carries the cross; after the cross the abbots, the bishops, the archbishops, the orators, the prelates, the vicechamberlain, if he be a bishop, other assistants of the pope, the cardinal deacons, priests, and bishops, all without mitres, then all the torches, which follow, two acolytes with candlesticks, and two with thuribles censing the sacrament continuously, then the pope in the middle between the two cardinal deacon assistants under a canopy, as we have said, who one on each side lift up and hold the border of the pope's cope. Let the chief layman of the city bear his train. Let the auditor in charge of the mitre in the middle between two private chamberlains, the protonotaries and others without vestments, follow the pope. When the pope is at the place where the sacrament is to be reposed the cardinal who has celebrated, or the deacon assistant on the right of the pope, takes it from the hands of the pope, and reposes it in the coffer, and the pope retiring a little after making a reverence puts incense into the censer, the cardinal priest ministering it, and censes the sacrament again as before. Then the sacrist closes the coffer, and gives the key to the cardinal who will celebrate on the morrow[1].

When the pope himself celebrates we are told·

He puts away the body of Christ to be reserved for the morrow into the chalice prepared before he washes his fingers.

[1] *Sac. Caer sive Rit Ercles S Rom Eccles* lib. II. c xliv Ed Catalani, vol. II pp. 169–73

In olden times it was carried at once to the sacristy, which is near the altar of the blessed Peter, by the deacon or by the cardinal bishop assistant. But according to the decree of Sixtus it can be carried by the pope at the end of mass, all going in procession with candles as above; and when the sacrament is reposed and the candles extinguished they will go in the accustomed manner to read the processes[1, 2].

Of this decree of Pope Sixtus IV († 1484) Patricius and Marcellus speak more particularly elsewhere:

It is to be noted that before Pope Sixtus the processes were accustomed to be read and the solemn benediction given as a rule before mass. Then mass was said and the sacrament was carried after the communion to the coffer for the morrow by the deacon according to the common rubric and sometimes by the celebrant, the ministers of the altar only accompanying him with lights, and when they returned mass was finished, and at the end, if the processes had not been read, the pontiff set out thither in procession with all the ranks of the court and they were read, and at the end the Mandatum was performed, as has been said. But Sixtus before-mentioned, considering that our Saviour cannot be venerated with worthy enough praise, for this reason ordained the method aforesaid[3].

When the pope is absent the procession of the sacrament still takes place after the communion. We read:

If the pope is not present at the office of the Thursday all things being ready for the celebration of mass and the reservation of the sacrament for the morrow, as we have said above, the cardinal who is about to celebrate takes his vestments at the proper time and performs mass with the accustomed ceremonies until he has made his communion. Then before he purifies himself he puts away the sacrament to be reserved in the chalice, censes it and carries it in procession to the place prepared in this order.—The esquires of the cardinals, and if they are present of the pope, the advocates, the secretaries,

[1] I e the excommunications read out on certain days
[2] c. xlvii Catalani, p 188
[3] c xlvi § 3, Catalani, pp. 186-7.

the chamberlains go first, then the acolytes, the clerks of the closet, the auditors, the apostolic subdeacons, the nobles, the orators, the singers chanting *Pange lingua*, the chaplains of the celebrant with torches, the master of ceremonies with the thurible, or two masters of ceremonies with two thuribles, censing the sacrament continuously, then the celebrant without a canopy in the middle between the deacon and subdeacon, and following after him without vestments the cardinal bishops, priests, and deacons, and the prelates in their copes, and other officials. But if being prepared they wish to go in solemn procession the order described above when the sacrament is carried by the pope should be observed, except that the subdeacon of the chapel should carry the cross, and his own ministers should minister to the cardinal, and not the officials of the pope. The sacrament being reposed they return in the same manner to the altar, and mass is finished, and the benediction given, and the indulgences proclaimed if the pope does not make a process[1].

The directions of the book of ceremonies for cardinals and bishops drawn up by Paris de Grassis († 1528), but not published till 1564, require the procession of the sacrament always to be held after mass. We read.

The celebrant, his communion made in both kinds, before he purifies himself puts away the sacrament within the bowl of the chalice last brought, and not upon the paten, and covers the chalice first with the pall, then with the paten which he used at mass, and the deacon covers them with a small veil. At the end of mass *Ite missa est* is said, and the solemn benediction is given by the cardinal, but the indulgence is in no wise to be proclaimed, because when the sacrament has been put away it will be proclaimed in the place of the sacrament, as below. The celebrant when he says the gospel, *In principio*, does not sign the altar as at other times. And he puts off all his vestments at the side, and meanwhile all things are quietly prepared for the procession, and the torches lighted and given to the chaplains of the cardinal. And the canons take their

[1] c xlviii Catalani, p. 189.

customary vestments, and two who are to be the ministers a tunicle and dalmatic, and all when they are ready, holding lighted candles in their hands, come one by one to the altar, and there first of all genuflect....Then standing with biretta but without mitre he puts incense into two thuribles without blessing it...and two chaplains hold the two thuribles; and so he goes to the altar in the accustomed manner, and there with bare head he prays, kneeling upon the cushion: then taking one of the thuribles he censes the sacrament kneeling, swinging the censer thrice. Afterwards, as he kneels, the veil mentioned above is put on his shoulders by the ministers and fastened with pins. Then by the same canon-ministers who stand ready the sacrament is offered to him still kneeling, without any reverence on the part of the cardinal, and without kissing his hand. And when it has been offered to him the ministers genuflect and the cardinal rises and the choir sing there the hymn, *Pange lingua*....And two ministers ready for the purpose, one on each side, lift up the front borders of his cope, and a chaplain lifts up the hem of his vestment in the front. And the chief of the banner bearers of the people, or one of them, right excellent and honourable, but a layman, bears the cardinal's train, and he goes devoutly indeed but saying nothing under the canopy, which as I said the mansionaries, who are ready for the purpose, carry. And all the clergy with candles in their hands proceed singing the afore-mentioned hymn. And when the cardinal is before the place of repose of the sacrament the canopy is left outside and the clergy carry it back; and kneeling there the singers begin the most pious song, *O salutaris*, or, *Verbum caro*, or as they will, continuing until the sacrament has been censed by the cardinal[1].

In the post Tridentine missal of 1570, after the revision under Pius V, directions for the procession of the host after mass have been added to the older rubrics. We read:

Then let the communion take place and afterwards the mass be finished. The Communion, *Dominus Jesus*. The Post Com-

---

[1] *De Caer. Card. et Epis* 1564, lib. II 46, ff. 127-8.

munion, *Refecti*. And *Ite missa est* is said. Mass being finished torches are lighted and a procession is made in the accustomed manner. The celebrant genuflects before the altar, puts incense into two thuribles and with one censes the sacrament thrice. Then taking the chalice with the sacrament from the hand of the deacon and covering it with the ends of the veil with which his shoulders are covered he proceeds in the middle between the deacon on the right and the subdeacon on the left under a canopy, two acolytes continuously censing the sacrament until they come to the place prepared where it is to be reserved for the morrow. Meantime while the procession is made the hymn, *Pange lingua*, is sung. And after reposing the sacrament and censing it again let vespers be said in choir[1].

In the *Caeremoniale Episcoporum* first published by Clement VIII in 1600 we find in a modified form the directions of Paris de Grassis with regard to the ceremonial of Maundy Thursday. We read:

And having received the communion of the body and blood, before he purifies himself the bishop puts away the sacrament within the chalice, which the deacon covers with a pall and the paten placed over it, and finally with a silk veil, and reverently places it in the middle of the altar....*Ite missa est* being said the bishop without mitre, standing on the epistle side, will give the solemn benediction, but the indulgences will be proclaimed in the place where the sacramentis reposed. When after mass the bishop is about to say the gospel, *In principio*, he will not make the sign of the cross over the altar as at other times, and when this is finished, returning to his throne he puts off the sacred vestments as far as but exclusive of the stole, and puts on a white cope. Meanwhile the canons when they are ready take lighted candles, and the senior of the beneficed, or of the mansionaries who are ready in copes, take the posts of the canopy. The bishop, having put on his cope and mitre, standing puts incense into two thuribles without blessing it, and the priest assistant who ministers it not kissing the hand

[1] p 160 Lippe, vol. I p 158, vol. II. p. 73

of the bishop as at other times. And this done he returns to
the altar and there with bare head, kneeling upon the cushion,
taking one of the two said thuribles from the assistant priest
censes the sacrament with a triple swing. Then the veil is put
over his shoulders and fastened with pins, and the deacon
assistant and no other with due reverences takes the sacrament
from the altar, and standing offers it to the bishop kneeling,
without any reverence towards the bishop and without kissing
him, though after he has left it in the hands of the bishop he
genuflects. And the bishop rises with the sacrament and
immediately the singers begin the hymn, *Pange lingua*. The
assistant ministers one on each side lift up the front borders
of his cope, and the master of ceremonies or some chaplain,
when the bishop ascends or descends steps, lifts up the edge of
his inner vestment in the front, and some right worthy layman,
or someone else who is present according to the custom of the
place, lifts up his cope at the back. The bishop enters under the
canopy carrying the sacrament devoutly. The canons being
ready with candles go before in the accustomed order. When
they have arrived at the chapel where the sacrament is to be
placed the canopy is left outside and the singers in pious and
devout song sing *O salutaris* or *Tantum ergo* until the sacrament
has been reposed by the bishop and censed. When the bishop
is before the highest step of the altar let a deacon, kneeling
without kissing his hand, take the sacrament from his hand as
he stands, and put it down on the altar in the place prepared,
covering the chalice with a veil all round. And meanwhile the
bishop retiring a little puts incense into one of the thuribles
standing, and kneeling again he will cense the sacrament with
a triple swing, and ascending to the altar and kissing it with
a genuflection will give the solemn benediction, standing
without mitre on the epistle side, holding his pastoral staff
while he says *Pater et Filius*; and the priest assistant will then
proclaim the indulgences of forty days in the accustomed
manner, and the canons put off their vestments, and return into
the choir for vespers[1].

[1] Lib. II. c. 23, pp. 227–30.

ON MAUNDY THURSDAY

The directions of the modern *Caeremoniale Episcoporum* are almost verbally identical.

In the missal of 1604, after the revision of Clement VIII, practically the rubrics of the modern missal appear, few changes having been made since. We read:

Today the priest consecrates two hosts one of which he consumes, the other he reserves for the following day on which the sacrament is not consecrated. He reserves also other consecrated particles if there be need for the sick But the whole of the blood he consumes and before the ablution of his fingers he puts the reserved host into another chalice which the deacon covers with the pall and paten, and over it he spreads the veil, and places it in the middle of the altar. Then the communion is made, and mass is finished. And the priest genuflects whenever he approaches or departs from the middle of the altar, or crosses before the sacrament reserved in the chalice, and when he has to say *Dominus vobiscum* he does not turn towards the people in the middle of the altar that he may not turn his back upon the sacrament, but on the gospel side, and at the end he gives the blessing from the same place. The Communion, *Dominus Jesus*. The Post Communion, *Refecti*. And *Ite missa est* is said. The blessing is given, and the gospel of St John is read, at the beginning of which the priest does not sign the altar but only himself. Today let a suitable place be prepared in some chapel of the church, or on an altar, and let it be adorned as fairly as possible with veils and lights that the chalice with the reserved host as above may be reposed there. And mass being finished torches are lighted and a procession is made in the accustomed manner, but with another subdeacon who is in readiness bearing the cross. The celebrant wearing a white cope stands before the altar and puts incense into two thuribles without blessing it. Then genuflecting in the middle with one of them he censes the sacrament thrice, and taking the chalice with the sacrament from the hand of the deacon who stands, and covering it with the ends of the veil with which his shoulders are covered, he proceeds in the middle between the same deacon on the right and the subdeacon on the left under the canopy, two acolytes continuously censing the sacrament, until they come to the place prepared where it is to be reserved for the morrow. Meantime while the procession is made the hymn, *Pange lingua*, is sung. And when they have come to the place prepared the deacon genuflects and takes the chalice with the sacrament from the priest who stands, and puts it first on the altar where it is censed by the priest kneeling as above. Then he reposes it in the coffer and vespers are said without chant in choir[1].

A few notes on the Ambrosian and Mozarabic customs on Maundy Thursday may finish our enquiry.

At Milan in the twelfth century according to the *Ordo* of Beroldus the sacrament remained on the altar until the end of mass. We read.

Let the archbishop communicate with the clergy and people. So let mass be finished according to custom. Afterwards...let the pontiff go into the sacristy, where he bids the subdeacons diligently guard the sacrament of the body and blood of the Lord[2].

The modern Ambrosian missal has adopted the Roman rubrics, and they are practically identical with those of the missal of 1604, so that the sacrament is still not removed until the close of the service.

The early Mozarabic books make no mention of any reservation of the sacrament on Maundy Thursday. In the *Missale Mixtum* of Cardinal Ximenes of 1500 we find an elaborate procession of the host, with bell-ringing and the strewing of branches, and it follows the priest's communion immediately[3]. The order in many ways is similar to that of Patricius and Marcellus, and from a literary point of view is probably derived ultimately from the same source

We have now traced out the development of the pro-

---

[1] pp 93-4.
[2] Magistretti, *Beroldus*, p 104
[3] Lesley, *Missale Mixtum*, p 165 *P L* LXXXV col 418-9

cession of the blessed sacrament on Maundy Thursday from its commencement to the present day. Our enquiry seems to have made it clear that except at Rome, or in the papal chapel at certain periods, the custom was as a rule that the holy sacrament which was to be reserved from the mass of Maundy Thursday for use on Good Friday, should remain on the altar until the end of mass, in accordance with what appears to have been the primitive custom on all occasions, and then put away, with little or no ceremonial in the earliest days, and afterwards with very much. The contrary Roman custom, which was imitated in other places, and particularly among the religious orders, as the Carmelites and Augustinians, seems to have descended from the practice of sending the Fermentum before the end of the station mass to the titular churches of Rome for use when mass was celebrated by another than the pope, and on Maundy Thursday for the communion of the faithful throughout the city on Good Friday. New ideas at Rome after the return from Avignon, and particularly the notions that out of honour to our Lord the procession should be a very elaborate ceremony, and that the pope or celebrant only should carry the sacrament on this occasion, brought about a different practice, and Sixtus IV ordained that when the pope was present the procession of the host to the place of repose should not take place until mass was finished, and that the pope himself should bear the host. Consequently, at a later date, it became once more the custom at Rome, as in other places, whoever was the celebrant, that the sacrament should remain on the altar until the end of the mass, and there was thus though not intentionally a reversion to primitive practice.

CHAPTER VII

IN LATER DAYS IN THE WEST

WE are now in a position to return to a further consideration of the rules of the church in the West, and particularly those of later times, and in liturgical documents of different sorts, for dealing with what was left of the consecrated elements after the communion, whether intended for the purpose of reservation, or because too much was consecrated.

In the letter of the pseudo Clement already noted we have the foundation of the later rules. According to the usual translation it reads:

But if any (hosts) remain let them not be reserved until the morrow, but be carefully consumed by the clerks with fear and trembling[1].

In the Synodical Admonition ascribed to Leo IV (847–55), and at any rate belonging to about his period, though probably Gallican in origin, this direction becomes·

Consume the body and blood of the Lord with fear and reverence[2].

By itself this injunction is perhaps ambiguous, but the visitation articles of Regino of Prüm († 915) bring out the original meaning. We read:

Mass being finished (expleta missa), does the priest himself with fear and reverence consume what is left of the body and blood of the Lord[3]?

The exact meaning of "mass being finished" may

[1] *P G* I. col. 484   See p 12   [2] *P.L* cxxxii. col 456
[3] *P L*. cxxxii. col 190

perhaps be determined by the occurrence of the same phrase in another of the same articles of enquiry, where it is the equivalent of "post missam" in the Admonition:

Mass being finished, does he distribute eulogiae to the folk from the oblations which are offered by the people on Sundays and feast days[1]?

The eulogiae were not distributed until the conclusion of the liturgy, and so unless the phrase is used in two different senses in the same articles, the probability is that the consumption of the remains also took place when mass was completely ended; and this agrees with the other evidence about the earlier days. In other documents, however, we do sometimes find "expleta missa" used with a wider meaning, as in the Appendix to Roman *Ordo I* for the consecration[2], but this would not fit the context in either of Regino's articles.

In the description of mass given by John of Avranches (c. 1065) the consumption of the remains takes place before the end of the service. We read:

The particle which remained in the chalice let the priest consume, and afterwards let him give the chalice to the deacon to cleanse and consume what is left; and let him carry away the chalice with the paten to the left corner of the altar, and there receive part himself and give part to the subdeacon.... After the cleansing of paten and chalice let an acolyte hold each wrapped in a napkin until the end of the first Post Communion[3].

The earlier Roman *Ordines*, apart from the mention of the piece left on the altar till the end of mass, say nothing about what is done with the remains of the sacrament after the communion, but the suggestion is that they remain on the altar till the conclusion of the service.

---

[1] *P L* cxxxii col 190 Cf col. 457
[2] Mabillon, vol II p 32 See pp 54, 75 above.
[3] *De Off Eccles*, *P L* cxlvii col. 37.

Perhaps there may be a reference to a different custom in the Gallican *Ordo VI* (eleventh century?) where we read:

> The same archdeacon must be very careful that nothing of the blood or body of Christ remain in chalice or paten[1].

Unfortunately nothing is said about the way in which he is to carry out this duty.

At a later date Durandus († 1296), commenting on a Roman *Ordo*, gives more precise information:

> And then the subdeacon consumes the rest of the blood with the particle put into the chalice....The part dipped in the chalice...the lord pope does not receive...but the ministers consume it...and in particular the subdeacon consumes it for him, because he communicates last, and it is the business of the last to consume the remains and purify the chalice[2].

In an *Ordo*, printed by Martene, giving the duties of the cardinal deacon on feast days, and in an *Ordo* printed by Gattico, both presumably of the fourteenth century, though based on earlier materials, we read:

> And when all the communicants have received the blood, the cardinal deacon gives the reed to the subdeacon for him to suck at both ends, and afterwards the chalice to consume what is left over of the blood of Christ[3].

The rules for the general communion on Easter Day in *Ordo XV* incorporate the same directions. We read

> It is to be noted that our lord the pope on this day is not accustomed to wash his fingers with wine, nor to consume the wine, as he is accustomed, after he has communicated the subdeacon, but when all have communicated. And not only so, the subdeacon does not drink the wine until all have communicated, and this because, if anything of the body of Christ remain on the paten, the pope alone ought to consume it, and,

---

[1] Mabillon, vol II. pp 75–6

[2] *Rationale Div Off* lib IV cap. liv *De Communione Sacerdotis*, f lxxvii

[3] Martene, vol I lib I cap iv Art XII p 247. Gattico, *Acta Caerem.* vol I p 42

if anything of the blood of Christ in the chalice, the subdeacon ought to consume it....And when all the communicants have received the blood the lord deacon gives the tube or reed to the subdeacon for him to suck at both ends, and afterwards the chalice to consume what is left over of the blood of Christ[1].

All the evidence with regard to details of what was done at Rome with the remains of the consecrated elements is comparatively late, and unfortunately there is very little information about earlier days to be found elsewhere. In Ulrich's Constitutions of Cluny (*c.* 1080) we read·

All being communicated who wish and last of all the subdeacon, who always by custom ought to communicate at the high mass, except on those days on which only one host is consecrated, and when he is communicated who holds the scutella[2], if the body of the Lord remain over, or if it seem good to him, it is covered with the scutella[3].

What exactly is done with the remains we are not told here, but the writer makes it clear in his description of what has been the previous custom on Good Friday, and what he wishes for the future:

Formerly there was great care that after all had communicated whatever was left over should be consumed by the same priests who brought it in, with great reverence and attention, and nothing at all remained until the morrow. And indeed I never knew it otherwise, although, to speak generally, there may be another custom in other churches—but about that we are not here greatly concerned—that on this day as on another, if anything be left over from the communicants, it is reserved[4].

The same custom was observed on Good Friday, and it would seem also on other days, at the monastery of St

---

[1] Mabillon, vol II pp 506–7
[2] A tray or dish used to catch any small fragments of the sacrament of the Lord's body which might fall in the act of communion.
[3] Martene, vol. IV lib II. cap. IV. § xv. p. 63
[4] *P L* CXLIX. col 662

Benignus at Dijon, the constitutions of which were based on those of Cluny. We read on Good Friday:

Then the priest communicates first from the Sancta, and afterwards distributes to all in order. Whatever is left over of the body of the Lord is taken up carefully by the priests who perform all the service in church on this day, and consumed[1].

On other days we are told similarly:

If the body of the Lord be left over, or if it seem good to him, he gives it to the subdeacon to consume, or he puts it away in a pyx[2].

We see here the original meaning of the words "if it seem good to him," which have become meaningless in Ulrich's version of the constitutions, according to which what is left is always reserved, and no mention is made of its being consumed. We find also an earlier custom surviving at Dijon with regard to the remains in the chalice. According to Ulrich the priest alone communicates with the blood, save by intinction; in the Constitutions of Dijon we read much as in the Roman *Ordines* quoted above·

All those being finished who are to receive the blood of the Lord, the subdeacon also approaches and receives it. The deacon also afterwards, lifting the tube from the chalice and putting it to his mouth, when he has emptied it of the blood by sucking it at both ends, commits it to the subdeacon to keep for the time, and he himself consumes the rest of the blood, with that particle of the Lord's body which the priest had put into it, from the front part of the chalice[3].

In the Constitutions of Hirshau compiled by the abbot William from those of Cluny towards the end of the eleventh century we find a curious modification of the rules for the communion of the subdeacon and the minister who held the scutella, suggesting that the compiler did not

---
[1] Martene, vol IV lib. III. cap xiv § xlii. p. 140.
[2] Martene, vol IV. lib II cap IV § xv. p 64.
[3] Martene, vol IV lib II cap IV § xv p 64

understand the document he was using as the basis of his own work. We read:

And then the subdeacon receives the body of the Lord and after him all who wish, and last of all the minister who holds the scutella, if any remain....After all who have received the body of the Lord have communicated with the Lord's blood it is brought last of all to the minister that he too may drink of the same blood of the Lord, but only if he has received the body of the Lord, for by custom he does not communicate unless some part of the body of the Lord remain over[1].

According to Ulrich's Constitutions the consecrated hosts left over from the communion are reserved for another day. In another place he gives detailed instructions about the renewal of the reserved sacrament.

It should be known also that the body of the Lord is changed every Sunday. While the priest proceeds to the pax the newly consecrated is placed by the deacon in a cork pyx, and what was consecrated the previous Sunday is taken out and divided by the same deacon, and the brethren thence communicated; only the two particles of that host which the priest divided are not changed. And while the familiar psalms[2] are being said after terce the deacon takes the aforesaid pyx from the dove which hangs continually over the altar, wiping well the dust from the outside with a small linen cloth, and places it upon the right corner of the altar under a veil, and when mass is finished puts it back in the same place[3].

In the Cistercian rules of the twelfth century the directions for reserving the sacrament and the disposal of the remains are combined. We read:

And let him thus receive the body of the Lord over the chalice, and then the blood. And then having put down the chalice uncovered upon the corporal let him turn to the right

---

[1] *P L* CL. col 1013-4.
[2] Additional psalms said after the regular office on behalf of benefactors
[3] *P L* CXLIX. col. 722-3.

corner of the altar, and putting down there the paten with the hosts, let him take the host from the vessel put ready by the deacon, and place it upon the paten, and one, or more when it shall be necessary, of those which are there let him put away in the vessel: but let this be done only on Sundays and Maundy Thursday. And let the vessel be put down on the altar until after mass. This being done let the priest communicate the deacon and subdeacon from the third part (of his host), and then from the other hosts the rest of those about to communicate. But let him be as careful as possible that no other part of the Lord's body remain....If any of the blood be left over let him (the deacon) drink it from the chalice after he has returned the tube to the subdeacon. And before he returns the tube let him empty it as far as possible of the blood of the Lord by sucking it at both ends, and return the chalice to the priest without kissing his hand....But before the priest receives the chalice let him place in the vessel any whole hosts which have been left over from those who communicated[1].

In a thirteenth century version of the Cistercian Customs belonging to the convent of Val des Choux in Burgundy we find considerable alteration and curtailment, due chiefly to the fact that in 1198 the General Chapter had limited the communion in both species to the deacon and subdeacon only[2], but the rule that the hosts left over should remain on the altar until after mass is still retained[3]. The earliest evidence of a different custom seems to be in the rules for the Dominican mass belonging to the thirteenth century, and there we find that the deacon not only brings the reserved sacrament to the altar during the service, but, unless the communion is deferred, carries it away again likewise, the last relic of the old rule with regard to the third part of the priest's obley having thus disappeared. We read

[1] Martene, vol IV lib II. cap IV § xv pp. 64–5
[2] Séjalon, *Nomasticon Cisterc.* (Lib Antiq Definit), p 406
[3] Birch, *Ordinale Conventus Vallis Caulium*, p. 40

LATER DAYS IN THE WEST

When the time of communion has arrived let the deacon, candlebearers going before him with candles, bring the aforementioned pyx with the body of the Lord, and open it upon the altar....And it should be known that if there is a great company present awaiting the end of mass, the communion can be put off until after mass, if it seems good to the prior, except on Maundy Thursday. Otherwise it must be finished before the communion is said....But if before the end of the communion the priest sees that too great a number of hosts has been prepared he can give them to the brethren two at a time, so that he need not reserve too great a number. But let those which remain, being placed by the priest in the pyx, be carried with honour to the proper place by the deacon, candlebearers going before, and the brethren making a genuflexion[1].

The Carmelites likewise according to the 1312 constitutions removed the hosts for reservation from the altar after the communion and before the end of mass. We read

Let the priest also after receiving the body of Christ and before the reception of the blood consume likewise the consecrated hosts brought to him by the deacon, putting two others into the pyx, after which the pyx being closed, let the deacon, first genuflecting, carry back the sacrament to its place, candlebearers going before him as before....But if on the day when the sacrament has to be renewed the brethren are to be communicated the priest can give the reserved hosts upon the altar in communicating them, placing others in their place as before. And then after the communion of the brethren the deacon can carry back the sacrament to its place as above[2].

The Carmelite rule for the removal of the sacrament to be reserved is thus the same on ordinary days as on Maundy Thursday. That there should be a tendency to assimilate the practice of Maundy Thursday and other

---

[1] *Missale Conventuale* Legg, *Tracts on the Mass* (H B S), pp 85-6

[2] Zimmerman, *Ordinaire de l'ordre de Notre Dame du Mont Carme* (1312), XLIV. p. 87.

days is quite natural, and we can hardly regard this as independent of the custom on that day which we have already noticed as being connected with that described in *Ordo X*. The ceremonial of the Dominicans at mass is closely allied with that of the Carmelites, and they appear to have a common origin.

It may be useful to quote other rules of various dates which indicate the time of the removal from the altar of the hosts which are to be reserved. With the Carthusians (*c.* 1130) the customary place of reservation was over the high altar, and so it is scarcely surprising that the sacrament should be put away immediately. We read:

And on Sundays the deacon, making a genuflexion on the right side of the altar, puts down on the paten the host which was reserved from the preceding Sunday, and putting back another whole host instead of it in the pyx restores the pyx to its place, and communicates with the first mentioned host on his knees at the right corner of the altar. And whoever takes the pyx in which is the body of the Lord, and whenever, in taking it from behind the altar he genuflects[1].

The directions in the Soissons ritual are similar, though as the place of reservation is no longer behind the altar but in a hanging pyx, the action is not so simple:

Meanwhile let the priest proceed as far as the communion and then let the deacon bring to him the vessel which hangs over the altar in which the eucharist is reserved from Sunday to Sunday. And let the priest, receiving it, place within it a host newly consecrated, and take out that which was reserved, and communicate with it. And let the deacon carry back the vessel with the fresh host to its place[2].

At Bayeux in the fourteenth century though the sacrament is reserved in a chest over the altar, the procession of the Dominicans and Carmelites has been adopted, and the new hosts are carried back immediately. We read.

[1] Martene, vol I lib I cap IV Art XII Ordo XXV p 228
[2] Martene, vol I lib I cap IV Art XII Ordo XXII. p 220

Every Sunday while the priest communicates let the deacon take the linen cloth placed on the left part of the altar, and two candlebearers going before him, fetch the Lord's body from its place over the right corner of the altar, bearing it aloft in a pyx with great reverence. And this being received by the priest, and two new hosts put back by him, let the deacon with the same solemnity carry back the pyx with the body to the place where it was before[1].

Though the new practice, adopted it would seem in imitation of the Maundy Thursday custom, first evidenced in the Sixth Roman *Ordo*, of removing the sacrament from the altar before the end of mass, became very widespread, the older usage, by which the hosts left over from communion, or set apart for reservation, remained on the altar until the end of the service, survived at Rome on ordinary days until almost the close of the sixteenth century, thus continuing in a manner the ancient rule with regard to the third part of the priest's obley. In the book of *The Sacred Ceremonies and Ecclesiastical Rites of the Holy Roman Church*, published in 1516, we read:

The communion being done the pope rises if he sat for the communion and makes his reverence to the sacrament, and the subdeacon puts back the hosts, if any remain, upon the altar where they stay until the end of mass[2].

In order to show how persistent was this practice where Roman influence was strong it may be well to give further particulars about this book. It was compiled by Patricius, Bishop of Pienza, and dedicated to Pope Innocent VIII in 1488, not being intended for publication. It was published with slight alterations by Marcellus, Bishop of Corcyra in 1516, much to the indignation of Paris de Grassis, Bishop of Pesaro, the papal Master of Ceremonies, who resented its appearance as likely to be

---

[1] Martene, vol. I lib I cap. IV. Art XII Ordo XXIV p. 227.
[2] *Sac Caer sive Rit Eccles S. Rom Eccles* lib II cap 1. § 6. Ed. Catalani, vol II. p 269.

derogatory to the dignity of the pope by making public what would better be kept private, and also because it was published as though it were Marcellus's own work. Its popularity, however, was very great, and its influence must have been enormous for between 1516 and 1582 at least eight editions of it were printed at Rome, Florence, Venice or Cologne, besides other editions later. Paris de Grassis († 1528) himself also indeed prepared a similar work concerning the ceremonial to be observed by cardinals and bishops in their dioceses, giving in particular the customs at Bologna, but it was not published until after his death. Of this there were editions at Rome in 1564 and 1580, and at Venice in 1582. With regard to the removal of the hosts left over after a general communion to the place of reservation the rule is the same as that given by Patricius, and they remain on the altar until the end of mass. We read:

The communion being finished the torches will be carried away, and the cardinal will rise if he sat for the communion, and the chalice with the remainder of the hosts being put back and covered he will purify his fingers in the accustomed manner and consume the ablution. Then if there shall be hosts upon the altar he will wash his hands on the epistle side without mitre and finish mass. And at the end, if there shall be hosts upon the altar, he will give the blessing without mitre, and when he says *Initium Sancti Evangelii* he will not sign the altar, and as often as he shall go or return from the book to the middle of the altar let him always genuflect, and he will not be precisely before the middle of the altar when he sings *Dominus vobiscum* that he seem not to turn his back directly on the sacrament[1].

The conditional form of the directions appears to be due not to the possibility of the chalice with the rest of the hosts being carried away, but to provide for the case when every host would be used in the communion. Though

---

[1] *De Caer. Card. et Episc.* lib. II cap. 49, t. 141

details of ceremonial are given with some minuteness there is no direction that the hosts which remain should be removed from the altar before the end of the mass. The normal thing would be that after a general communion and on some other occasions at least a few would be left over, and this the rule for the benediction makes clear. We read·

If the body of Christ be on the altar, as on Easter Day, Corpus Christi, Maundy Thursday, or whenever it may be, then the blessing ought to be given with bare head[1].

Patricius tells us that he had called in the help of John Burchard in compiling the second book of his work. In 1502 while Master of the Ceremonies at Rome Burchard published his well-known *Ordo Missae*, and in this the ancient rule is still observed, and the hosts which are to be reserved remain on the altar until after mass. When the priest has said *Quid retribuam* and before *Calicem salutaris* we are told:

If there are consecrated hosts on the corporal to be reserved for another time, making due reverence to them, he places them in a vessel provided for the purpose[2].

After the benediction at the end of mass we read

If there is a vessel with consecrated hosts to be reserved for another time to be put back, due reverence being made to the sacrament with bare head, he carries it away and puts it down in its place and safely closes it, and this being done he returns to the middle of the altar[3].

Nothing is said about any hosts which might be left over from the communion, but presumably they were added to those in the pyx, as in other rites.

That the ancient practice of keeping any hosts which were to be reserved on the altar till the end of mass was

---

[1] Lib I cap xlii f. 54.
[2] Legg, *Tracts on the Mass* (H B S), p 163
[3] Legg, p 168.

universal where Roman influence was at work is proved by the popularity of Burchard's *Ordo Missae*, even more than by the book of Patricius and Marcellus. No work is of greater importance for the history of the ceremonial of the mass in the Roman Church than this book, for it gives the order of service, not simply as performed in the basilicas of Rome, but as carried out in the ordinary church. The rules about the sacrament for reservation, though in accordance with the most ancient usage, do not appear in the first draft of the *Ordo* in the missal of 1501, but they are to be found in numerous editions published during the sixteenth century. There appear to have been at least nine Latin and two Italian editions of it as a separate book, the latest being in 1589. It is included in seven editions of the *Liber Sacerdotalis*, in one of the *Liber Familiaris Clericorum*, in eight editions of the Roman missal and in two local missals, and probably this list is not exhaustive[1]. There can be no doubt about its widespread influence, and it found its way into England. A copy now in the British Museum was in England at an early date, for the title-page shows that it once belonged to the Pardoner's Churchyard at St Paul's, and as it bears also the name "Lumley" it may have belonged to Cranmer[2]. Perhaps it may have suggested the mixing of the chalice at the offertory as ordered in the First English Prayer Book, for this is in accordance with Roman, not with old English custom, though it is the more ancient usage, and is found elsewhere.

In 1570 a new edition entitled *Ritus Servandus in Celebratione Missarum*, or *Ritus Celebrandi Missam*, appeared after emendation under the authority of the council of Trent in the Missal of Pius V, which henceforth was the only authorised missal of the Roman rite. The rule about the hosts for reservation being placed in the pyx still remained practically as before, as indeed it does to

[1] Legg, pp. xxv ff [2] Legg, p. 121.

the present time, but the order to put the pyx back in its place after the blessing has disappeared. In the *Caeremoniale Episcoporum* first published by Clement VIII in 1600 we read in the directions for Easter Day:

The communion being finished the torches which up to this point have been burning are carried away, and the celebrant, having put back the vessel or chalice with the hosts upon the altar, if any remain, covers it,—or he also (vel etiam) consigns it to some priest ready with stole and cotta or cope, and he carries it under a canopy, if it can be done conveniently, clerks going before with torches and certain of the clergy accompanying, to the place where the sacrament is kept[1].

The practice prescribed for Maundy Thursday in the Tenth Roman *Ordo*, and adopted by the Carmelites and Dominicans and others even on ordinary days, is thus officially sanctioned for the Roman rite as an alternative to the older and more general custom described by Patricius and de Grassis, so that now the remains of the sacrament may be removed from the altar immediately after the communion and before the end of mass. The reason for the change seems to emerge quite plainly from what we are told by Paris de Grassis. In his description of a general communion we have noted that the ceremonial is to be different for the conclusion of the mass when the sacrament remains on the altar. He tells us also that when the bishop is about to celebrate the sacrament should be removed from the place over the altar where it is usually reserved[2]. His reason, as given in another place, is as follows

In the presence of the sacrament neither the pope nor the celebrating bishops can properly sit, nor can they retain the mitre on their head nor receive the censing themselves until after the sacrament has been censed[3].

[1] Lib II. cap xxix pp 263-4
[2] *De Caer Card et Episc* lib. I. cap 28, f. 34.
[3] Mabillon, vol. II. p. cxliii.

We notice here a quite different attitude towards the sacrament from that of the ancient *Ordines*, where frequently we are told that the pope sits in its presence and this indeed is the posture still retained for the communion, not only in the ceremonial of Patricius and Marcellus, but in the book of Paris de Grassis himself, though nowadays it is no longer the custom, as Catalani said, "out of reverence for the sacrament[1]." The explanation of the removal of the reserved sacrament from over the altar on the occasion of a solemn pontifical mass affords also a reason for taking away what remained after communion immediately. As the practice of removing the sacrament before the bishop celebrates appears to have been adopted in the days of Leo X (1513-21) it is not surprising that by the time of Clement VIII in 1600 there should be a further development, and provision should be made for the remains to be taken away after communion. In Innocent X's edition of the *Caeremoniale Episcoporum* in 1651 the new ideas of reverence have prevailed entirely over ancient custom, and by the change of "vel etiam" into "et" the alternative usage is disallowed, so that the breach with antiquity is complete[2], and the rule mentioned in *Ordo I* that "while the solemnities of mass are being performed the altar should not be without the sacrifice[3]," when a bishop celebrates can no longer be observed.

According to the *Ritus Celebrandi Missam* of 1570 it was still possible to keep the ancient rule when a priest celebrated, though it seems seldom to have been done in practice except when communion was given after mass, for which special provision was made in the 1570 order, or when there was no tabernacle over the altar where mass was said. The Brescia *Rituale* of 1570 provides an

---

[1] Catalani, *Caeremoniale Episcoporum*, vol II cap xxix § viii n 2, p 354
[2] Lib II cap xxix p 364 Cf Ed Catalani, p 354
[3] See p 63 Mabillon, vol. II. p 14

LATER DAYS IN THE WEST

example of it when the communion was postponed until the end of mass:

The consecration being completed, if there be a number of consecrated particles which hinder those things which remain to be done for the completion of the sacred mystery of the altar, let him put them a little on one side until the reception of the body and blood, and this being finished let him put them back again in the middle of the altar, or put them away in the tabernacle if the communion of the people be deferred to another day: afterwards let him wash his fingers according to custom. The consecration being finished so long as the most holy body of Christ is on the altar let two lighted candles at least burn there continually, and when it is given to the faithful let there be also a burning taper[1].

The Peru *Manuale* of 1607 has a modified form of these directions and the change from "the consecration being finished" to "mass being finished" brings out even more clearly that the sacrament remains on the altar until after the end of mass[2].

In the 1604 missal of Clement VIII the same rule about placing the hosts in the pyx still appears as in Burchard's *Ordo Missae* and the *Ritus Celebrandi Missam* of 1570, and we find the rubric of the modern Roman missal with regard to the sacrament remaining on the altar for the first time·

If any particles remain on the altar in a chalice or other vessel until the end of mass let those things which are prescribed for the end of mass on Maundy Thursday be observed.

In the Brixen *Sacerdotale* of 1609 which gives directions for saying mass "according to the Roman rite and the use of the diocese of Brixen," the remains of the sacrament after communion are plainly ordered to remain on the altar until after mass. We read:

The communion being finished, if any particles are left over

[1] ff 12, 13.   [2] p. 20.

let them be kept upon the altar, and after mass the sign of the cross being first made towards the people, let them be transferred to the tabernacle of the venerable sacrament. If only one or so be left over the celebrant can either give them all together to the last communicant, or himself consume them up to the time of the ablution[1].

The chief reason however according to modern practice for the hosts to remain on the altar until the end of mass on ordinary occasions is the absence of a tabernacle where mass is being said. We may perhaps close this part of our enquiry with the words of a modern writer with regard to the usage of the Roman Church:

If no particles remain he does not genuflect on returning but if any remain he immediately genuflects, placing his hand on the corporal, and if they are not to be reserved he consumes them reverently; if they are to be put into the tabernacle, he covers the pyxis,...puts it into the tabernacle, genuflects, and then closes the tabernacle. If there be no tabernacle on the altar, so that the pyxis must be left on the corporal, to be afterwards removed, the priest should be careful to observe the reverences prescribed by the missal for the case in which the pyxis containing the blessed sacrament remains on the altar till the end of mass[2].

Unfortunately we have little information about the details of ancient English practice with respect to the reservation or consumption of the remains of the sacrament after communion. Among the canons of the council of Durham in 1220 we read:

And therefore we straitly decree that priests be careful with regard to those things which pertain to the essence of the sacrament of the body and blood of the Lord, providing that the eucharist be reserved in a clean and well fastened pyx and let not consecrated hosts be reserved more than seven days Let the reserved hosts be consumed before the consumption of

---

[1] p 111
[2] O'Kane, *Notes on the Rubrics of the Roman Ritual* p 446

the blood of the Lord by him who celebrates the mass or by some other person of clean and honest life[1].

The rule found among the *Cautelae Missae* of the printed Sarum and York Missals is rather different:

And if he has to consume other hosts, as when the host is to be renewed, let him first consume that which he has consecrated and the blood: afterwards the others which are left over. Let him consume his own host before the others, because about his own he believes and knows, about the others he believes and does not know; at last after all the ablutions, and not before[2].

Nothing is said about the hosts left over after a communion of the faithful, but presumably if not reserved they would be consumed at the same point before the ablutions.

Our somewhat lengthy enquiry in this chapter has shown that at the beginning of the tenth century at any rate as in the earliest days the remains of the sacrament after the communion were not consumed until the end of mass. In the eleventh century, however, in Gallican circles, if not elsewhere, the custom, which is perhaps that alluded to in the Roman *Ordo VI*, of consuming what was left in the chalice and the hosts not required for reservation immediately after the communion, was firmly established. Relics of the older practice survived in the fact that the priest's host was still broken into three pieces, though the third part was no longer laid down on the altar until the end of the service, and in the almost universal custom of retaining the hosts to be reserved on the altar until after mass, which continued to be the most general usage both at Rome and elsewhere until the end of the sixteenth century. The Dominicans, however, as early as the thirteenth century, imitating the practice of Maundy Thursday on

[1] Wilkins, *Concilia*, vol. I. p 579.
[2] Dickinson, *Sarum Missal*, col. 650. Henderson, *York Missal*, vol II. p. 224.

ordinary days, had begun to remove the sacrament from the altar to the place of reservation immediately after the communion, and the custom was imitated in other churches. In the *Caeremoniale Episcoporum* of 1600 the newer practice was allowed at Rome as an alternative to the older, apparently because of the impossibility, with the later ideas of reverence due to the sacrament, of carrying out the full ceremonial of a pontifical mass in its presence. In the edition of 1651 the more recent alternative has become the only practice allowed. The rule for putting away the sacrament for reservation after the ordinary mass, found in Burchard's *Ordo Missae* of 1502, disappeared in the official *Ritus Celebrandi Missam* of 1570, and though a rubric added in the Roman missal of 1604 provides for the custom, since the publication of the reformed missal of Pius V there has been no positive order on the subject. In practice as a rule the hosts are placed in the tabernacle immediately after the communion so that the primitive custom survives only on certain days in the year when communion is deferred until after mass, or when mass is said at an altar where there is no tabernacle, and some of the sacrament has to be reserved.

About ancient British custom with regard to putting away the hosts for reservation on ordinary days, no directions seem to have survived. The probability, however, is that any hosts which remained after the communion would remain upon the altar until mass was ended as on Maundy Thursday according to Salisbury use and according to the Roman books both on Maundy Thursday (save for a time) and other days. The fact that in England the method of reserving the sacrament was in a pyx hanging over the high altar points to the same conclusion. It is unlikely that the lowering of the dove as described in the Constitutions of Cluny[1] would as a rule take place in the middle of mass immediately after the

[1] See p. 103.

communion, even though something of the sort seems to have been prescribed at Soissons[1]; at any rate it would be improbable when the priest celebrated without assistant ministers, and there seems no hint that such an awkward practice obtained on any occasion in England. We can hardly conclude otherwise therefore than that in England as in Rome and other places with few exceptions the sacrament remained on the altar until the end of the service. Even the adoption of the more Roman custom of employing tabernacles for reservation instead of the hanging pyx in Mary's reign as at Hereford, Gloucester, Durham and other places[2], would hardly alter the existing custom, for the Roman practice was identical with it, and evidence of no other usage in England seems to be known.

[1] See p 106
[2] Frere, *Visitation Articles*, vol. II pp. 393, 408, 414.

CHAPTER VIII

THE DEVELOPMENT OF THE ABLUTIONS

HAVING discussed the disposal of the remains, great or small, of the consecrated hosts after the communion we turn to a consideration of the means adopted to ensure that the whole contents of the chalice also should be reverently treated and consumed. This desire to avoid any sort of irreverence in dealing with the remains of the cup led to special care in the manner of washing it, and ultimately to the ceremony of the ablutions.

In the letter of the pseudo Clement (seventh century) we saw that it was the duty of the "minister" to prepare the chalice for mass, and to see that it was thoroughly cleansed, and therefore presumably to wash it after use. We read:

The chalice...let the minister prepare, lest if the chalice be not well washed, it become sin to the deacon who offers it[1].

Nothing is said about what should be done with the water afterwards, but perhaps it was disposed of in the same manner as the ashes of the palls of the altar and other sacred things, which were burnt when too old for use. We read·

Let their ashes also be taken into the baptistery where no one has to pass, or be put into the wall, or into holes in the floor, that they may not be defiled by the feet of those who enter[2].

At Rome according to *Ordo I* (*c.* 770) the washing of the chalice used for the consecration must have taken place where it had been prepared, apparently in the

[1] *P.G* I. col. 486. See p 13   [2] *P.G.* I. col. 485.

sacristy, and hardly before the end of mass. After the chalice has been emptied into the large cup used for administering the communion we are told:

But the subdeacon attendant takes the chalice and gives it to an acolyte who puts it back in the sacristy (paratorium)[1].

The same direction is found also in *Ordo II*, and with verbal alterations in *Ordo III*[2].

In the Synodical Admonition ascribed to Leo IV (847-55), and plainly not unconnected with the letter of the pseudo Clement, there are much fuller instructions with regard to the cleansing of the sacred vessels, and here it is the duty not of any of the inferior ministers but of the priest. We read:

Consume the body and blood of the Lord with fear and reverence. Wash and wipe the sacred vessels with your own hands....Let a place be provided in the sacristy or near the altar where the water can be poured when the sacred vessels are washed, and let a fair vessel stand there with water, that there the priest may wash his hands after the communion[3].

The Admonition is either repeated in or used as a basis of a number of documents which appeared within the next hundred years or so, and in particular we may note the Capitular of Hincmar, Archbishop of Rheims, of the year 857, the synodical charges of Ratherius, Bishop of Verona († 958), and of Ulrich, Bishop of Augsburg († 973), and also the so-called *Eutychiani papae exhortatio*[4]. It is also the foundation of certain visitation articles of about the year 906 ascribed to Regino of Prüm. We find however in these documents some progress in the way of addition and interpretation. Hincmar's enquiry runs:

Has he a place provided where the water can be poured when the vessels of the altar are washed, or the mouth or hands

---

[1] Mabillon, vol II pp 14, 15   [2] Mabillon, vol II pp. 50, 60
[3] *P L* cxxxii col 456
[4] *P L* cxxv col 779   *P L* cxxxvi col. 559   Gerbert, *Vet Lit Alem* vol I pp 397-8   *P L.* v. col. 165

after the reception of the sacred communion? Or does the priest himself with his own hands wash the corporal for the first time, or his deacon or subdeacon[1]?

Still more important is an enquiry of Regino, part of which we have already quoted in the previous chapter:

Mass being finished (expleta missa), does the priest himself with fear and reverence consume what is left of the body and blood of the Lord? And if he has no deacon or subdeacon does he himself with his own hand wash and wipe the chalice and paten[2]?

We have already noticed that apparently the mass is to be completely ended before the remains are consumed, and therefore of course before the washing of the sacred vessels, which may now be entrusted to the deacon or subdeacon, as in the letter of the pseudo Clement.

The Admonition of the pseudo Leo clearly refers to a washing of the vessels after the communion comparable with the washing of the priest's hands. The water employed for the ablution of the vessels was to be poured into the place provided for the purpose, and it would presumably be the same with the water used for washing the priest's hands, as Hincmar's enquiry makes plain. The alternative "in the sacristy or near the altar" seems to show the beginning of the custom of consuming the remains at the altar instead of in the sacristy as prescribed in the letter of the pseudo Clement. If so, since according to the original text of the Admonition the vessels were to be washed with the priest's own hands, not by the deacon or subdeacon, as allowed by the pseudo Clement, or anyone else, the reference must be to an ablution after the service was over rather than to one immediately after communion. This was almost certainly the case later according to Regino's articles, and it would seem to have been the traditional custom at the period.

[1] *P.L.* cxxv col 779   [2] *P L.* cxxxii col. 190

In the *Missale Francorum* belonging to the latter part of the seventh century, and in kindred documents, in the allocution to the subdeacon at his ordination we read. And the palls which are spread upon the surface of the altar ought to be washed in one vessel, the corporals in another. Where the corporals have been washed no other linen cloth ought to be washed in the same place. The water ought to be poured away in the baptistery[1].

We notice that only the washing of the linen cloths of the altar is mentioned, and that nothing is said about the sacred vessels. The order to pour away the water of ablution in the baptistery reminds us of the direction in the letter of the pseudo Clement, where this is one of the places suggested, as we have noticed, for the disposal of the ashes of worn-out palls and other things when burnt. Both the allocution to the subdeacon and the Admonition of the pseudo Leo are obviously based to some extent on the directions of the pseudo Clement. The mention of the washing of the corporal in Hincmar's Capitular, as well as of the sacred vessels, seems to show the beginning of a process which was to combine the requirements of the two documents and change the significance and scope of some of the directions in later versions of the Admonition, applying them to the washing of sacred things in general. In later days too the consumption of the body and blood of Christ referred to appears to have been interpreted of the priest's communion, not, as in the Visitation Articles of Regino of Prüm, of what was left over from the administration. In the version given in the first printed Roman Pontifical of 1485 as revised by Patricius, Bishop of Pienza, we find both these modifications. We read:

In it (i.e. at mass) consume the body and blood of our Lord Jesus Christ with all reverence and fear....The corporals and palls...and other linen cloths and the sacred vessels with your

[1] Thomasius, *Opera Omnia*, vol VI p 343 Martene, vol II. lib. I. cap. VIII Art XI Ord II, iii, IV, XIV, XVII pp 34, 38, 42, 70, 84, etc.

own hands wash and wipe carefully....In the sacristies or secretaria, or near the high altar, let there be a suitable place for pouring the water after washing the corporals and linen cloths, the vessels and other sacred things and the hands after you have touched the holy chrism, or the oil of catechumens or of the sick. And let a vessel stand there with clean water to wash the hands of the priests and others who are about to perform a holy function, and the divine office, and near by a clean linen cloth to wipe them[1].

The Admonition is still found in the modern Roman Pontifical for use at a synod in a form more or less dependent on Patricius, though in some particulars there is a return to the original, and we no longer hear of wiping linen cloths.

The Admonition required the priest to wash and wipe the sacred vessels with his own hands. Whatever may have been aimed at, the practice of entrusting their cleansing to the deacon or subdeacon, which is found in the letter of the pseudo Clement, is again allowed in Regino's articles. Until quite a late date this washing of the chalice and paten with the consumption of the small portions of the remains was still performed after the conclusion of the service, as we shall see later, in the Cistercian Customs and in the rule of the monastery of St Victor at Paris of the twelfth and thirteenth centuries[2].

It may be interesting to see how the requirements of the letter of the pseudo Clement and the Admonition of the pseudo Leo with regard to the washing of the sacred vessels, etc., were carried out in practice, and the directions given in the Constitutions of Cluny compiled by Ulrich († 1093) are specially valuable, though not directly concerned with the ablutions after mass. We read:

The subdeacon washes his hands beforehand that he may

[1] *P L* cxxxii col 458
[2] See pp. 133–5 Martene, vol III lib IV App *Ant Const S. Vict. Paris* cap 1. p 277 Vol. IV lib II. cap IV. § xx. p. 65.

be ready to perform his office with the chalice, and taking it
with the corporal and paten while the gospel is being read he
looks to see if any water has been left in it from the washing,
and he pours it into a hollow place made in the brick of the
tiles near the altar, just as another has been made a little
further away that the same subdeacon and the other inferior
ministers may wash their hands over it[1].

Elsewhere each of these "hollow places" is called a
piscina. We read:

And as soon as the subdeacon and ministers have received
the Pax they do not neglect to wash their hands in the piscina
which is near the altar[2].

For this purpose let there be provided very deep vessels of
brass, devoted to no other use, and in these after vespers in
church let the corporals be dipped twice in cold water, and
rubbed in the hands. Afterwards water is poured over them
a third time, and so they remain all night. And in the morning
it is poured, as also before, into the piscina over which the
chalices are washed[3].

As there appear to be no wall piscinas in France belonging to a time much before the end of the twelfth
century[4], presumably piscinas in the floor took the place
of the earlier use of the baptistery, and as we shall see, it
was the same in England.

In the Admonition of the pseudo Leo the washing of
the priest's hands and of the sacred vessels are closely
connected and we shall find it convenient to discuss them
together. In Roman *Ordo I* we read only of an ablution
of the pope's hands at an ordinary mass after the receiving
of the oblations at the offertory, and likewise of the archdeacon's:

After this the pope...returns to his throne, and washes his

[1] Lib. II cap xxx. *P L*. CXLIX. col 717.
[2] Lib II cap xxx *P.L* CXLIX. col 720.
[3] Lib III cap xiv. *P L*. CXLIX col 758
[4] Viollet le Duc, *Dict. de l'Arch Franc*. vol. VII. p 189.

hands. The archdeacon standing before the altar after finishing the reception washes his hands[1].

The same order with regard to the washing of the pope's hands is found in *Ordo II*, but nothing is said about the archdeacon's. In *Ordo III*, on the other hand, there is no mention of the washing of the pope's hands, but that of the archdeacon's is still prescribed[2]. In *Ordo I* and in the Appendix on Maundy Thursday there are washings of the pope's hands before the service begins and after the blessing of the oils before the communion of the faithful, in each case after handling the oils. We read:

And let the other ministers hold the ampulla when full, and the pope having washed his hands proceeds with the seven taper bearers to mass[3].

After finishing this (the benediction of the oils), and having washed his hands the pope goes to the altar, and all the people communicate in order[4].

In *Ordo I*, and similarly in *Ordo II*, we read at the communion·

After these things all return to the pope's throne, the caller of the names, the treasurer, the acolyte who holds the paten, he who holds the towel, and he who ministers the water, and communicate, and the archdeacon confirms them after the pope[5].

Nothing is said about the acolytes who have the towel and water performing their functions after the communion, and in view of the careful mention of the different washings of hands on other occasions it is unlikely that any further ablution took place before the end of mass, and it is probable that the washing of the hands after the communion was as yet confined to Gallican circles. The earliest evidence of any such thing comes from Gaul,

---

[1] Mabillon, vol II. pp 11, 47. [2] Mabillon, vol. II. p 57.
[3] Mabillon, vol. II pp. 20, 33. [4] Mabillon, vol. II. pp. 21, 34.
[5] Mabillon, vol II pp. 15, 50.

THE ABLUTIONS

being found in the *Ordo* of St Amand (*c.* 830) which is a Gallicanized version of *Ordo I*.

We read there at the conclusion of the communion.

Then the pontiff descends from his seat and goes to the altar, and the taper bearers return after him. And meanwhile the priests or deacons wash their hands[1].

We note that it is not said that the pope washes his hands after the communion, but only his assistants, and it may be that here as also after the offertory in *Ordo III* there was no ablution of the pope's hands. The references to handwashing in the *Ordo* of St Amand are somewhat peculiar, and are apparently derived from a document now represented by a ninth century St Blasien manuscript. At the offertory it is before receiving the oblations of the people that the pope washes his hands, and not afterwards as is usual[2]. It seems somewhat extraordinary that the pontiff should be the only one who omitted to wash his hands after the communion, but the presumption is that the writer of the *Ordo* did not intend it.

In *Ordo VI* (eleventh century?) the ceremony is very distinctly described, and it is one of some elaboration. Though the document appears to be Gallican in origin it appeals to Roman custom as set out in some earlier Roman *Ordo* known to the writer. We read:

Afterwards when all have now communicated, the acolyte who carries the paten goes to the left part of the altar, and stands with the subdeacon. And the bishop sitting according to the aforesaid *Ordo*, three acolytes kneeling before him minister water for his hands. Having washed his hands, the bishop rises, turns to the people, and says, *Dominus vobiscum*[3].

---

[1] Duchesne, *C W* p. 463
[2] Duchesne, *C.W.* p 459   Cf Gerbert, vol II p 173   Elsewhere however (p 169) the St Blasien MS orders it at both points; so also the *Codex Ratoldi* of Corbie (tenth century)   Martene, vol. I. lib. I. cap. IV. Art. XII. Ordo XI pp. 203-4.
[3] Mabillon, vol. II p. 76

We notice that though it is in this *Ordo* that we are told that "the archdeacon must be very careful that nothing of the blood or body of Christ remain in chalice or paten[1]," nothing is said about any ablution of the vessels during the service.

Directions very similar in many ways are to be found even earlier in the tenth century *Codex Ratoldi* († 986) of the abbey of Corbie. We read:

At the nod of the bishop the cantor begins the Communion, *Pascha nostrum*. This being completed, let the bishop sit on his throne and having washed his hands for the third time return to the altar and say the collect *Ad complendum*[2].

Ivo of Chartres († 1115) describes the washing of the priest's hands after communion at length, and compares it with the ablutions of the Levitical priests. After the reception we read ·

After these things the priest returns to the right part of the altar, and there completes the office of the mass....It should be noted that after the handling and consumption of the sacraments before the priest returns to the assembly of the church, though he ought to have been cleansed by partaking of such great holiness, he washes his hands as from the touch of an unclean and deadly thing, and the water is poured into a sacred place provided for this purpose....Therefore they wash their hands and treat the water of ablution fittingly, in which way they honour the dignity of the sacrament, and by such an ablution call to mind their own unworthiness....Afterwards there follow prayers in which there is a remembrance of benefits received and a giving of thanks...and all these things being finished, the priest or the deacon says, *Ite missa est*[3].

Though the water with which the celebrant's hands were washed is disposed of so carefully nothing is said

---

[1] Mabillon, vol II pp 75–6 See p 100
[2] Martene, vol. I lib I. cap IV Art. XII. Ordo XI p. 204
[3] *De Rebus Eccles. Sermones.* Hittorp, col 808

VIII]   THE ABLUTIONS   127

about any ablution of the vessels, or precaution against irreverence with regard to what remains.

In the description of mass written by John of Avranches (*c.* 1065) when appointed archbishop of Rouen, describing the ceremonial of Rouen, we find further development, though the date is earlier:

The particle which remained in the chalice let the priest consume, and afterwards let him give the chalice to the deacon to cleanse and consume what is left; and let him carry away the chalice with the paten to the left corner of the altar, and there receive part himself and give part to the subdeacon. Afterwards let each take a share in cleansing each. And let an acolyte bring another chalice to the priest to wash his fingers. And let the subdeacon help the deacon to cleanse the chalice and paten. After the cleansing of paten and chalice let an acolyte hold each, wrapped in a napkin until the end of the first Post Communion[1].

For the first time we find details not only of the washing of the priest's fingers, but also of the sacred vessels, which takes place in church after the communion and the consumption of the remains, and before the end of the service. Nothing is said about the disposal of the water in which they were washed, and presumably it was poured away. The priest's hands are washed, not in the fair vessel of the Admonition of the pseudo Leo, nor in the chalice used at the mass, but in another chalice. We note that the whole ceremony of consuming the remains, washing the vessels and the priest's hands, which originally had taken place in the sacristy, has now come to be performed, presumably from motives of greater reverence, near the altar and during the service. If the cleansing could be performed by some one else besides the priest it is not surprising that sooner or later it should be carried out by the deacon or subdeacon immediately after the communion of the

[1] *De Off Eccles*, P L CXLVII col. 37

people, and while the priest concludes the service. It would be a great convenience that the vessels clean and dry should thus be put away at the end of mass on the departure of the ministers from the altar.

In a letter of Peter Damien († 1072) to the priest Ubertus we find a further development:

With regard to the celebration of the solemnities of masses we have both learned and hold this rule according to the custom in well-ordered churches, that we put off pouring into the chalice at the end of mass if we hope ourselves to offer the sacrifice again the same day. Otherwise whenever we offer the sacred hosts at the end we always besprinkle the chalice according to custom. Further whether we are fasting or not, we do not change this rule of besprinkling[1].

Peter Damien appears to be the first to mention a ceremonial pouring into the chalice, but he does not tell us whether it is identical with the pouring over the priest's fingers, or even mention the latter at all, nor does he say whether the ablution is of wine or water. It seems more probable that wine was used, and this was certainly the custom later, but in view of the omission of the sprinkling when the priest had to celebrate again it is improbable that there was any pouring over the priest's fingers into the chalice or other vessel, apart from the final washing of his hands; but however this may have been the ablution was consumed by the priest and not poured away, or the ablution need not have been omitted before a second mass. The ceremony is clearly a preliminary to the necessary washing of the vessels which must take place later and after the service, at any rate when there was no minister. The ablution he says is already traditional in well-ordered churches, but as yet it is not universally regarded as an essential feature of mass.

In Roman *Ordo X* (eleventh century) we get the sug-

---

[1] *Epis.* lib VIII ep. xviii, *P.L.* CXLIV. col. 370.

gestion of further elaboration. In the description of the Good Friday ceremonies we read:

And the pontiff alone communicates without the ministers, not solemnly at his throne, but on this day only before the altar out of humble reverence for God and the passion of Christ. And on the present Friday, and when mass is celebrated for the dead, he makes the ablution in the chalice and consumes it himself, and afterwards washes with water in the bowls[1].

We note that it is only at requiems and the communion of the presanctified on Good Friday that the ablution is made in the chalice, apparently that used at the mass. As this is a preliminary to the washing of his hands it seems that the ablution in the chalice was made over his fingers, and in view of later practice probably of wine. At requiems and on Good Friday the ablution is consumed by the pope, on ordinary occasions presumably by other of the ministers.

In the Carthusian Statutes (c. 1230) we are told:

After consuming the blood the priest on every occasion consumes the first ablution immediately without any interval.... When the priest washes his fingers in water *Agnus Dei* is begun....On every occasion when mass is sung he who assists the priest, whether he communicates or not, takes the chalice, washes it with wine and consumes it, but only when he communicates. Otherwise the wine is poured into the sacrarium, and the chalice as in other masses is turned over upon the paten[2].

As the chalice is afterwards washed with wine the first ablution can hardly be of anything else. Presumably it is made into the chalice and consumed by the priest. The washing of the fingers in water must be in another vessel, and as the wine with which the chalice is washed is not necessarily consumed, the water of ablution is probably poured into the piscina.

[1] Mabillon, vol II p 103
[2] Martene, vol I lib I cap IV Art XII Ordo XXV p 228

Innocent III (1198–1216) in a work on *The Sacred Mystery of the Altar* written before his elevation to the papacy, describing the practice of his time, bases his words on those of Ivo of Chartres.

After the consumption of the sacrifice of the eucharist the priest washes and besprinkles his hands lest anything remain unawares after touching the most divine sacrament, not that he has contracted any uncleanness in touching the sacrament, but rather that he may remember his own unworthiness who has judged himself unworthy of celebrating so great sacraments...and indeed account it unfitting that the hands which have handled the incorruptible body should touch a corruptible body until they are carefully washed. But the water of ablution ought to be poured away honourably into a clean place that the dignity of the sacrament may be more reverently esteemed[1].

About the year 1212 the Bishop of Maguelonne and the clergy of his cathedral of St Peter wrote to Innocent III asking for a ruling with regard to the ablutions. In the pope's letter of reply we read:

You desire to be instructed by letters apostolic when a priest ought to besprinkle at mass. To which we thus make answer. The priest ought always to besprinkle with wine after he has received the whole sacrament of the eucharist except when on the same day he has to celebrate another mass, lest if by chance he received the wine of ablution, he should be hindered from another celebration[2].

We notice that no information is given about what is to be besprinkled or washed, whether the chalice, the priest's mouth or fingers, or all three, but the ablution is evidently in the chalice and clearly quite distinct from the washing with water mentioned in the previous extract, for the wine is to be consumed but the water poured away in a

---

[1] *De Sacro Altari Mysterio*, lib VI 8, *P L*. CCXVII col 910-11
[2] *P L* CCXV col 442 Cf *Decret Greg IX*, lib III tit xli *De celebratione*, c v *Corpus Juris Canonici*, Pars II Ed Friedburg, 1881, col. 636

clean place. In the version of this letter used and commented on by St Thomas Aquinas († 1274) we read: "The priest ought always to rinse (besprinkle) his mouth with wine[1]," but there is no reference to the mouth in the authentic text, and more probably the ablution of the chalice is intended.

In the Order of the Offices of the church of Siena compiled in 1213 by Orderic, a canon of the church, we find interesting directions with regard to the ablutions:

The communion being received by the priest, and all the ministers and those who were to be communicated communicated, the deacon folds the corporal and puts it back in its place, and if any of the body remains he puts it away with the greatest care. And this done the priest washes over the chalice the tips of the fingers of each hand with which he has consecrated the body of the Lord, the deacon near the altar holding the chalice from underneath, and the subdeacon pouring the wine. And afterwards he washes the same fingers over a bowl with water given by an acolyte. Then wiping his fingers with a towel which was put on the corner of the altar he drinks up the ablution of wine which is in the chalice, and so all things being arranged the deacon and subdeacon return to stand in their place behind the priest[2].

Only one ablution is mentioned, of the priest's fingers, and nothing is said about a washing of the chalice. Wine is used, and the ablution is over the chalice, but afterwards there is a washing of the same fingers with water over a bowl.

Alexander of Hales († 1245) gives a paraphrase of the directions of Innocent III[3], but as he was an Englishman we may perhaps reserve it for consideration later when dealing with the history of the ablutions in Britain.

[1] *Summa*, Pars III Quaes LXXXIII *De ritu eucharistiae*, Art. v 10, *P L* IV (Second Series), col 848.
[2] Trombelli, *Ordo Off Ecc Senensis*, Pt II. § 68, p. 472.
[3] *Tractat. de Officio Missae*, Pars II. *Summa Theol.* 1622, vol III p. 327 See pp. 150-1.

The remarks of Durandus († 1296) on the ablutions in his *Rationale of the Divine Offices* are clearly based on the paraphrase of Ivo of Chartres by Innocent III. We read:

After the consumption of the sacrifice of the eucharist the priest washes and besprinkles his fingers lest anything by chance remain unawares, or adhere after touching the divine sacrament, not that he has contracted any uncleanness in touching it, but rather that he may remember his own unworthiness who judges himself unworthy of celebrating so great sacraments....It is indeed unfitting that his hands which have handled the incorruptible body should take hold of a corruptible body, or approach and touch common things until they are carefully washed. And on account of this also some, when mass is finished and they have put off the sacred vestments, wash their hands again. And the water of ablution ought to be poured into a clean and honourable place that the dignity of the sacrament may be reverently esteemed....And the priest besprinkles his fingers and consumes the ablution at the right corner of the altar, or at least turning towards it....Some having drunk the ablution put the chalice on its side[1].

In the ancient *Rituale* of the church of Soissons we find a reminiscence of Roman *Ordo X*. We read·

The Communion is so called because it is sung at the time of communion. And so to complete (ad complendum) the mystery of our salvation let the subdeacon pour wine into the chalice. At the ablution of the hands let the clerks minister water in bowls let this ablution also be poured into the piscina which is reserved for the use of the high altar[2].

Again there is no mention of the pouring of wine over the priest's fingers, but it could hardly have been omitted.

In the Roman *Ordo* printed by Martene describing the duties of the cardinal deacon when he assists the pope at mass on festivals only one ablution is mentioned. We read

---

[1] *Rationale*, lib IV cap lv *De Perfusione*, f lxxviii
[2] Martene, vol I lib. I cap IV Art XII Ordo XXII pp 220–21.

And after the subdeacon has sucked the reed at both ends the same cardinal places the reed upon the paten, and the subdeacon afterwards consumes what is in the chalice. Then the same cardinal turns to the cardinal bishop who brings to him the ablution which the pope had made after receiving the body and blood, and he takes it and drinks a little and gives the rest to the subdeacon to drink[1].

As the ablution made by the pope is brought to the cardinal while the subdeacon is in the act of consuming what is left in the chalice, it must be that of the pope's fingers made in another vessel, not that of the chalice. There is no mention of the washing of the pope's hands in the bowls as elsewhere.

In the statutes of the monastery of St Victor in Paris (thirteenth century) we find a description of the ceremonial ablutions in a developed state, but when there is a communion of the people they are only a preliminary to the more thorough cleansing of the sacred vessels with the consumption of the smallest fragments of the consecrated hosts which still takes place after mass at the altar. We read:

And when all have communicated let the brethren who are in the choir sing the Communion, and then let the deacon with the chalice and the subdeacon with a cruet of wine cross to the corner of the altar, and let the priest take the chalice and wash his fingers in it, and then do the rest in the accustomed manner. But it should be known that as often as the body of the Lord is administered from the paten, and as often as the blood from the chalice, to another besides the priest, the deacon ought when he returns with the subdeacon to the altar after mass, having first washed his hands, to wash the paten itself and to pour the ablution into the chalice, and he or the subdeacon to consume it then the subdeacon pouring water let him wash the chalice both within and without, and the paten

---

[1] Martene, vol. I. lib. I. cap. IV. Art. XII p 246.

in the piscina, and wipe it with a towel provided for the purpose[1].

The priest washes his hands in the piscina after the first ablution in the chalice, for we read:

And after the Pax has been received each will turn to the altar, and they will so stand until the priest goes to the piscina. Then the Communion will be begun[2].

The Customs of the Cistercians (c. 1120) likewise provide for the more ancient manner of making the ablutions after the service, and though earlier in date than the statutes of the monastery of St Victor the directions are more elaborate, and show really a more advanced stage of development. We read:

Receiving the chalice let him besprinkle his fingers within it, and placing it upon the altar go to the piscina to wash his fingers in water. Wiping them on the moderate sized linen cloth provided for him for the purpose let him return to the altar to consume the wine which he has poured into the chalice. After receiving it let him again besprinkle the chalice with wine. Having drunk this let him place it, not on its side, upon the altar next the paten....After *Benedicamus Domino* or *Ite missa est* has been said let him (the deacon) bow, and then going to the altar let him take away from it the chalice and the paten upon a salver, consuming there with his tongue anything which may have been left over of the body of the Lord upon the paten. And afterwards taking the tube let him wash it with wine, and afterwards the paten. After drinking this let him pour other wine into the chalice rinsing the inside, and let him again receive it. Let him a third time pour in wine, rinsing it in the same manner, and this let the subdeacon finish. And if it shall be necessary let him pour in wine still another time, and having washed and wiped them on the towel on which

---

[1] Martene, vol III. lib IV. App. *Ant Cons. S Vict. Paris*, cap 1. p 277
[2] Cap. lxviii p 283

THE ABLUTIONS

a little before the priest wiped his fingers, let him put them away, and the corporals with the chalices[1].

At Cluny ceremonial elaboration took place at an early date, and already in the eleventh century we find not only the ceremonial ablutions after the communion but also that the necessary cleansing of the vessels, which also has become an elaborate ceremony, has been transferred from after the service to the same place. We quote Ulrich's version, but practically the same directions are to be found in the Constitutions of the monastery of St Benignus at Dijon, which appear to be based on an earlier text of the Cluny statutes[2]:

If the body of the Lord remain over, or if it seem good to him (the priest), it is covered with the scutella, and he who holds it does not move away thence until the priest after taking the chalice from the subdeacon consumes the blood and the wine with which he afterwards washes the chalice, which is poured by the same subdeacon who holds the cruet in one hand, and with the other, which is wrapped in a linen cloth, which he had placed with the paten upon the altar, lifts up the foot of the chalice. The deacon after receiving the communion goes near the armariolum that he may wash with wine in another chalice his fingers, with which he has handled the Lord's body, the minister who is serving pouring the wine from the cruet and lifting the foot of the chalice. And after washing he first wipes them on the chalice and then puts it to his face, and that part which he wiped to his mouth, and consumes the wine turning to the east....And the subdeacon, as soon as the priest has consumed the blood and the wine with which he afterwards washed the chalice, takes from him the chalice kissing his hand, and from the deacon the paten belonging to the chalice, which he had taken from the altar, one of the corporals being always put upon it,—for the other he puts back into its place upon the altar—and then he who holds the scutella lifting it on high

[1] Martene, vol IV lib II cap IV §§ XV, XX p 65.
[2] Martene, vol IV lib II cap IV § XV p 64

goes to the left corner of the altar, and the subdeacon remains with the chalice on the right, holding the chalice in one hand behind the priest, the paten with the corporal being lifted up for a short time with the other And towards them the whole convent genuflects out of reverence for the body and blood of the Lord. And as soon as the minister who is serving has poured the wine on the fingers of the deacon he approaches towards the foot pace (reclinatorium) bringing the other smaller chalice with the cruet, with which he has ministered to the deacon and which he afterwards took from him, that the priest also may wash his fingers with which he has handled the Lord's body, which he is never allowed to wash in the chalice of the high mass. After taking this wine is again poured into the chalice, that the chalice itself may be washed a little, and it is consumed by the priest. And as often as he consumes either the blood or the wine which is left he turns his face towards the altar or towards the east. And he who carries the candlestick, after the priest has returned from the pax, immediately takes it and holds it lifted up before the step, and does not put it down before *Per Dominum nostrum* of the first Post Communion collect is said. At the same time both the subdeacon with the chalice and the minister with the scutella depart....
And after the subdeacon and minister have departed from before the altar each carries his own things to the armariolum, and there although it be bright day both, that is to say the paten upon which the body of the Lord was broken and the chalice, are most carefully examined with a taper by the subdeacon and minister lest by chance even the most minute portion of the Lord's body remain, and if he should see anything remain he does not presume to touch it with his hand but lifts it with his tongue only and consumes it, if it be a particle such as he can conveniently consume, but if it be very minute and as one may say indivisible and like an atom, if he can he takes it with wine in the chalice in which the priest and deacon wash their fingers, and lifts it and removes it. But if it so adhere that this cannot be done with wine, he puts his tongue lightly on the place where he saw it and consumes it, and afterwards again pours wine

upon the paten. But even if he has discovered that nothing of any size remains there, yet let him not because of this omit to pour wine upon it very carefully at any rate once, and consume entirely what was poured; and afterwards he washes the same chalice in which he consumed the wine which was poured upon the paten with other wine, or he puts that other wine, with which either he or the minister washed the chalice of the high mass inside, into that chalice and consumes it, and puts other wine into the chalice of the high mass, and washes it all round inside, and if the minister has communicated he will drink it, but if not the subdeacon, after he has consumed the wine poured upon the paten, puts it, as was said, into that chalice on which the same paten was placed and consumes it, and then does not wash it with other wine unless by chance he discovers that something remains there afterwards....And if they are able to finish a little before the end of mass neither of them ought because of this to unvest. And when the priest leaves the altar he gives the missal to the deacon that it may be carried back by him[1].

In comparison with this very complicated account the description of what is done at low mass is quite simple:

Then he consumes the blood. Then his companion pours wine into the chalice for the first time, and the third time pours it over the first four fingers which have handled the body of the Lord, and these after the ablution he ought to wipe on the front part of the chalice whence he consumed the blood. Then he puts the chalice to his own mouth, and does likewise for his companion if he has communicated, and he receives it, and his companion kisses his hand when he returns the chalice to the priest[2].

The description of low mass is, as we should expect, based on that of high mass, for it is high mass which is properly the norm of any rite, and low mass is merely a

---

[1] Martene, vol IV lib II cap IV § XV pp 63–4. *P L.* CXLIX col. 721–3

[2] Martene, vol. IV. lib II cap IV. § XX p. 71

convenient curtailment. We note that the pouring of wine into the chalice is distinct from the pouring over the priest's fingers, and this ablution of the chalice takes place twice before the ablution of the fingers. If he has communicated the server assists in the consumption of the ablutions.

From the beginning of the thirteenth century references to the ablutions are plentiful, but there was great variety of practice. About this time we begin to find rules about what is to be done when a priest duplicates, but the fact that it was necessary for councils so frequently to make decrees on the subject shows clearly that as yet there was no rule which was generally accepted and absolute. Various British councils considered the question, and made canons dealing with it, as those of Westminster in 1200, Durham in 1220, Oxford in 1222, and Aberdeen in 1230[1]. We find similar rules also in the constitutions of Richard le Poor of Salisbury (c. 1220), of Archbishop Langton in 1222, and of Archbishop Edmund of Abingdon in 1236, and elsewhere[2]. Reserving these for the present we may note a canon of the council of Cologne in 1280. We read·

And now in the first mass after the reception of the blood let him not take the ablution of wine and water, but reserve it in a safe and proper place, and receive it at the second mass, or let him give it to a proper person who is fasting and whom he knew to be ready for the purpose[3].

At the council of Nîmes in 1284 we find what was to become the ordinary practice of the West.

We decree also that in the chalice there be placed more wine than water, and that after the priest has received the whole

---

[1] Wilkins, *Concilia*, vol I. pp 505, 579, 586 *Registrum Aberdonense*, vol II p 27

[2] Spelman, *Concilia*, vol II p 148 Wilkins, vol I p 594 Spelman, vol II pp 206, 232 See pp 151-4

[3] Harduin, vol VII col 825

THE ABLUTIONS

of the sacrament of the body and blood of Christ, he shall make two receptions according to the custom of the church of Nîmes, the first of pure wine only, the second of wine and water; and with the second let him at the same time besprinkle his fingers over the chalice and afterwards receive it, except when he has to celebrate another mass the same day, and then he ought not to receive it but only the blood. And if he receives it, it prevents the second celebration[1].

In Roman *Ordo XIV* the ceremony of the ablutions is mentioned several times, and as these directions form the basis of the modern Roman rules, we must give the chief of the accounts in full. We note the influence of the Admonition of the pseudo Leo in the phraseology, and so ultimately of the epistle of the pseudo Clement·

Afterwards the chalice being uncovered by the deacon, he will be able to wipe the paten over it a little with his right thumb, so that if anything of the host remains on it, it may fall into the chalice, and let him say the verses, *Quid retribuam, Calicem,* and the other things which are to be said before the consumption of the blood, as they are contained in the book. And then let him consume the blood with the portion of the host which is in the chalice with all reverence and care. After consuming it let him take a little wine in the chalice, the subdeacon pouring it, and consume it to wash his mouth Afterwards saying the prayers, *Quod ore sumpsimus* and *Corpus tuum,* let him hold the fingers of each hand, with which he has touched the host, over the chalice and wash them a little, the subdeacon again pouring the wine. And before he consumes it let him wash his fingers again in water, which a chaplain pours into the bowls, and let this water be thrown away in a clean place. Having washed his fingers in water in the aforementioned manner let the pontiff wipe his mouth with a towel, which he who keeps the mitre offers to him. Afterwards having drunk the wine which was in the chalice let him wipe his mouth with the same cloth. Meanwhile let the deacon,

[1] Hardouin, vol. VII. col 916.

having washed his fingers, fold the corporals and put them away in the place in which they ought to be kept[1].

In Roman *Ordo XV* we have already mentioned the washing of the pope's hands in the great bowls. More details are given with regard to the ceremony of the ablutions on Good Friday, the description being based on that in *Ordo X*. We read·

And the pope communicates alone without the ministers... and he consumes the blood not with the reed, but from the chalice, and after the consumption of the blood wine is poured into the chalice by the sacristan, or other bishop who serves him in the mass, and it is consumed from the chalice at the corner of the altar; and in the same place he washes his hands in water in the bowls brought by one of the soldiers, or servants of the household[2].

On Maundy Thursday there was no reference to any ablution of the chalice or of the priest's fingers over it. On Good Friday though there is mention of the former all reference to the latter is still omitted. On Easter Day there is no mention of any ablution of the chalice, and presumably it is performed by the subdeacon to whom both chalice and tube are delivered that he may consume whatever remains, not by the pope. We read:

And after all have communicated the confessor of the pope if he be a bishop approaches, but if not another bishop of the papal household brings the golden chalice covered with one end of the linen cloth, the other end hanging over his left shoulder according to custom. And after the bishop the senior of the acolytes carries the cruets of wine and water with two cups covered with the cloth with which the altar-pall is covered. And the afore-mentioned bishop comes with the said acolyte to the pope, and the second bishop washes the small cup of gold with wine. Then he pours wine over the fingers of the pope and the second bishop carries the perfusion of his fingers to the altar, and the cardinal deacon with the subdeacon

---

[1] Mabillon, vol II pp. 307-8.   [2] Mabillon, vol II. pp 494-5.

drinks it according to custom. The confessor, having washed the chalice, pours wine and the acolyte water into the chalice, both kneeling before the pope, and the lord pope washes his mouth, and consumes the wine in the afore-mentioned chalice; and if any remains the subdeacon consumes it over the altar. Then the pope washes his hands in the great golden bowls, and having washed them he goes to the altar and so finishes mass[1].

It may be interesting to trace the development in the later Roman printed books.

In the earliest printed Roman missal of 1474 the rubric with regard to the ablutions is quite short.

After the consumption of the blood let him say *Quod ore*. Then while purifying he says *Corpus tuum*[2].

In the 1505 edition the first part of this becomes·

The blood being drunk he afterwards besprinkles his fingers, saying *Quod ore*[3].

In 1558 there is a further enlargement:

The blood being drunk let him afterwards besprinkle his fingers with wine and water, saying *Quod ore*[4].

In a Roman missal printed at Venice in 1501, probably for Franciscan use, we find an introduction by John Burchard on the order to be observed in saying mass With regard to the ablutions we read·

He reverently consumes the whole of the blood with the particle put in the chalice, and having consumed these he says *Quod ore* (another prayer, *Corpus tuum*), holding out the chalice meanwhile to the minister who pours wine into it, and with it the priest purifies himself. Then the same minister pouring wine the priest washes his thumbs and forefingers over the chalice and consumes this ablution also. Then he wipes his mouth and fingers and the chalice, he folds the corporals, and puts them down in the middle of the altar[5].

[1] Mabillon, vol II pp 506–7   [2] Lippe, vol. I p. 211
[3] Lippe, vol I p 211, vol II p 114   [4] Lippe, vol I p 211, vol II p 114.
[5] Legg, *Tracts on the Mass*, p 164.

In 1502 Burchard published an enlarged version of his *Ordo missae*, and in this form, as we have noticed, it was reprinted many times, either as a separate tract, or as an introduction to various missals, or incorporated in other works. We now read

And standing he reverently consumes the whole of the blood with the particle put in the chalice. And having consumed these he says secretly *Quod ore*, holding out the chalice meanwhile to the minister who pours wine into it, and with it the celebrant purifies himself. And if there are any to be communicated he communicates them before he washes his fingers, the order on the time and manner of communicating the people given in the *Presbyterale* being observed. Then purifying himself and the rest of those who have communicated he says secretly *Corpus tuum*. The same minister again pouring wine, the celebrant washes his thumbs and forefingers over the chalice, and consumes the ablution also. Then he also wipes his mouth and the chalice with the purificator, and puts the purificator over the chalice, and over it the paten, and places it as seems best to him on the right side or left, or puts it down in the middle of the altar[1].

We see here the distinction clearly drawn between a "purification" and an "ablution," the former referring to the rinsing of the priest's or communicant's mouth after partaking, the latter to the washing of the chalice or the priest's fingers. Usually the first pouring is both.

Burchard's directions about what is to be done when a priest duplicates are also interesting. We read.

These or any other priests in cases permitted by law wishing to celebrate twice in a day ought not in the first mass after the consumption of the blood to purify themselves or to consume the ablution of the fingers, but after the consumption of the blood to wash his fingers over the chalice, and to put away this ablution into some clean vessel, and to purify himself with it another day on which he has celebrated one mass only

[1] Legg, p. 164.

after the consumption of the blood, or on the same day after the said second mass, or to consume it after the purification and ablution of the same second mass. But more than two masses in one day it is not lawful to celebrate, save only on the day of the nativity of our Saviour Jesus Christ, on which any priest otherwise disposed to celebrate is able to celebrate three masses And also when intending to do this he ought not in the first or second mass to purify himself, or to take the ablution of his fingers, but to put it away in some clean vessel, and to consume it after the purification of the third mass. But if anyone intending to celebrate more masses on the same day has purified himself in the first or second mass or consumed the ablution, he ought not to celebrate again that day[1].

In the Book of Ceremonies of Patricius and Marcellus of 1516 we read after the communion·

Then the pope sits and an acolyte approaches with two cups, one of gold for the pope and the other for the credence, carrying in his hands ampullae of wine and water, and with him comes the chief of the cardinal priests who pours wine over the golden cup, and the pope without mitre washes his fingers. Then taking his mitre he washes his hands in the accustomed manner. Then he descends to the altar and mass is finished[2].

The directions of de Grassis († 1528) are shorter:

He will purify his fingers in the accustomed manner and consume the ablution. Then if there shall be hosts upon the altar he will wash his hands on the epistle side without mitre and finish mass[3].

In the post Tridentine missal of 1570 the rubric dealing with the ablutions has become much more detailed:

He consumes the whole of the blood with the particle. And when he has consumed it if there are any to be communicated let him communicate them before he purifies himself. Afterwards he says *Quod ore*. Meanwhile he holds out the chalice

---
[1] Legg, p 172
[2] Lib II cap 1 § 6 Ed Catalani, vol. II pp 269–70.
[3] Lib. II 49, f 141. See p. 108.

to the minister who pours into it a little wine with which he purifies himself. Then he proceeds *Corpus tuum*. He washes his fingers, wipes them and consumes the ablution. He wipes the chalice, and having folded the corporal covers it in the accustomed manner. Then he proceeds with mass[1].

In the *Ritus Servandus in Celebratione Missarum* prefixed to this missal we read:

Standing he reverently consumes the whole of the blood with the particle put in the chalice. And when he has consumed these he says secretly *Quod ore*. Afterwards he holds out the chalice over the altar to the minister at the epistle corner, and on his pouring in wine he purifies himself. Then he washes his thumbs and forefingers over the chalice and wipes them with the purificator: saying meanwhile *Corpus tuum* he consumes the ablution. Then he wipes his mouth and the chalice with the purificator, and having done this spreads the purificator over the chalice, and over it the paten and over the paten the small pall, and covers it with the veil, folds the corporal and puts it back in the burse which he puts over the chalice, and places it on the altar as before. If there are any to be communicated during mass, let him communicate them before he takes the purification and before he washes his fingers; and when they are communicated he says *Quod ore*, and then purifying himself and those who have communicated he says *Corpus tuum*, and does the rest as above.

In the revised missal of Clement VIII of 1604 the rubric is altered but little. The chief modification is that the priest "wipes his mouth and the chalice" before folding the corporal. In the first part of the *Ritus servandus* there is likewise very little change, but we are told that the priest "washes his thumbs and forefingers with wine and water over the chalice." The directions when there are communicants are much more precise and may be quoted. We read.

[1] Lippe, vol II. p 246.

THE ABLUTIONS

If there are any to be communicated during mass the priest after the consumption of the blood before he purifies himself, makes a genuflexion and puts the consecrated particles in a pyx, or, if there are few to be communicated, on the paten, unless they have been put in a pyx or another chalice from the beginning....When all are communicated he returns to the altar saying nothing, and does not give them the blessing because he will give it at the end of mass. If the particles were put on the corporal he wipes it with the paten, and if there were any fragments on it, he puts them into the chalice. Then he says secretly *Quod ore* and purifies himself saying *Corpus tuum*, and does the rest as above. And a minister holding a vessel with wine and water in his right hand and a napkin in his left, a little behind the priest, offers them the purification and the napkin to wipe their mouths.

The changes made in the Roman missal by Urban VIII in 1634 had practically no effect on the directions dealing with the ablutions, and they are almost verbally identical with those which appeared in the edition of 1604.

With some few exceptions the reformed missal of 1570, which was revised under the authority of the council of Trent, was imposed upon the whole Roman communion by the bull of Pius V, and in ordinary churches no deviation from this standard was allowed. It was the same also with the editions of the missal as revised by Clement VIII and Urban VIII. Pius V however in his bull did except those churches which could show a prescription of two hundred years for their own local uses, and it was continued after the later reforms. Consequently the ancient customs of such churches as those of Rouen, Lyons, Chartres, as also of the Carthusian, Carmelite and Dominican orders still survived. At Rouen as late as the beginning of the eighteenth century the ceremonial at the ablutions was still much the same as that described by John of Avranches in the eleventh century.

De Moléon gives some interesting particulars of ancient

ceremonial still surviving when he wrote in 1718 in various French churches. We read:

In all the missals of Rouen printed up to last century...there is only one purification or ablution with wine as at Lyons and among the Carthusians. The last ablution with water and wine was not then practised and they did not compel the priest to drink the rinsing of his fingers. He went to wash his hands at the piscina or lavatory which was near the altar (sacerdos vadat ad lavatorium). The same thing is seen in the missal of the Carmelites of the year 1574, and the Ritual of Rouen requires that there should be one near every altar as in the church of St Etienne des Tonneliers at Rouen[1].

A similar custom prevailed also at that date at Chartres. We read:

The deacon brings the cruets and pours the ablutions. This is the only place where the deacon serves the priest, since a boy gives him water to wash in a bowl, as at the lavabo, and pours it into the piscina, so that he is not obliged to drink the rinsing of his fingers. Formerly this was practised everywhere, and it is still practised to this day at Lyons and among the Carthusians who have continued to maintain their ancient customs[2].

Nothing is said, we may note in conclusion, in any of the Mozarabic service books about the ablutions, but in practice those usual in the rest of the Western Church, of the chalice and of the priest's fingers, have been adopted[3]. The modern Ambrosian rite has taken over not only the Roman practice, but the Roman rubrics also.

We have now traced out from the various documents the chief points in the history of the ceremony of the ablutions from the time that we first hear of any such thing until the present day, reserving, however, the consideration of specifically British authorities for separate

[1] De Moléon, *Voyages Liturgiques de France*, p 315
[2] De Moléon, p. 230.
[3] Lesley, *Missale Mixtum*, p 233 P L LXXXV col 566

THE ABLUTIONS

treatment. In the earliest days and for many centuries there appear to have been no ceremonial ablutions at all, either of the chalice or of the priest's hands after the communion, during mass, but only a necessary and reverent washing of them afterwards in the sacristy. By about the ninth century however, if not earlier, the washing of the priest's hands had been introduced into the ordinary course of the service and took place immediately after the communion. At about the same period we find that the washing of the vessels was transferred, at any rate in some churches, from the sacristy to a place near the altar, the water employed being reverently poured away in a place provided for the purpose. Generally it seems to have been performed by the deacon and subdeacon, not by the priest, but still apparently after the service was over. The next century we read of the washing of the priest's hands immediately after communion as a firmly established custom. In the eleventh century we hear of an ablution of the chalice, presumably with wine which is consumed by the priest, and that it is traditional in well-ordered churches. This takes place before the final cleansing of the vessels, which also in some churches has now begun to take place during the service. There is also before the washing of the priest's hands in bowls or at the piscina, an ablution of his fingers, sometimes in another chalice, but sometimes in that of the mass, whether with wine or water is not mentioned, but presumably with the former, and it is consumed by the priest or ministers. In the twelfth century we find it clearly stated that the ablution of the priest's fingers is with wine which is consumed, though we hear also after a first ablution of a sprinkling with water. There is a cleansing of the chalice with wine during the service by the minister, and this is sometimes consumed and sometimes poured away. The water in which the priest's hands were washed is always put into the piscina. By this time it seems that the method of making the ablutions is becoming more or less fixed. With elaborations on occasions, such as the ablution of the priest's fingers by the subdeacon or other minister, practically the same use persists for some centuries. In different places there was variety of detail, sometimes wine was used for the ablutions both of the chalice and of the priest's fingers, but sometimes water for the latter. In some churches there were more than two ablutions, and two of the chalice before that of the priest's fingers, one being regarded as for the purification of the mouth. Any ablution of the chalice or of the priest's fingers during the service is of late introduction according to the evidence, and was interpolated for the sake of additional reverence, being intended as a preliminary to the actual cleansing of the hands and vessels after mass was over. In some places however this necessary cleansing of the vessels came to be performed during the service immediately after the ceremonial ablutions, but in others the older practice of postponing it until the end of the service continued at any rate till the thirteenth century, the smallest fragments of the host being consumed at the same time, a survival from the days when all the consecrated remains were consumed after mass.

CHAPTER IX

THE ABLUTIONS IN BRITAIN

IT may be interesting to supplement our general enquiry into the historical development of the ceremony of the ablutions by giving also its outline as found in documents which illustrate English or British usage.

The Admonition of the pseudo Leo with its rules for the washing of the sacred vessels and the priest's hands was evidently known and regarded as authoritative in England as well as on the continent at an early date. It is found in Cotton MS., Tiberius C. I, of the British Museum[1], a manuscript belonging to the diocese of Salisbury, and written in the latter part of the eleventh century, perhaps in the episcopate of St Osmund, or even earlier, and as in later days it is for use at the Provincial Council of the bishop. The earliest examples of a piscina or "clean place" as required by the Admonition in England as elsewhere appear to have been in the floor and similar to what is described in the *Consuetudines* of Ulrich of Cluny, specimens which date perhaps from the early thirteenth century still surviving in two of the chapels of Lincoln Cathedral, and other places. Of wall piscinas there appear to be no examples in England any more than in France before the middle of the twelfth century, but Norman examples exist at St Martin's, Leicester, Ryarsh, Kent, in the crypt of Gloucester Cathedral, and two at Romsey Abbey, while at Jesus College, Cambridge, there is one approaching early English[2]. The work of John of Avranches *De Ecclesiasticis Officiis* giving the use of Rouen was

---

[1] f 191 b Cf Chambers, *Divine Worship in England*, p 11.
[2] Parker, *Glossary of Terms used in Architecture*, p. 164

known and used at the abbey of Llanthony in the twelfth century[1], and so it is not improbable that his elaborate ceremonial for the ablutions was imitated as well as other things. The ceremonial of Rouen evidently had considerable influence in Britain, the *Lay Folks Mass Book* being a description of an adaptation of it[2], while the Hereford Holy Week ceremonial is also derived from it[3]. The *Lay Folks Mass Book* in its present form belongs to the thirteenth century, and in its original text, which appears to have been in French, to the twelfth[4]. In a manuscript of about the year 1375 in the British Museum we read:

> Loke pater-noster thou be sayande,
> I-whils tho preste is rynsande.
> When tho preste has rinsynge done,
> Opon thi fete thou stonde up sone[5].

There is also a shorter text of later date (*c.* 1450):

> Whanne the prest hath the rensynge don,
> He wol make an ende son[6].

Nothing is said whether the rinsing is that of the chalice or of the priest's fingers, but probably the reference is to both. In a manuscript at Gonville and Caius College, Cambridge, also of the middle of the fifteenth century, we find "receyuande," "receuyng" instead of "rinsing[7]," and as the reference must be to the same ceremony, the ablution was evidently consumed.

Alexander of Hales († 1245), who was an Englishman, speaks of the washing of the priest's hands, as we have already noticed, and practically reproduces the remarks of Innocent III. We read:

These things being done, the priest washes his hands, not that he has contracted any uncleanness in touching the Lord's

---
[1] Bishop, *Liturgica Historica*, pp. 299, 300.
[2] Simmons, *Lay Folks Mass Book*, p xxxii.
[3] Bishop, pp. 276–300.   [4] Simmons, pp xxxi, xli–xliii
[5] Simmons, p. 54   [6] Simmons, p. 55.   [7] Simmons, p. 55.

sacrament, but rather out of reverence for the sacrament and that he may remember his own unworthiness, and that he may account it unfitting that the hands which have handled the incorruptible body should touch a corruptible body, or anything unclean until they are carefully washed, and also in order that if anything has by chance adhered to his hands in touching the sacrament it may be washed away. And the water of ablution ought to be poured away honourably into a clean place, that the dignity of the sacrament may be more reverently esteemed[1].

The Consuetudinaries of Salisbury (thirteenth century), Wells (thirteenth century), and Exeter (fourteenth century), all ultimately Sarum, also mention only the earlier washing of the hands:

After the reception of the sacrament, while the priest goes to wash his hands, let the deacon fold the corporals[2].

It is the same also in the Vernon MS. of the thirteenth or fourteenth century,—*A treatise of the manner & mede of the mass*. We read:

> Whon he hath used, he walketh riht
> To lauatorie, ther hit is diht
> For to wassche his hende.
> So gostly he comes a-geyn
> Un-to god for-to preyen
> Sum special grace[3].

The question of the ablutions and particularly what was to be done when a priest celebrated twice in the same day, occupied the attention of various British councils about the beginning of the thirteenth century. Among the canons of the council of Westminster in 1200 we read:

When the same priest celebrates twice in one day after the first celebration and the consumption of the blood let nothing

---

[1] *Summa Theol* vol. III p 327 See p 131
[2] Frere, *The Use of Sarum*, vol I p 88 Reynolds, *Wells Cathedral*. *Ordinale et Statuta*, p. 38 Dalton, *Ordinale Exon* (H B S) vol. I p. 298
[3] Simmons, p 145

be poured into the chalice, but of course let the drainings of the chalice be most carefully swallowed after the first celebration, and the fingers sucked, or licked with the tongue, and washed, the ablution being reserved in a clean vessel provided specially for the purpose, and let this ablution be consumed after the second celebration. Let these things be so done unless at the first celebration a deacon or other proper minister be present who can consume the ablution[1].

At the council of Durham in 1220 we find a washing of the paten also, and now any innocent person is allowed to consume the ablutions. Two of the decrees read.

And if he receives it (the host) from the paten as some do after the celebration of mass let him cause both paten and chalice to be besprinkled with water, or if he does not receive it from the paten, the chalice only. And let the priest have near the altar a most clean cloth wrapped all round in another cloth, fitly and properly covered, on which after the reception of the healthful sacrament, he may wipe his fingers and his lips, when he has washed them....Also if the priest has of necessity to celebrate twice by any chance in a day—which except on Christmas Day, or Easter Day, or when a corpse is present in church for burial, or some evident necessity compel we forbid to be done—after the first celebration let the drainings of the chalice be most carefully swallowed, and what was poured over his fingers into the chalice be reserved in a clean vessel specially provided for the purpose, and be consumed after the celebration of the second mass, unless by chance at the first celebration a deacon or other proper minister, or some innocent person, be present who can consume the ablution without hurt to conscience[2].

The repeated expression "after the celebration" does not mean apparently after the conclusion of the service, but only after the communion, the remainder of the liturgy being considered presumably of negligible importance.

[1] Wilkins, vol. I p. 505   [2] Wilkins, vol I p 579

THE ABLUTIONS IN BRITAIN

In the Constitutions of Richard le Poor (c. 1220), Bishop of Salisbury, we find the same provision for the washing of both paten and chalice, and for the consumption of the ablutions, and use of the purificator, expressed in identical words, and again, "some innocent person" is allowed to take the ablutions[1].

At the council of Oxford in 1222 we have again the same rule to be observed when a priest duplicates:

And let the priest after he has consumed the Lord's body and blood at the altar, if he has himself to celebrate the solemnities of the mass a second time on the same day, not presume to consume the wine poured into the chalice, or over his fingers[2].

We find an almost identical order in the Constitutions of Archbishop Langton, also in 1222, though water is allowed as an alternative to wine

After the priest has consumed the body of Christ and the blood let him not dare to consume the water or wine put into the chalice, or poured over his fingers, if on the same day he has of necessity to celebrate the solemnities of the mass again[3].

The council of Aberdeen in 1230 repeated with but slight alteration the directions of the council of Durham in 1220, ordering the ablution of the priest's fingers to "be consumed by some person of good conscience," or reserved until after the second celebration in a clean vessel, and adding words from the decree of the council of Westminster in 1200—"after the first celebration and the consumption of the body and blood let nothing which is consumed by the celebrant be poured into the chalice, but only after the following celebration[4]."

The Constitutions of Edmund of Abingdon, Archbishop of Canterbury, of the year 1236, have the same order about the ablution of the paten and chalice, and the use of the

---
[1] Spelman, vol II p 148 [2] Wilkins, vol I p 586
[3] Wilkins, vol I p 594
[4] *Registrum Aberdonense*, vol II p 27

purificator, but the direction about what is to be done when a priest duplicates is omitted[1]. Both the Durham decrees with regard to the ablutions reappear with slight modifications in certain anonymous constitutions of perhaps a little later date[2].

By the beginning of the thirteenth century the ablutions had evidently become a regular feature of the liturgy in Britain, and at the end of the century we find references to them in the service-books. In the pontifical of Anianus, Bishop of Bangor (1267–1305), there is a mention of the threefold ablution, though no particulars are given. After *Corpus et sanguis* we read:

After the first effusion let him say *Quod ore*, after the second effusion *Haec nos communio*, after the third effusion *Gratias tibi*. After the completion of mass let the priest say *Placeat tibi*[3].

No distinction is drawn between the different ablutions, but perhaps the first and third are of the chalice, and the second of the priest's fingers in the chalice.

In a manuscript Sarum missal (perhaps earlier than 1300), formerly belonging to the Earl of Crawford, and now in the John Rylands Library at Manchester, we read:

Then let the body and blood be consumed, and afterwards let this prayer be said, *Gratias tibi*. Then let him proceed to wash his fingers and the chalice, and meanwhile say *Haec nos communio, Benedicta, Quod ore*. Mass being finished, with head bowed before the altar and hands joined, let the priest say *Placeat tibi*[4].

The three prayers suggest that there are three washings, perhaps two of the chalice and one of the priest's fingers, but nothing is said about wine or water.

A manuscript Sarum missal of about the same date, now

---

[1] Spelman, vol II p 206   [2] Spelman, vol II p 232.
[3] Henderson, *York Missal*, vol. I p 335
[4] Legg, *Sarum Missal*, p 228

THE ABLUTIONS IN BRITAIN

at the library of the Arsenal in Paris, has the same rubrics at this point, save for the omission of that before *Placeat tibi*[1].

In a manuscript containing the order for a nuptial mass, probably of the first half of the fifteenth century, and now in the British Museum, we have a rearrangement of the Crawford form of the rubric which makes nonsense, due, it would seem, to an unintelligent attempt to make *Gratias tibi* the final prayer, as it is according to another Sarum tradition. We read:

Then let him proceed to wash his fingers and the chalice, and meanwhile say *Quod ore, Haec nos communio*. Then let the body and blood be consumed, and afterwards let this prayer be said, *Gratias tibi*[2].

In a manuscript Sarum missal of a little later date than the Crawford book, now in the University Library at Bologna, the rubrics with regard to the ablutions are contradictory, for though prayers are provided for three ablutions, where the liquid to be used is prescribed they are as distinctly limited to two, due apparently to a combination of two different sets of rubrics without the necessary adjustment. We read:

At the first washing *Corpus tuum*, at the second washing let him say *Quod ore*, at the third washing let him say *Haec nos communio*. The prayer being said let the priest take the chalice and go to the right corner of the altar, and let the subdeacon minister to him wine once and water once, and let the priest say these prayers following. At the first washing of his hands in the chalice let him say *Gratias tibi*. Then let the priest turn the chalice over on the paten, and with hands joined say before the altar *Perceptio corporis*. Then let him go to the sacrarium to wash his hands, and again with hands joined let him return to the altar to say the collects; and so let mass be finished[3].

---

[1] Legg, *Sarum Missal*, p 228.
[2] Legg, *Tracts on the Mass* (H.B.S), p 266.
[3] Legg, *Sarum Missal*, p. 228.

In a manuscript Sarum missal of perhaps the beginning of the fourteenth century in Cambridge University Library (ff. 4. 44), in a manuscript manual of slightly later date belonging to the Rev. Edmund McClure, and also in a manuscript manual of the fifteenth century which belonged to the late Dr Rock, we find different rubrics again. We read·

Then let him receive. After this let the minister approach and pour wine or water into the chalice, and if it be necessary that the priest should celebrate again let him receive nothing of the effusion, but put it in the sacrarium. After the first effusion let him say *Quod ore*, after the second effusion *Haec nos communio*, after the third effusion let him say with great devotion this prayer, *Gratias tibi, Adoremus crucis, Lavabo inter innocentes*. After the completion of mass let the priest, with body bowed before the altar and hands joined, say this prayer, *Placeat tibi*[1].

Nothing is said about the liquid to be used for particular ablutions. We note the addition of *Adoremus crucis* after *Gratias tibi*, and of *Lavabo inter innocentes* presumably at the washing of the hands.

In the Sarum Customary, given in manuscripts of the Ordinal of the end of the fourteenth century, we find much more elaborate rubrics, incorporating those of the more ancient Consuetudinary and of the missals, and also the substance of the decree of the council of Westminster in 1200 on duplication. We read according to the manuscript at Corpus Christi College, Oxford:

Then let him consume the blood, and having consumed it let the priest go to the right corner of the altar with the chalice between his hands, his fingers still joined as before, and let the subdeacon approach and pour into the chalice wine and water, and let the priest rinse his hands lest any remnants of the body and blood remain on his fingers or in the chalice. But when

[1] Legg, *Tracts on the Mass*, pp 267–8 Cf Rock, *Church of our Fathers*, Ed. Hart and Frere, 1905, vol. IV p. 193.

any (priest) has to celebrate twice in one day then he ought not to receive any ablution, but to put it in the sacrarium or in a clean vessel until the end of the second mass, and then let each ablution be consumed. After the first infusion let this prayer follow, *Quod ore*. Then let him wash his fingers in the bowl of the chalice with wine poured by the subdeacon. And this being drunk this prayer, *Haec nos communio*, follows. Then let the subdeacon pour water into the chalice, and this being drunk let the priest go to the middle of the altar and bow and say with devotion this prayer, *Gratias tibi*. And with this prayer let the priest go to the right corner of the altar and wash his hands. Meanwhile let the deacon fold the corporals. Let the subdeacon carry the book to the right corner of the altar. And let the deacon take the chalice which lies on the paten, and when the priest returns to the right corner of the altar if any of the infusion remain let him hold it to the mouth of the priest for him to consume. After the reception of the sacrament, while the priest goes to wash his hands, let the deacon fold the corporals and put them back in the case. And afterwards let him place the corporals on the chalice with the chalice veil, and commit the chalice also to the acolyte until the Post Communion is said, and when *Per omnia saecula saeculorum* is said after the prayer let him carry it away with the same solemnity with which he brought it in. When he has washed his hands let the priest return to the right corner of the altar, and say the Communion with his ministers[1].

The passage "After the reception...brought it in" is taken verbatim from the Consuetudinary.

Apparently the ablution of the chalice like that of the priest's fingers is with wine, but the third pouring into the chalice is now of water. According to another text of the Ordinal, however, in a manuscript at Salisbury Cathedral, the third pouring also is of wine. This text omits, probably by an error of the copyist, the statement that when the priest goes to the right corner of the altar he "washes his

[1] Frere, *Use of Sarum*, vol. I. pp 87–8. See p 151 above.

hands" while the deacon folds the corporals, though the second reference to this washing still remains[1].

In a missal written for Colewich[2] about the year 1400 and now in the British Museum we find the directions of the Customary according to the text of the manuscript at Corpus Christi College, Oxford, incorporated with but few alterations in the ordinary of the mass instead of the shorter rubrics. Water is prescribed for the third ablution, and when the priest washes his hands at the sacrarium he says *Lavabo inter innocentes*. At the end we read. "After the reception of the sacrament, etc., as above on the First Sunday of the Advent of the Lord," the details not being repeated[3].

In another missal of about the same date, which was presented to Oswestry church in 1554, and regarded by Maskell as perhaps belonging to the use of Bangor, we find another version of the rubrics from the Sarum Customary. As in the Roman missal the priest is directed to consume "the whole of the blood." It then continues.

And having consumed it and put the chalice down upon the altar, bowing with great veneration in the middle of the altar and looking at the cross, let the priest say this prayer following *Gratias tibi*, and this being said let the priest go....

We notice that *Gratias tibi* here follows the consumption of the elements immediately, as in the Crawford missal. There are only two ablutions, the first of the priest's fingers with wine, the second of the chalice with wine or water, the different uses of the two manuscripts of the Customary being thus made alternatives, and both may be poured by the subdeacon "or some other minister." The words "After the first infusion let this prayer follow, *Quod ore*," are omitted, and *Quod ore* takes the place of *Haec nos* in the text as given in the Customary, while

---

[1] Frere, vol I pp 87–8   [2] Probably Colwich, Staffs.
[3] Harl MS. 4919 Legg, *Tracts on the Mass*, pp 266–7

Haec nos is now said after the final ablution before the priest returns to the middle of the altar. At this point there is an insertion and we read.

The prayer being finished, let the priest go to the middle of the altar and putting the chalice down there so as to lie upon the paten, and bowing with great veneration, and looking at the cross, let him say in memory of the Lord's passion *Adoremus crucis*.

The reference to the cross is thus repeated in similar words. The section "Meanwhile let the deacon...to consume," is omitted, as also the section "and give the chalice ...brought it in." We read also that the priest places the corporals "with the chalice veil or napkin" on the chalice[1].

In a manuscript Sarum missal of about the middle of the fifteenth century now in the Bodleian Library, Oxford (Rawl. Liturg. C 2), we find another form of the directions of the Sarum Customary, akin to those of the Oswestry missal, *Gratias tibi* being said after the priest's communion and before the ablutions, but with various other alterations, and without the lengthy omissions of the Oswestry manuscript. We read

Then let him consume the blood, and having consumed it and put down the chalice on the right corner of the altar, bowing with great veneration before the middle of the altar, and looking at the cross let him say, *Gratias tibi...Jesu Christi*, (then let him retire from the altar) *et precor...in vitam eternam*. Then let the priest go to the right corner of the altar, and take the chalice again between his hands, his fingers still joined as before, and the subdeacon approaching let him pour wine into the chalice, and let the priest rinse his fingers in the bowl of the chalice, lest any remnants of the body and blood remain on his fingers or in the chalice. But when any priest has to celebrate twice in one day then he ought not to receive any ablution, but to put it in the sacrarium, or in a clean vessel until the end

---

[1] Maskell, *The Ancient Liturgy of the Church of England*, pp. 184-196.

of the second mass, and then let him consume each ablution. And so the said infusion of wine being consumed let the priest say this prayer, *Quod ore*. Then the fingers with which the sacrament is handled ought to be besprinkled by the subdeacon in the bowl of the chalice, with wine, which is consumed by the priest himself. And this being drunk the prayer, *Haec nos communio*, follows. And afterwards let the priest lean the chalice over on the paten and bow in the middle of the altar and say with devotion this prayer looking at the cross, *Adoremus crucis*. Then let the priest go to the sacrarium, or to the right corner of the altar, and wash his hands, an acolyte ministering to him. And meanwhile let the deacon fold the corporals and put them back in the case. And let the subdeacon carry the book to the right corner of the altar. And when the priest returns to the right corner of the altar after the washing of his hands let the deacon take the chalice which lies on the paten, and if any of the infusion remain in it, let him hold it to the mouth of the priest for him to consume. Then let him place the corporals on it with the chalice veil, and commit it to the acolyte until the Post Communion is said, and when *Per omnia saecula saeculorum* is said after the prayer let him carry it away with the same solemnity with which he brought it in. When he has washed his hands let the priest return to the right corner of the altar, and say the Communion with his ministers[1].

We notice that here again there are only two ablutions, but it is the third and not the second as in the Oswestry missal which is omitted. Wine is prescribed on both occasions. The order to turn the chalice over on the paten is almost verbally identical with that in the early fourteenth century Bologna manuscript. The direction to look at the cross is repeated as in the Oswestry book. It is the second reference to the deacon folding the corporals while the priest washes his hands which is here omitted.

In another fifteenth century Bodleian manuscript (Laud. Misc. 164) we have another version of the directions of the

---

[1] f 123 Cf. Legg, *Tracts on the Mass*, p. 267.

ix] THE ABLUTIONS IN BRITAIN 161

Customary akin to that of the last named missal, but the influence of the rubrics of the Oswestry book is also apparent. There are three ablutions and an attempt has been made to combine the two conflicting types of Sarum rubric, and to put back *Gratias tibi* so as to follow the third ablution; for where it is found in the preceding manuscript immediately after the consumption of the elements the priest is directed to say this "prayer," though no prayer is given. There is only one reference to looking at the cross when he says *Adoremus crucis*. We read:

Then let him consume the blood, and having consumed it and put down the chalice on the right corner of the altar let him say this prayer. Then let the priest go to the right corner of the altar and take the chalice between his hands, his fingers still joined as before. And this being done let the deacon pour wine into the chalice. And this being drunk let him say *Quod ore*. Then let him wash his fingers in the bowl of the chalice with wine poured by the subdeacon. And this being drunk let him say *Haec nos communio*. Then let the subdeacon pour water into the chalice, and this being drunk let the priest go to the middle of the altar and bow and say with great veneration, looking at the cross, *Adoremus crucis*. Let *Gratias tibi* follow. Then let the priest go to the sacrarium, and there wash his hands in the sacrarium, and having washed and wiped them let him return to the right corner of the altar and say the Post Communion; and this being said let him say *Ite missa est* towards the people[1].

We notice that it is the deacon who pours the first ablution, though the subdeacon still pours the other two, and that the third ablution is of water.

In the missal presented to Westminster Abbey by Abbot Lytlyngton (1362–86) we read:

Prayer of the priest at receiving before taking (the ablutions), *Corpus et sanguis*. When the minister pours wine into the

[1] Cf. Legg, p. 266.

chalice for the ablutions let the priest say *Domine Jesu.* After the washing of the hands *Corpus Domini.* Another prayer after the washing, *Quod ore*[1].

Apparently there is only one ablution, which is of wine

In a late fourteenth century manuscript missal which belonged to the church of Sherborne, and is now at Alnwick Castle, we read

After the reception of the body and blood of the Lord, and after the first infusion say *Quod ore,* after the washing of the fingers within the chalice *Haec nos communio.* Bowing let him say *Gratias tibi.* Mass being finished let the priest bow before the altar and say *Placeat tibi*[2].

In a manuscript missal of Hereford use of the fourteenth century in the library of University College, Oxford, we read·

Then let him sign himself with the blood. Then let him go with the chalice to the right corner of the altar and make three infusions. While the first is made let him say *Quod ore,* while the second infusion is made over his fingers *Haec nos Domine,* while the third infusion is made *Tres sunt.* Then let the chalice be put on the paten. Then let the priest bow before the altar, and say on this wise *Corpus tuum.* Then let him wash his hands at the sacrarium, and say *Lavabo inter innocentes.* Then let him go to the altar, and having said the collects with *Ite missa est* let the priest before the altar, with head or body bowed and hands joined, say this prayer, *Placeat tibi*[3].

We notice a resemblance to the later directions of the Bologna Sarum missal. As at Sherborne nothing is said whether the ablutions are with wine or water, but in addition to the washing of the hands at the sacrarium there are plainly three pourings into the chalice, *Tres sunt* (1 John v. 7) supplying a mystical interpretation.

[1] Legg, *Missale Westmonast* vol II col 520–1
[2] Legg, *Liturgical Notes on the Sherborne Missal,* pp 8, 9. Cf Simmons, *Lay Folks Mass Book,* p 306
[3] Henderson, *Hereford Missal,* pp 134–5

In a fourteenth century manuscript missal of the use of York now in the Minster Library we have only two prayers, *Quod ore* and *Haec nos communio*, followed by *Placeat tibi*[1], so that probably only two ablutions are intended, but there are no rubrics.

In another copy of about the same date now at University College, Oxford, we read.

Quod ore, Haec nos communio, Tres sunt. After mass let him bow. *Placeat tibi*[2].

Here there are probably three ablutions corresponding to the number of the prayers, the third again providing the mystical meaning.

In a manuscript breviary of the use of York of the fourteenth century, now in the Minster Library, we find also the canon of the mass, etc., and as given here the rubrics are somewhat more elaborate. We read.

When first the wine is poured into the chalice after the reception this prayer is said, *Quod ore*. Secondly after the infusion of the water into the chalice let the priest say *Haec nos communio, Tres sunt*. Then let him bow his body in the middle of the altar and say as he goes to the lavatory this prayer, *Gratias tibi*. After the completion of mass let the priest, with body bowed and hands joined before the altar, say this prayer, *Placeat tibi*[3].

We note that the first of the ablutions in the chalice is of wine and the second of water. If a third is intended by the prayer, *Tres sunt*, this also would probably be of water.

In another manuscript York missal of the fifteenth century (*c.* 1470), written for use in the cathedral itself, as is plain from a number of points, and now at Sidney Sussex College, Cambridge, we find a version of the rubrics of the Sarum Customary. We read:

Then let him consume the blood, and having consumed it

---
[1] Henderson, *York Missal*, vol 1. pp. 203–5.
[2] Henderson, vol 1 pp 203–5   [3] Henderson, vol. 1. pp. 203–5.

let the priest go to the right corner of the altar with the chalice between his hands, his fingers still joined as before, and let the thurifer approach and deliver to the subdeacon a phial with wine that he may pour into the chalice, and let the priest rinse his hands lest any remnants of the body and blood remain on his fingers, or in the chalice. But when any priest has to celebrate twice in one day then at the first mass he ought not to receive any ablution, but to put it in the sacrarium in a clean vessel until the end of the second mass, and then let each ablution be consumed. And after the first ablution let a prayer follow in this wise, *Quod ore*. Then let him wash his fingers in the bowl of the chalice with wine poured by the subdeacon. And this being drunk let the prayer, *Haec nos communio*, follow. Then likewise let the subdeacon pour wine into the chalice, and this being drunk let the priest go to the middle of the altar and replace the chalice upon the paten, and bow and say *Gratias tibi*. And with this prayer let the priest go to the right corner of the altar that the thurifer may give the priest water at the sacrarium, the candlebearer holding the bowls. And while these things are being done let the deacon fold the corporals, and afterwards carry the book to the right corner of the altar. Then let the deacon take the chalice which lies on the paten, and if any of the infusion remain in it let him hold it to the mouth of the priest for him to consume when he comes from the right corner of the altar. And afterwards let him cover the chalice on the north part of the altar, and put on it the corporals, and deliver it to the subdeacon, or acolyte, as is noted above in the rubric before the preface. After the reception of the sacrament, and the ablution of his hands, let the priest turn towards the people at the right corner of the altar, and say the Communion, and the rest. Mass being finished, let the priest, with body bowed and hands joined, silently before the middle of the altar say this prayer, *Placeat tibi*[1].

We notice that here there are plainly three ablutions in the chalice each of wine in addition to the washing of the

---

[1] Henderson, vol. I pp 202–4

IX]   THE ABLUTIONS IN BRITAIN   165

priest's hands at the sacrarium. The word "likewise" in the case of the third shows that the practice of using water for the last ablution was known and disallowed. Among the modifications of the Sarum order we note the addition of the words "Let the thurifer approach and deliver to the subdeacon a phial with wine," the directions to "replace the chalice upon the paten" before saying *Gratias tibi*, and "that the thurifer may give the priest water at the sacrarium, the candlebearer holding the bowls," and the statement that the chalice is to be covered "on the north part of the altar." Also it is when the priest comes "from the right corner of the altar," not when he goes to it, as in the Customary and other books, that the drainings of the chalice are to be consumed. The reference to the bowls suggests the Roman *Ordines*.

Certain notes of the canonist Lyndwood in his *Provinciale*, begun in 1422, are interesting as illustrating English custom with regard to the ablutions, and the liquid used. We read:

Digitis superfusum. From these words it can be gathered that the first ablution ought to be in the chalice, and the second over the fingers also in the chalice, and each of wine. Therefore they err who first pour over their fingers, and they also who use water at the second pouring[1].

Ablutos. By the pouring over of wine into the chalice, or by the ablution made at the lavatory. But today according to the usual custom this is not observed, except that a towel is kept near the lavatory[2].

Apparently Lyndwood knows nothing of a third ablution. Though he prefers that the ablutions of the chalice and of the priest's fingers should both be with wine, he is witness to the prevalence of a contrary custom, by which water was used at the second ablution, as we noticed in

[1] Lib III Tit 23, *De celeb. miss* Constitutio, *Stephanus*, Ed Oxford, 1679, p 227
[2] Constitutio, *Edmundus*, p. 235.

the Oswestry missal (*c.* 1400) (as an alternative), in the rubrics of the York breviary text of the fourteenth century, and in the Constitutions of Archbishop Langton as early as the thirteenth, where indeed water is allowed apparently even for the first ablution. It is only for the third ablution that water is prescribed in the Corpus Christi College, Oxford, text of the Sarum Customary and texts dependent on it, and this Lyndwood does not mention. He tells us that in most places the hand-washing at the sacrarium after the ablutions in the chalice was obsolete, though a vestige remained in the provision of a towel, but the rubric derived ultimately from the Consuetudinary is repeated in all missals at a much later date, showing it would seem that the existence of rubrics is not necessarily evidence that in practice they are obeyed.

In the manuscript missal written by James Sibbald († 1507), Vicar of Arbuthnott in the diocese of St Andrews, really a book of Sarum use, we find another version of the directions derived from the Customary according to the original text in which *Gratias tibi* is said at the end of the ablutions and not after the consumption of the elements. It agrees generally with the Corpus Christi College Oxford, manuscript, water being ordered for the third ablution, but the section derived from the Consuetudinary "After the reception...he brought it in," is omitted at the end. We notice also that as in the York missal with the Sarum rubrics, now at Sidney Sussex College, Cambridge it is when the priest comes "from the right corner of the altar," not when he goes to it, that the last drainings of the ablutions are to be consumed[1].

The rubrics of the York printed missal of which five editions are known to have existed, 1509 (?), 1516, 1517, 1530 and 1533 are in marked contrast as regards length with those of the Sidney Sussex manuscript, yet they are plainly derived from them by a process of curtailment,

---

[1] Forbes, *Missale de Arbuthnott*, p. 163.

IX]   THE ABLUTIONS IN BRITAIN   167

much of the characteristic phraseology, here and elsewhere, being retained. We read after *Corpus et sanguis*:

After the first ablution let this prayer be said *Quod ore*. Then let him take the chalice and put it upon the paten and afterwards bowing let him say *Haec nos communio*. Then let the priest, with body bowed and hands joined, silently in the midst of the altar say this prayer, *Placeat tibi*[1].

The directions are obviously incomplete for only one ablution is actually mentioned, but as this is called the first and two prayers are provided, probably two are intended—of the chalice and of the priest's fingers. The rubrics of a missal, Sarum in many points though drawn up for the use of York Minster, are adapted not very skilfully to the requirements of an ordinary parish church with few assistant ministers and simple ceremonial.

The rubrics of the Hereford printed missal as published in 1502, are longer and somewhat more elaborate. We read·

After he has communicated let him go to the right corner of the altar with the chalice and wash it with wine saying *Quod ore*. Then let him wash his fingers over the chalice with wine or water saying *Haec nos Domine*. Then let him wash it with water and return to the middle of the altar with that ablution, and there consume it, and let him say again *Corpus tuum*. Then let him put the chalice so as to lie on the paten, and bow to the altar and go to the sacrarium and wash his hands, and as he goes let him say *Lavabo inter innocentes*. Then let him return to the altar and say the Communion. This being said let him sign himself and turn to the people and say, *Dominus vobiscum*. And let him say the Post Communion. And at the end of the prayer let him join his hands and go to the middle of the altar saying *Per Dominum*....Then with hands joined let him bow to the altar saying *Placeat tibi*[2].

We notice that there are three ablutions, that the second may be of wine or water, and the third of water. The

[1] Henderson, *York Missal*, vol. I pp 202–4
[2] Henderson, *Herefore Missal*, pp. 134–5.

rubrics show considerable expansion and modification of the manuscript missal, and a comparison seems to show the influence of the Sarum rubrics, though there is much curtailment; and the use of water is here authorised, not condemned as by Lyndwood.

In the various editions of the printed Sarum missal which appeared between 1487 and 1557 there is little change in the rubrics, which are a modification of the version of the rubrics of the Customary found in the Bodleian manuscript, Rawl. Liturg. C 2. With respect to the ablutions we read:

Then let him consume the blood, and having consumed it let the priest bow and say with devotion the following prayer, *Gratias tibi*. And having said this let the priest go to the right corner of the altar with the chalice between his hands, his fingers still joined as before, and let the subdeacon approach and pour into the chalice wine and water, and let the priest rinse his hands lest any remnants of the body or blood remain on his fingers, or in the chalice. But when any priest has to celebrate twice in one day then at the first mass he ought not to receive any ablution, but to put it in the sacrarium or in a clean vessel until the end of the second mass; and then let each ablution be consumed. After the first ablution this prayer, *Quod ore*, is said. Then let him wash his fingers in the bowl of the chalice with wine poured by the subdeacon. And this being drunk let the prayer, *Haec nos communio*, follow. After the reception of the ablution let the priest put the chalice on the paten so that if anything remain it may drain. And afterwards bowing let him say *Adoremus crucis*. Then let him wash his hands. Meanwhile let the deacon fold the corporals. When he has washed his hands and the priest returns to the right corner of the altar let the deacon hold the chalice to the mouth of the priest for him to consume, if anything of the infusion remain in it. And afterwards let him say the Communion with his ministers[1].

---

[1] Dickinson, *Missale Sarum*, col. 626–8.

THE ABLUTIONS IN BRITAIN

The final text of the rubrics of the Sarum missal with regard to the ablutions thus agrees with the earliest known, that of the Crawford manuscript, in placing *Gratias tibi* immediately after the communion and before the ablutions. Apparently as in the Bodleian manuscript, Rawl. Liturg. C 2, there are only two ablutions, and though we are told that the subdeacon will pour wine and water into the chalice the second ablution is to be of wine, and all reference to the third which was frequently of water has vanished.

The rubrics for the ablutions of the Sarum Customary reappear in the Manual of 1554, and it is the text of the Corpus Christi College, Oxford, manuscript which is followed. Three ablutions are prescribed and water for the third. We notice that it is the deacon not the subdeacon, as is usual, who ministers both the wine, as in the Bodleian manuscript, Laud. Misc. 164, and also the water, while the subdeacon, not the acolyte, as in the Bodleian manuscript, Rawl. Liturg. C 2, ministers the water when he washes his hands at the sacrarium. The words "after the first ablution," which properly indicate when *Quod ore* is to be said, have been joined to the previous sentence so that when a priest duplicates we are told that each ablution should be consumed "after the first ablution." After the third ablution the priest is directed to "turn the chalice over upon the paten," as in the Bodleian manuscript, Rawl. Liturg. C 2, and in the earlier Bologna manuscript, and as suggested in the printed missals at this point[1].

Our investigation has shown that the history of the ablutions in England and Britain generally was much the same as elsewhere. In the earliest days the rules of the Admonition of the pseudo Leo with regard to the washing of the vessels and the priest's hands were observed, as we see in Cotton MS. Tiberius C. I of the eleventh century, now in the British Museum. The washing of the priest's fingers

[1] Dickinson, col 626-8.

was the earliest form of ablution to be moved so as to take place during the service, exactly as on the continent, and it is found in the Consuetudinaries of different cathedrals, the oldest of which, that of Salisbury, dates from the beginning of the thirteenth century, and is the basis of the rest. About the same time we find various councils laying down rules for the ablutions, as for a practice which, though now well established, was still uncertain in detail, and particularly with reference to what is to be done when a priest duplicates. There is to be a rinsing both of the chalice and of the priest's fingers. The influence of Rouen on English ceremonial as seen in the *Lay Folks Mass Book* and elsewhere suggests that the customs of that church were imitated in this as in other matters. By the end of the thirteenth century directions for the ablutions are included in the service books, and we find them in the pontifical of Anianus of Bangor. In the Sarum Customary of the first half of the fourteenth century, which is an elaboration of the older Consuetudinary, we find a big development, and the complicated directions contained in it became the norm of later days, and appear with various modifications not only in all the later Salisbury missals, where the cross influences are extremely complicated, but also at York, Hereford, and St Andrews.

CHAPTER X

THE ORDER OF COMMUNION AND THE FIRST PRAYER BOOK

THE first change in the traditional method of giving communion in England is to be found in the *Order of Communion* published in 1548, a form of prayer in English by which the holy sacrament in both kinds was to be given to the people, to be interpolated in the Latin mass. The preliminary rubric runs.

The time of the communion shall be immediately after that the priest himself hath received the sacrament, without the varying of any other rite or ceremony in the mass (until other order shall be provided), but as heretofore usually the priest hath done with the sacrament of the body, to prepare, bless, and consecrate so much as will serve the people, so it shall continue still after the same manner and form, save that he shall bless and consecrate the biggest chalice, or some fair and convenient cup or cups full of wine with some water put into it, and that day not drink it up all himself, but taking one only sup, or draught, leave the rest upon the altar covered, and turn to them that are disposed to be partakers of the communion, and shall thus exhort them as followeth.

After the confession and absolution and *We do not presume*, we read·

Then shall the priest rise, the people still reverently kneeling, and the priest shall deliver the communion, first to the ministers if any be there present that they may be ready to help the priest, and after to the other And when he doth deliver the sacrament of the body of Christ he shall say to everyone these words following,

The body of our Lord Jesus Christ, which was given for thee, preserve thy body unto everlasting life.

And the priest delivering the sacrament of the blood, and giving everyone to drink once and no more, shall say,

The blood of our Lord Jesus Christ, which was shed for thee, preserve thy soul to everlasting life.

If there be a deacon or other priest then shall he follow with the chalice, and as the priest ministereth the bread so shall he for more expedition minister the wine in form before written. Then shall the priest, turning him to the people, let the people depart with this blessing,

The peace of God which passeth all understanding keep your hearts and minds in the knowledge and love of God, and of his Son Jesus Christ our Lord.

To which the people shall answer, Amen.

The new *Order of Communion* was not in many ways such a very great innovation. Numerous such orders for use when communion was given out of mass are in existence, and since the twelfth century a form of confession and absolution had been frequently interpolated in the service on the occasions when the sacrament was distributed in its proper place after the communion of the priest. Also the insertion of a confession and absolution in the vernacular into the mass after the sermon had been common on the continent, at any rate from the eleventh century, and many forms exist[1], so that the absolutely new elements in the *Order of Communion* were not so very numerous. Allowing for other influences we note that the words used at the actual delivery of the sacrament are very similar to what we find in the order for the visitation of the sick in the lost St Remi codex of the Gregorian Sacramentary (c. 800). After preparatory devotions we read:

Then let him communicate the sick man saying,

The body of our Lord Jesus Christ preserve thee unto everlasting life.

---

[1] Mulhenhoff and Sherer, *Denkmäler deutscher Poesie und Prosa*, p 200 ff

The blood of our Lord Jesus Christ redeem thee unto everlasting life.

The peace of our Lord Jesus Christ and the communion of the saints be with thee and with us unto everlasting life, Amen.

Prayer in consummation[1].

The Pax at the giving of the sacrament privately came usually before communion as at mass, and was indeed a duplication of the Pax given in church, but the practice of giving it after the words of adminstration, if not after the actual reception, seems to have been not uncommon, and survives in various orders of communion. In the *Codex Tilianus* of the Gregorian Sacramentary and in a twelfth century pontifical of Salzburg, which retains the Gregorian rubrics, in the service for the communion of the sick we read:

A prayer at (before, Salz.) the reception of the eucharist,
The body and blood of our Lord Jesus Christ preserve thy soul unto everlasting life. Amen.
(And then, Salz.)
The peace and communion of the body and blood of our Lord Jesus Christ preserve thy soul unto everlasting life.
After the consumption of the eucharist,
O Lord Jesu Christ...[2].

In a tenth or eleventh century German form only the Pax in its modified form has survived. After the unction and collects we read:

Here let him be communicated,
The peace and communion of the body and blood of our Lord Jesus Christ preserve thy soul unto everlasting life. Amen[3].

The English *Order of Communion* according to the rubric was to be inserted in the order of the mass immediately after the priest's communion, and therefore before the

---

[1] Menard, *Gregorian Sacramentary*, pp. 550-1 *P L* LXXVIII col. 537 Cf Freestone, *The Sacrament Reserved*, p 243

[2] Menard, p 542 *P L* LXXVIII. col 528 Martene, vol I. lib VII. Art IV Ordo XV p 325

[3] Gerbert, *Mon. Vet. Lit Alem.* vol. II p. 33.

prayer *Gratias tibi* according to the printed Sarum missal. When there were communicants the order of the Crawford missal would probably be that adopted, and in this we read before *Gratias tibi,* "Then let the body and the blood be consumed," so that after the *Order of Communion* the consumption of the remains would precede *Gratias tibi,* the remains ordinarily being the contents of the chalice with the particle, and sometimes reserved hosts from the pyx.

The prayer, *Gratias tibi,* begins.

I give thee thanks, O Lord, holy Father, almighty everlasting God, who hast refreshed me with the most sacred body and blood of thy Son our Lord Jesus Christ, and I pray thee that this sacrament...[1].

A longer version of this prayer, *Gratias tibi,* to be said by the priest after mass is also found in the printed Sarum missal. This begins:

I give thee thanks, O Lord God, almighty Father, who hast vouchsafed to satisfy me with the body and blood of thy dear Son our Lord Jesus Christ. I beseech thy great clemency, almighty and merciful Lord, that this holy communion...[2].

In the Bobbio and Stowe missals and in the ninth century Irish fragment, St Gall MS. 1394, practically the same form is found as the last prayer at mass[3], and the text is now seen to be derived from certain Post Communion collects of the Leonine Sacramentary[4]. We note the beginning·

We give thee thanks, O Lord, holy Father, almighty everlasting God, who hast satisfied us with the communion of the body and blood of Christ thy Son, and we humbly beseech thy mercy, O Lord, that this thy sacrament...

---

[1] Dickinson, *Sarum Missal,* col 626–7.
[2] Dickinson, col. 639
[3] Neale and Forbes, *Ancient Gallican Liturgies,* p. 209. Warren, *Liturgy of the Celtic Church,* pp 243–4, 179
[4] Feltoe, pp 71, 111.

In the Bobbio missal the prayer, *Gratias tibi*, which is so widespread in different versions is headed "The consummation of mass," so that by the combination of the *Order of Communion* with the Sarum mass we have an almost exact reproduction of the sequence of the St Remi order of clinical communion.

The communion Pax according to the new English Order, in which the original Pax of the mass also survives, is the concluding act in the distribution of the sacrament and the ratification of the communion of the recipients with one another "in the knowledge and love of God, and of his Son Jesus Christ our Lord," which is effected in that holy action. It is a development of the idea of peace and communion (pax et communicatio) found in the forms quoted above, and in the Ambrosian missal, and with an addition in the Stowe missal and St Gall MS. 1394[1]. As part of the act of communion the Pax, though following the reception of the sacrament, naturally precedes the consumption of the remains, and in the *Order of Communion* it marks the dismissal of the communicants from the altar, not the end of the mass which has still to be completed. The sequence would thus be, the communion of the people in both kinds, the communion Pax in English at the dismissal of the communicants, the consumption of the remains, the thanksgiving, *Gratias tibi*, and then the ablutions, after which the mass was concluded.

In 1549 was published the first English Prayer Book. The order of communion is now no longer a separate thing from the usual order of mass, but the two are joined inseparably. The dismissal of the communicants and the dismissal of the rest of the congregation are united, and the blessing which had commonly been given at the end of mass is added to the new communion Pax. The idea of thanksgiving after communion, not always included in the old Latin Post Communion collects, has now become a

[1] Warren, pp 242, 177.

regular feature of the service, and unlike *Gratias tibi*, the form is said publicly and before the new Pax. Yet its connection with the old thanksgiving is obvious, for it begins:

Almighty and everliving God, we most heartily thank thee, for that thou hast vouchsafed to feed us in these holy mysteries with the spiritual food of the most precious body and blood of thy Son our Saviour Jesus Christ....And we most humbly beseech thee, O heavenly Father....

The thanksgivings after communion in Hermann's *Consultation* begin similarly, and may have suggested the provision of the English form, but verbally this agrees rather more closely with the old English prayers[1].

The order of the latter part of the service is now somewhat modified, and we have the sequence, the communion of the people, the thanksgiving, the communion Pax and blessing for the dismissal of the whole congregation. Nothing is said about either the consumption of the remains of the sacrament or the ablutions. It was quite natural, however, that priests accustomed to the Latin service should continue the ceremony of the ablutions, adapted of course slightly to the new conditions, and now that the chalice was delivered to all communicants it would generally be necessary to deal with what was left of the consecrated wine, as in the earliest days, as well as of the consecrated bread, so that the performance of the ablutions, particularly when there was more than one cup, as suggested in the *Order of Communion*, would no longer be quite so simple a ceremony. That the ceremony of the ablutions was continued to the annoyance of certain of the bishops and others who favoured the new ideas we have considerable evidence. In a draft of "Articles to be followed and observed according to the King's Majesty's Injunctions and Proceedings," compiled it would seem in 1549, we read:

[1] Hermann, f 96 b.

For an uniformity that no minister do counterfeit the popish mass as to kiss the Lord's table, washing his fingers every time in the communion...laying down and licking the chalice of the communion...or setting any light upon the Lord's board at any time, and finally to use no other ceremonies than are appointed in the King's Book of Common Prayers[1].

In 1550 Ridley put forth a somewhat expanded form of these requirements in his diocese. We read:

That no minister do counterfeit the popish mass in kissing the Lord's board, washing his hands or fingers after the gospel, or the receipt of the holy communion, shifting the book from one place to another, laying down and licking the chalice after the communion...or setting any light upon the Lord's board, and finally that the minister in the time of the holy communion do use only the ceremonies and gestures appointed in the Book of Common Prayer and none other, so that there do not appear in them any counterfeiting of the Popish mass[2].

In 1551 Hooper put forth the same directions with regard to the ablutions, etc., in his diocese of Gloucester[3].

We note that though the Articles appeal to the Injunctions of 1547 they forbid what they allowed—the lights on the altar—because of the silence of the Prayer Book.

Bucer in his *Censura* on the First Prayer Book presented to the Bishop of Ely in 1551 includes washing the chalice among the numerous superstitions still rife among those who used the Book. He says.

There are some who by whatever signs they can study to counterfeit their never sufficiently hated mass, both by vestments, lights and bowings, by crossings, by washing the chalice and other gestures of the missal, by breathing over the bread and cup of the eucharist, by transferring the book on the table from the right side to the left, by placing the table in the same place in which the altar stood, by showing the

---
[1] Frere, *Visitation Articles*, vol II pp 191–3.
[2] Frere, vol II pp 241–2.   [3] Frere, vol. II p 276.

bread and chalice of the eucharist to adoring old people and other superstitious folk, who do not communicate with the sacraments[1].

We notice that here there is condemnation of what is required or allowed by the Prayer Book—the vestments and crossings—as well as of that which is not mentioned.

Though the ablutions were thus performed still in the old manner, there must have been on some occasions at any rate a change in the time of performing the action.

Following the example of the Brandenburg Order of 1540, provision is made in the First Prayer Book for the communion of the sick or those in danger of death with the reserved sacrament in both kinds, and this is evidently intended to be the normal method of giving communion. We read:

And if the same day there be a celebration of the holy communion in the church, then shall the priest reserve at the open communion so much of the sacrament of the body and blood as shall serve the sick person, and so many as shall communicate with him, if there be any. And so soon as he conveniently may, after the open communion ended in the church, shall go and minister the same, first to those that are appointed to communicate with the sick, if there be any, and last of all to the sick person himself. But before the curate distribute the holy communion the appointed general confession must be made in the name of the communicants, the curate adding the absolution with the comfortable sentences of scripture following in the open communion, and after the communion ended the collect, *Almighty and everliving God, we most heartily thank thee*, etc.

There is also another rubric at the end of the office dealing with the question of reservation:

And if there be more sick persons to be visited the same day that the curate doth celebrate in any sick man's house, then shall the curate there reserve so much of the sacrament of the

---

[1] *Scripta Anglicana*, pp 493-4

body and blood as shall serve the other sick persons, and such as be appointed to communicate with them, if there be any, and shall immediately carry it and minister it unto them.

These rules clearly involved the remains of the consecrated elements in both kinds, or some of them, remaining on the altar until the conclusion of the mass. Nothing, however, is said about what is to be done with what is left after all have communicated in the sick man's house, and as the sick man is to communicate last that something would frequently be left is plain. The consumption of any such remains and anything in the nature of ablutions must certainly have been postponed, and could not well follow immediately after the communion. The words "last of all" seem decisive against this, and preclude the consumption by the priest or neighbours at this point, and by the sick person it would in many cases be impossible. That whatever was left over was reserved until the conclusion of the service appears to be the only possible thing, and it is not improbable that the same order was intended to be observed at ordinary celebrations of the holy communion in church.

According to the *Order of Communion* after the distribution of the sacrament there followed the new communion Pax, the consumption of the remains, the thanksgiving, *Gratias tibi*, said secretly, and then the ablutions. It seems unlikely that now the thanksgiving is said publicly the consumption of the remains would come before it and the ablutions afterwards Indeed it seems clear from a comparison of the wording in the *Order of Communion* with that in the thanksgiving, and elsewhere in the new communion service, that the disposal of what was left was not intended to take place before the saying of the thanksgiving. To Cranmer, whatever might be his views at the moment, the eucharistic elements were rightly called "the mysteries" of the body and blood of Christ, and in this sense he uses the word "mysteries" very many times in his book on *The true and catholic Doctrine and Use of the Sacrament of the Lord's Supper.* In the exhortation in the *Order of Communion* to be said after the consecration in the presence of the holy sacrament we read: "meet partakers of *these* holy mysteries," "he hath left in *these* holy mysteries as a pledge of his love." In the First Prayer Book, where the position of the exhortation has been changed to a point before the elements are placed on the altar, immediately after the sermon, we find instead "meet partakers of *those* holy mysteries," "he hath left in *those* holy mysteries as a pledge of his love." Similar changes may be noted in the use of other expressions as "*this* holy communion," "*this* holy sacrament," "*this* most blessed bread." In spite of the care shown however in making these alterations we find in the thanksgiving which appears for the first time in the First Prayer Book, "thou hast vouchsafed to feed us in *these* holy mysteries," words which certainly seem to imply the presence of the sacrament. The doctrine of the First Prayer Book with respect to our Lord's presence in the eucharist is declared in the final rubric, continued from the *Order of Communion,* and derived perhaps ultimately from Gratian[1]. After requiring the eucharistic breads to be broken it continues·

And men must not think less to be received in part than in the whole, but in each of them the whole body of our Saviour Jesus Christ.

If the mysteries remained in part, the sacrament would continue in its completeness, and this is suggested by the wording of the thanksgiving. Otherwise in view of the care shown in correcting the adjectives in the exhortation it is difficult to understand the deliberate introduction of the word "these" which seems to suppose the sacrament present.

[1] Gratian, *Decretum,* Pars III, *De Consec* Dist. II c 77, *P.L* CLXXXVII. col 1772–3

If the consumption of the remains of the sacrament came after the thanksgiving it must certainly have come after the new communion Pax and blessing also, and this would agree with what was apparently the original intention of the new Pax, as the seal of the fellowship in Christ assured in the act of communion, as explained in the thanksgiving, for which purpose it was placed as closely as possible to the distribution of the elements, and before the consumption of the remains.

It will be useful also to note the importance attached to the idea that every celebration of the Lord's Supper should be as far as possible something approximating to a general communion, though the extreme opinion of some of the reformers, which prevented all communion of the sick, that under no other conditions could the sacrament be administered, was not adopted. An examination of the language of the Prayer Book shows that a distinction was intended to be drawn by the compilers between receiving "the sacrament of Christ's body and blood" and the receiving of "the holy communion of the body and blood of our Saviour Christ." The latter always supposes the fellowship of the communicants about the Lord's table, and though the idea itself is not absent, in no single instance, it would seem, is the word "communion" intended to refer to the communion with our Lord, but only with the fellow worshippers. The meaning of the noun is in exact agreement with that of the phrase "to communicate with," and is used of fellowship with other men. For the reception of the sacrament to be a communion it was necessary to communicate with other persons, and as many as possible. The rubric required that there should be no celebration of the Lord's Supper "except there be some to communicate with the priest." To secure as general a communion as possible on every occasion there were only two days in the year on which provision was made for more than one celebration. The multiplication of masses with few or no communicants was intended to cease, and this was a point insisted on by the authorities as Bishop Bonner found when he tried to introduce a number of masses or "communions," as of our Lady and the apostles, in the chapels of St Paul's cathedral[1].

From this fact that every celebration of the Lord's supper was intended to be something akin to a general communion we may draw another argument with regard to the point at which the remains of the sacrament were consumed and the ablutions made, and it tends to the same conclusion. When communion had been given only in one kind the consecrated hosts which were left remained on the altar according to the almost universal custom of the church in the West, at Rome and elsewhere, and were not disposed of by being put away in the place of reservation until the end of mass, a relic of the primitive custom by which both the consumption of the remains of the elements in both kinds and the ablutions had taken place after the service. Now that communion was once more given in both kinds it would be quite what might be expected that the practice which had survived in the case of the hosts should be extended to the wine also, the practical reasons for it being even stronger than in the case of the bread, though now the method of disposal would normally be by consumption, as in the earliest days, and not by reservation in church. So far as we can see then, though there is no definite statement on the subject, all the arguments point to the idea that the compilers of the First Prayer Book intended a reversion to primitive usage, such as is mentioned in the letter of the pseudo Clement, and that the consumption of the remains of the sacrament should not take place until the conclusion of the service, and if so obviously the ablutions could not take place earlier.

[1] Foxe, *Acts and Monuments*, ed. Pratt, vol. v. p. 723. *Grey Friars' Chronicle* (Camden Society, 53), p. 59.

CHAPTER XI

THE SECOND PRAYER BOOK AND THE ELIZABETHAN SETTLEMENT

IN the Second Prayer Book, published in 1552 by the authority of parliament only, there was still further departure from traditional notions and practices than had been intended under the First Book, and particularly in the service for the administration of the Lord's Supper, and in the ideas with respect to it. A great many of the changes seem to be due to criticisms of the First Prayer Book by Bucer in his *Censura*. Some appear to be due to Swiss influence and particularly that of Zurich, probably through the influence of John Hooper who had just returned (in 1549) from that city, and was full of the ideas he had imbibed there during his exile. We may see examples of it in the insistence on the use of the full text of the ten commandments according to the twentieth chapter of Exodus, a favourite notion of Hooper's, as in the Zurich service books, and in such phrases as "remember the poor," found in all versions of the Zurich liturgy, and consequently in that of John a Lasco. The idea that at every celebration of the Lord's supper there should be a general communion is still further emphasised in the Second Prayer Book At Bucer's suggestion there is for the future to be only one communion even on Christmas and Easter Days. The rubric of the First Prayer Book is altered to read:

And there shall be no celebration of the Lord's Supper, except there be a good number to communicate with the priest according to his discretion. And if there be not above twenty persons in the parish of discretion to receive the communion, yet there shall be no communion except four or three at the least communicate with the priest.

Also there is to be no private celebration for a sick person except there be "a good number to receive the communion with the sick person."

The breaking up of the Canon in the Second Prayer Book and the removal of the confession and absolution, etc., were in accordance with Bucer's suggestions that the communion should follow the Great Thanksgiving immediately, so as to secure a closer conformity to our Lord's own practice. For the same reason presumably the Lord's prayer was made to follow the administration, though there was considerable precedent for this in the various orders for giving communion apart from mass. Since the Lord's prayer has always been regarded as belonging to the communion, and not to the consecration, as we see in all the liturgies, though Gregory the Great wished it to be said over the oblation, the difference was not of vital importance.

The new position of the *Gloria in Excelsis* after the thanksgiving for communion opens out a wider problem, and here we seem to recognise the influence of Zurich. In the Zurich liturgy the *Gloria* had been moved from the beginning of the service, and was sung between the epistle and gospel. The idea of our Lord as the Lamb of God, and the Lord's supper as the Christian passover, is a feature of the Zurich service. After the communion we read in the 1535 edition:

And he reads (John xiii) as long as is required until the breaking of the bread is entirely ended, and all the ministers have come back again to the table with the cups. Then the pastor says, *Let us kneel down and praise God and give him thanks.* Then he begins the following psalm which the Jews always say at their passover, the deacons saying one verse and then another. The pastor says, *Praise the Lord, ye servants*... (Ps. cxiii)[1].

As an alternative to this psalm, the beginning of the Jewish Hallel, there is another hymn of thanksgiving, a Christian Hallel as it were, made up partly of psalm verses, and partly it would seem of a paraphrase of the ancient proper preface for Easter Day, which speaks of Christ as the paschal Lamb. We read·

I will magnify thee, my God, and will praise thy name for ever and ever....He gave us his only Son, that we through him might live. He hath made his flesh and blood to be our proper food, and by his death hath brought us to everlasting life. He is the Lamb of God, the pardon for our sins, the one and only pledge of mercy[2].

Zwingli in his *Fidei ratio* of July 8, 1530, gave his belief with regard to our Lord's presence in this supper as follows:

I believe that in the holy eucharist, that is in the supper of thanksgiving, the true body of Christ is present by the contemplation of faith, that is, that those who give thanks to the Lord for the benefit He has conferred upon us in His Son, recognise that He took upon Him true flesh, in that flesh truly suffered, truly washed away our sins by His blood, and thus everything wrought by Christ for them becomes as it were present by the contemplation of faith[3].

The same idea is expressed in an exhortation added to the 1525 edition of the Zurich service in Zwingli's own hand[4], and repeated with but slight modifications in later editions. We read.

Now remembering, dear brethren and sisters, what we have now performed according to the commandment of our Lord, namely that with thankful remembrance we have borne witness

---
[1] Wolfensberger, *Die Zurcher Kirchengebete*, p 55
[2] Wolfensberger, p 56
[3] Kidd, *Documents of the Continental Reformation*, p 474
[4] Smend, *Die Evangelischen Deutschen Messen*, p 201

to our faith, that we are all miserable sinners, but by his body given and his blood poured forth we have been cleansed from sin, and redeemed from everlasting death...we ought also truly to pray God to grant unto us all to hold with firm faith within our hearts this remembrance of his bitter death, and bear it steadfastly with us, and therewith die daily to all wickedness... God be merciful unto us and bless us and shed forth the light of his countenance upon us, and be merciful unto us[1].

The presence of our Lord, dramatically represented in the supper, and manifest to the eye of faith in the act of communion as crucified for us, is something very real and abiding, so that throughout the concluding portion of the service He is worshipped as exhibited to the faithful in the sacrament, "the Lamb as it had been slain," "present by the contemplation of faith," and prayer is made to Him that His presence may be shown in our lives. With a thanksgiving to Jesus the service concludes:

O God, we thank thee for all thy gifts and goodness, who livest and reignest God for ever and ever. Amen[2]

This seems to suggest a reason, if not the only one, for the removal of the *Gloria in excelsis*, which had already been moved from its ancient place at the beginning of the service in the Zurich liturgy, to its present position in the English service, not only because it would thus be an act of thanksgiving for participation in the Christian passover, a Christian Hallel, but because it was an act of worship of Jesus, Who is both outwardly exhibited as the Lamb of God, and also specially manifest to the hearts of the faithful, in the sacrament. In the First English Prayer Book before *Ye that do truly*, and the confession and absolution the priest thus addresses the people and invites them to the feast

---

[1] Richter, *Evangelisch Kirchenord* p 138 For 1535 edition see Wolfensberger, p 57
[2] Richter, p 138 Wolfensberger, p 57.

XI] AND THE ELIZABETHAN SETTLEMENT 187

Christ our Paschal Lamb is offered up for us, once for all, when he bare our sins on his body upon the cross, for he is the very Lamb of God that taketh away the sins of the world. Wherefore let us keep a joyful and holy feast with the Lord.

A similar form is found at the same point in a Lasco's service, really a version of that of Zurich, for the Strangers' Church in London, published in 1551, and probably the two are not unconnected. We read:

Standing in the midst of the ministers, turning towards the people, he recites that joyful and saving message to the whole church from Paul, concerning that victim, the most innocent in the whole world, now offered up for our sins, Christ Jesus, in these words:

Behold now, dear brethren, Christ our Passover is sacrificed for us, therefore let us keep the feast, not with the old leaven nor with the leaven of malice and wickedness, but with the unleavened bread of sincerity and truth. Through the same Jesus Christ our Lord and Saviour. Amen[1].

In the First English Prayer Book, as in the liturgy of Hermann's *Consultation*, the *Agnus Dei* was sung during the communion. Originally according to the *Liber Pontificalis* it had been sung during the breaking of the bread, by order of Pope Sergius I (687–701)[2]. It was evidently intended as explanatory of the symbolical action of the Fraction, an idea quite in accord with the Zwinglian notion of the Lord's Supper as a dramatic representation of redemption and an exhibition of Jesus to the faithful as the Lamb of God. Both the invitation and the *Agnus Dei*, however, were omitted from the Second Prayer Book, presumably out of regard for Bucer's suggestion and to avoid what he called "bread worship." The worship of our Lord as manifest to the eye of faith in the sacrament, or in Zwingli's words "present by the contemplation of

---

[1] J a Lasco, *Forma ac Ratio tota Ecclesiastici Ministerii*, pp 252–3.
[2] Duchesne, *Liber Pontificalis*, I p. 376

faith," is retained in what apparently was considered a less dangerous position in the *Gloria in excelsis*, which was now placed after the thanksgiving for communion to supply the idea of the adoration of the Lamb; and perhaps for this reason there was an augmentation of the text, which suggests the three-fold *Agnus*.

In accordance with Bucer's suggestions in the Second Prayer Book the invocation of the Holy Ghost over the elements, together with the sign of the cross and other manual acts, was omitted; and generally he would abolish all idea of consecration or benediction of material things, the water in baptism as well as the bread and wine at holy communion. His criticisms of the rubrics which deal with the quantity and kind of bread to be employed are particularly important. Commenting on the rubrics of the First Prayer Book at the offertory he says in his *Censura*:

> From the fourth paragraph of this order, in which it is prescribed that the minister ought to take only so much bread and wine as will suffice for those about to communicate, some make for themselves the superstition that they consider it unlawful if anything of the bread and wine of the communion remain over, when it is finished, to allow it to come to common use, as if there were in this bread and wine of itself anything of divinity, or even sanctity, outside the use at communion. Consequently however much bread and wine remain from the communion there are yet some who consider that the whole of it must be consumed by themselves. And so men must be taught that Christ the Lord is offered not to bread and wine but to devout minds by the words of the Lord and these symbols. Wherefore outside the use of the communion which the Lord instituted, the bread and wine, even if they have been placed on the table of the Lord, have nothing in them of sanctity more than have other bread and wine. It is true indeed that we read in the writings of the holy fathers that these remains in some churches at one time were consumed immediately after the communion or otherwise by the ministers, in others

xi] AND THE ELIZABETHAN SETTLEMENT 189

that they were reserved, until the following day, as Cyril reminded Calosyrius[1], by others were consumed by fire as Hesychius (Lib. II. *in Levit.*) is witness[2]. But when we see how Satan with powerful and pestilent trickery by his Roman antichrists has put forward for so many generations now bread instead of Christ for us to adore that he may take away from us all perception and adoration of Christ our Saviour, we ought whatever things seem to favour that bread worship and are used by the antichrists to retain the same in the hearts of the simpler folk, as far and as completely as possible to banish from our churches. Christ our Lord truly gives Himself indeed to His faithful people that they may enjoy the food of eternal life, employing for that purpose His words and the symbols of bread and wine; and so indeed whoever with true faith in Him communicate in these mysteries as He Himself instituted them truly receive Him by the apprehension of faith and spirit. And so in this use of giving and receiving instituted by the Lord, bread and wine are the symbols of the body and blood of Christ, by which He offers Himself to us. But outside this use they are what other bread and wine are, for nothing in their nature is changed, nor is Christ the Lord given to them but to faithful minds. These things it is fitting that the people be taught, as in word so also in deed, as diligently as possible, so that, although in former times so many masses and such horrible superstitions about this sacred matter have been introduced, men may both understand its true meaning and resume its use[3].

Bucer's doctrine is very similar to that of Zwingli. According to Zwingli Christ was present in the sacrament "by the contemplation of faith," according to Bucer, "by the apprehension of faith and spirit." Cranmer had expressed almost identical opinions in his work on *The true and catholic Doctrine and Use of the Sacrament of the Lord's Supper*, published the previous year, 1550. Two extracts are of importance. The first is Cranmer's comment on the letter of the pseudo Clement. We read:

[1] See pp. 6–7   [2] See p 9   [3] *Scripta Anglicana*, p. 464.

They allege St Clement, whose words be these, as they report.

The sacraments of God's secrets are committed to three degrees: to a priest, a deacon and a minister: which with fear and trembling ought to keep the leavings of the broken pieces of the Lord's body, that no corruption be found in the holy place, lest by negligence great injury be done to the portion of the Lord's body.

And by and by followeth:

So many hosts must be offered in the altar as will suffice for the people. And, if any remain, they must not be kept until the morning, but be spent and consumed of the clerks with fear and trembling. And they that consume the residue of the Lord's body may not by and by take other common meats, lest they should mix that holy portion with the meat, which is digested by the belly....Therefore if the Lord's portion be eaten in the morning, the ministers that consume it must fast unto six of the clock: and if they do take it at three or four of the clock, the minister must fast until the evening....

For by the same epistle appeareth evidently three special things against the errors of the papists. The first is, that the bread in the sacrament is called the Lord's body, and the pieces of the broken bread be called the pieces and fragments of the Lord's body, which cannot be understand but figuratively. The second is, that the bread ought not to be reserved and hanged up, as the papists everywhere do use. The third is, that the priests ought not to receive the sacrament alone (as the papists commonly do, making a sale thereof unto the people) but they ought to communicate with the people. And here is diligently to be noted that we ought not unreverently and unadvisedly to approach unto the meat of the Lord's table, as we do to other common meats and drinks, but with great fear and dread, lest we should come to that holy table unworthily, wherein is not only represented, but also spiritually given unto us, very Christ Himself[1].

---

[1] Cranmer, *The Sacrament of the Lord's Supper*, Book III. Chap xv. (Parker Society), pp. 141–2.

The phraseology of this extract in quite a number of particulars we shall find reproduced in the rubrics of the Second Prayer Book. We notice that what Cranmer understands to be condemned by the letter of the pseudo Clement is not the carrying of the sacrament to the sick after the service the same day, a practice provided for in the First Prayer Book, but the hanging of it up or continual reservation. In another place a little further on we find even closer agreement with the quotation from Bucer. We read:

When common bread and wine be taken and severed from other bread and wine to the use of the holy communion, that portion of bread and wine, although it be the same substance that the other is from the which it is severed, yet it is now called consecrated, or holy bread and holy wine. Not that the bread and wine have or can have any holiness in them, but that they be used to an holy work and represent holy and godly things. And therefore St Dionyse calleth the bread holy bread, and the cup an holy cup, as soon as they be set upon the altar to the use of the holy communion. But specially they may be called holy and consecrated, when they be separated to that holy use by Christ's own words, which He spake for that purpose, saying of the bread "This is my body," and of the wine "This is my blood." So that commonly the authors before those words be spoken do take the bread and wine but as other common bread and wine, but after those words be pronounced over them, then they take them for consecrated and holy bread and wine. Not that the bread and wine can be partakers of any holiness or godliness, or can be the body and blood of Christ, but that they represent the very body and blood of Christ and the holy food and nourishment which we have by Him[1].

We see that the ideas of Bucer, as expressed in his *Censura*, are little more than a reproduction of Cranmer's. It is not surprising then that Cranmer should fall in to some extent with Bucer's suggestions for the disposal of

[1] Book III Chap xv pp 177-8.

the remains of the sacrament after the communion, so that the rule adopted, though it did not, as we shall see, actually insist upon this being done, was such as to allow the residue of the bread and wine to return to something akin to common use, a practice it would seem already adopted by some, but scrupulously avoided by others, in Bucer's view out of wanton superstition. Another quotation from the *Censura* will make the reason for the new rubric in the Second Prayer Book still more obvious; it was to conciliate those who held opinions such as Bucer's. We read:

But lest any should fear that by conformity to this anything superstitious should be strengthened, as that it were lawful to use such bread and no other, it may be possible to add in one or two words that it must not be thought from this description of the bread that it is not lawful of itself to use in the eucharist leavened and usual bread, and that the matter and form of the bread which is described in the book is only proposed, as it is stated in words also in this section, "for avoiding of all matters and occasion of dissension," and also of offence to the simple and the contempt of this sacred ordinance, which is commonly wont to ensue[1].

That the rubric of the Second Prayer Book was intended to carry out this suggestion is plain. It runs:

And to take away the superstition which any person hath or might have in the bread and wine it shall suffice that the bread be such as is usual to be eaten at the table with other meats, but the best and purest wheat bread that conveniently may be gotten. And if any of the bread or wine remain, the curate shall have it to his own use.

In spite of later interpretations there can be little doubt but that the direction about what remains was intended originally to refer to the consecrated bread and wine as well as to what was unconsecrated, for it was not supposed, as we have seen, by either Cranmer or Bucer

[1] *Scripta Anglicana*, p. 459.

that consecration had made any real difference. And yet the rubric is to some extent a compromise, for it by no means goes the full length of Bucer's suggestions, and it might have been much more peremptory in requiring conformity to the new ideas. It is not directed that the remains of the sacrament, which presumably remain on the holy table until the end of the service, shall return to common use, or to that of the multitude, but only of the curate. Consequently the primitive and widespread custom by which the remains were consumed by the priest and other ministers in the sacristy, as prescribed in the letter of pseudo Clement, the language of which—and that according to Cranmer's translation—and of his comments upon it, the new rubric seems at several points to adopt, was in no way prevented, and it was probably the deliberate intention that it should be so, " for avoiding of all matters and occasion of dissension" as the First Prayer Book said when speaking of the kind of bread to be used. Such an interpretation at any rate would almost certainly be put upon the rubric by those who favoured the old ways. There must have been many who used the book under compulsion, even with scrupulous exactness and with no breach of rubric, who by no means assented to the principles of the revisers who had made it what it was.

Peter Martyr took much the same view of the value of consecration as did Bucer in his criticism of the First Prayer Book. Like the continental reformers generally he maintained that the recitation of the words of institution was for the edification of the hearers only, and consequently he objected to a second recital of these words in the event of the original supply of bread and wine not sufficing, and also to reservation of the sacrament. He wrote to Bucer·

And surely it is wonderful that they find it a burden to say those words in the presence of the sick man to whom they would be especially useful when they say them uselessly in the temple if the wine has happened to fail in the cup when the men who are present and are receiving the sacrament have already heard them[1].

We notice that the practice of a second consecration had evidently continued under the First Prayer Book, though no longer prescribed as in the *Order of Communion*. To meet the wishes of those who objected to this custom and who regarded the words as for the edification of the congregation, all reference to reservation, which would make the recital of the words in the presence of the sick person unnecessary, and assume some virtue in consecration, was omitted in the Second Prayer Book, though the practice is not forbidden as we might have expected.

In a paragraph following the public service of holy communion in Hermann's *Consultation* the opinions of Bucer in an earlier stage of development than what we find in the *Censura*, come out quite plainly, and we find a condemnation of reservation in marked contrast with what was allowed to appear in the Second Prayer Book. We read:

But since our Lord instituted His sacrament only that we should eat and drink of it in remembrance of Him, and in no wise that we should set it out, or carry it round to view, and because this sacrament has been brought to horrible superstition and impiety, from the fact that abuses of this sort have been introduced in the former use of the sacrament, to take away both that superstition and impiety and also the various scruples of the feeble and irreligious questions about these mysteries, pastors and those who minister the sacrament will give heed that as often as the supper has to be administered, whether in church or in private houses for the sick, they carefully reckon the number of those who are going to communicate, that in accordance with it they may take the particles of bread and the quantity of wine. But whatever of the remnants is

---

[1] Strype, *Memorials of Thomas Cranmer*, vol. II. Num. lxi p 899

left over, when the communion is finished, let them immediately consume it, and not reserve it, or put it away anywhere, or carry it away, or set it out to view[1].

There was little agreement, however, among the various reformed liturgies about what was to be done with what was left after the communion. Pullain in his order of service for the refugees at Glastonbury published in 1551, and representing it would seem the custom of the French church at Strasburg, says:

After all have communicated, and they have returned one by one to their places, the deacon puts down the chalice and returns to his place, and then the pastor leads the people in thanksgiving in these words[2].

The chalice was apparently put back on the holy table, as we saw also at Zurich, but nothing is said about what happens to what is left. Evidently it was not consumed before the end of the service if we may judge from the rule "for administering the eucharist to the sick." We read.

If a sick man asks for the eucharist on the day on which the supper is celebrated by the church, the deacon is sent with a few pious persons, that they may communicate with the sick man[3].

It would seem as if the "pious persons" communicate a second time with the sick man, and apparently the deacon also, a practice which appears to have been adopted also in the reign of Elizabeth under the rubrics of the Second Prayer Book. The custom by which the priest took with him some of the congregation who had been present at the celebration in church to the sick person's house was incorporated by Aless in 1551 in the rubrics of the order for the communion of the sick, in his Latin version of the First Prayer Book.

---

[1] Hermann, *Simplex ac pia Deliberatio*, f 97 a
[2] Pullain, *Liturgia Sacra*, f 11.   [3] Pullain, f 28

In 1551 John a Lasco put out in Latin the service used in his church for strangers in Austin Friars, a translation into French being published in 1556, into Dutch in 1563, into German in 1565, and also one into Italian. A special interest attaches to it in connection with the origin and interpretation of the order on the same subject in the present Book of Common Prayer. We read:

And the deacons at the doors of the temple collect the alms for the poor; and the remnants of the bread and wine, which were left over from the use of the supper, they bestow on the poor of the church as each one has need, especially if there are any who are infirm or aged[1].

It seems plain from the words "as each one has need" that what is intended is not a consumption of the remains at the door of the church, but only a distribution there, the remnants being taken out of the church for use at home.

It may be useful to quote the views of other reformers even though their influence on the Book of Common Prayer was not so direct. Bullinger in *The Fifth Decade of the Lord's Supper* takes much the same line as Bucer, and in his later days Cranmer, that there is no holiness in the elements apart from their use. There would thus be no point in such an administration to the sick with what was left over from the service in church as is provided for by the First Prayer Book and Pullain's Glastonbury liturgy. Indeed he refused, as we know, even a celebration for the sick on the ground that it is a public service. We read:

The remnants of the supper. Of these things before handled springeth another question: What is to be thought of the remnants and leavings of the Lord's Supper; and whether there ought any part of it to be reserved; and whether that which is reserved or shut up ought to be adored? This question seemeth to have no godliness at all in it, but to be altogether

---

[1] J a Lasco, *Forma ac Ratio*, p 269

superstitious and very hurtful. For who knoweth not that bread and wine, out of the holy and lawful use appointed, are not a sacrament [1]?

Thomas Becon in his *Comparison between the Lord's Supper and the Pope's Mass,* says·

Christ when the banquet was done, did not command His disciples that they should gather up and keep in store the fragments that be left and remained of the sacramental bread; which thing, notwithstanding, we read that He did often before concerning the common bread [2].

In his Catechism of the Sacraments, and also in *Certain Articles of Christian Religion,* he interprets the words of the pseudo Jerome already quoted, which speak of a feast being held in church from that part of the people's offerings which was not needed for consecration, as though they referred to what had been consecrated [3]. Jewel has the same wrong interpretation, and likewise others [4].

The reformers everywhere however did not disapprove of some special honour being paid to the remains of the sacrament and their reverent consumption. In the liturgy of the reformed church of Sweden, drawn up by Laurence Petri, a disciple of Luther at Wittenberg, and afterwards archbishop of Upsala, which was published in 1576, we find provision for an ablution also. This order for the celebration of mass as it is called, though it incorporates a number of the reformed ideas, is based on the Roman service, and contains many of the Roman prayers, some in a modified form, but there are also apparently reminiscences of passages in the communion service of the English Book of Common Prayer. A peculiarity is that as in the liturgy of SS. Adai and Mari the priest does not communicate until he consumes the remains of the sacrament,

[1] Bullinger, *Works* (Parker Society), vol v. p. 422
[2] Becon, *Works* (P S), vol III pp 372-3
[3] *Works* (P S), vol II p 251, vol. III p 456 See p 11
[4] Jewel, *Works* (P S), vol II pp 553-4 See p 207 Cf pp 209, 211

though this is not at the end of the service as with the Nestorians, but immediately after the communion of the people. We read:

When the celebrant himself is about to communicate, taking in his hands the blessed and sanctified bread, he reverently genuflects saying *Panem caelestem*. Then he says thrice *Domine non sum dignus*. When he is about to receive he says, *Corpus Domini nostri Jesu Christi*, etc. Having received the body of Christ with joined hands he keeps his thoughts occupied in meditation on the most holy sacrament, that its use may be salutary to us. Then when he is about to take the chalice into his hands he reverently genuflects saying *Quid retribuam*. Partaking of the chalice he says, *Sanguis Domini nostri Jesu Christi*, etc. Afterwards he says to himself *Quod ore*. Then he pours a little wine into the chalice, and when he drinks it up he says to himself *Corpus tuum*[1].

The Second English Prayer Book had been published with the authority of Parliament only in 1552, and was never officially sanctioned by the church. As it was abolished the next year on the accession of Mary it can hardly be said really to have been accepted in practice. The principles which had suggested the alterations found in it with regard to the Lord's Supper were never more than the private opinions of the compilers, and the book must have been used by many who entirely repudiated them. Though for whatever reasons it was the Second Prayer Book which was adopted under the Elizabethan settlement the views of the men who had made it what it was were by no means those of the authorities of the time. The idea that there was no such thing as any consecration of the elements in Holy Communion, but only a setting apart for a holy use, was deliberately and officially abandoned. One piece of evidence is the addition of the words of administration from the First Prayer Book to the newly invented forms found in the Second Book, so

[1] Assemani, *Codex Liturgicus*, vol VI. p lxxxiii.

xi] AND THE ELIZABETHAN SETTLEMENT 199

that they now began with the ancient and traditional confession of faith in the sacrament—"The body of our Lord Jesus Christ," "The blood of our Lord Jesus Christ."

Another piece of evidence of the same change of opinion in official circles is to be found in the fact that in the Latin version of the Prayer Book put forth by authority in 1560 the translator Haddon, who evidently based his work on Aless's version of the First Prayer Book, was able without contradiction to revert to some extent to the text of that book. In particular we find that the rubric about the priest having for his own use whatever is left of the bread and wine is omitted, and Aless's rendering of the rubric of the First Book, providing for reservation, is prefixed to the order for the communion of the sick with but few and slight alterations.

Further evidence of the change in belief among those in authority is to be found in the trial of Robert Johnson, a preacher at Northampton and chaplain to the Lord Keeper Bacon, which took place at Westminster Hall before the Queen's Commissioners, including the Lord Chief Justice, the Bishop of London, the Dean of Westminster and others, on February 20, 1573. The chief offence with which he was charged was that he had used fresh wine at a communion service without reciting over them the words of institution. He quoted Cranmer and Bullinger in his defence, and referred also to the opinions of Musculus[1], Peter Martyr and Calvin, arguing that the words were used for the edification of the worshippers only, not to effect any change in the elements, and that as they had been recited once that was sufficient. Parts of the examination may be quoted:

R. Johnson. I stand here indited for three points, the first is, that I have not repeated the words of the institution, or as they commonly say, I have not consecrated the wine when

---

[1] Otherwise Reginald Wolf, a public reader in divinity at Berne.

I delivered it to the communicants....For the first I answer under protestation that at no time in the celebrating of the communion have I omitted any prayer or words of institution which the order of the Book prescribeth, but have used them in as full and ample manner as they are appointed, but some times upon occasion when wine failed I sent for more which I delivered to the people with the words appointed in the Book to be said at the delivery of the sacrament, not again repeating the words of institution, partly for that it being one entire action and one supper, the words of institution afore spoken were sufficient as I do take it, and partly for that in the Book of Common Prayer there is no such order appointed, unto the which in this case I do refer myself.

* * * * *

R. Johnson. I pray you tell me one thing, whether be the words of institution spoken for the bread or for the receivers.

Dean of Westminster. For both.

R. Johnson. I deny that, for the evangelist doth testify that Christ "said to his disciples," to teach them to what end and use they should take the bread.

* * * * *

Master Garrard. Johnson, you confess in a manner as much as you are burdened with, for you confess that when the words of institution were recited you had no wine.

R. Johnson. I do not confess that, for I had both bread and wine.

Master Garrard. But you had not that wine.

R Johnson. No.

Master Garrard. Therefore it was not consecrated.

R. Johnson. The words afore were sufficient for the consecration.

Dean of Westminster. Then with those words you consecrated all the wine in the tavern.

R. Johnson. No sir. For the wine that was in the tavern was brought to the church, and of a common wine was appointed to be a sacramental wine, to represent Christ's blood, and this is consecration.

xi] AND THE ELIZABETHAN SETTLEMENT 201

Dean of Westminster. Why then the word is of no force with you.

R. Johnson. No, not of force to bring any holiness to the sacrament. I trust you do not think that the word maketh the bread the holier when it is a sacrament.

Doctor Wylson. Yes, it is *sacer panis.*

Bishop of London. It is *sacer panis,* a holy sacrament; for the sacrament is holy.

R. Johnson. That I confess, but that holiness is in the use and end and not in the substance: for otherwise you shall make a magical incantation and not a consecration. Master Cranmer in his book of the sacrament saith that there cometh no holiness to the bread by consecration [1,2].

It is plain that his views were identical with those of Cranmer, Bucer and Peter Martyr, in accordance with which the Prayer Book had been revised. The letter of the Prayer Book was also on his side, for there was no direction to repeat the words of institution when the bread or wine failed, Peter Martyr, indeed, having objected strongly to this very thing, and interpreted the words of institution as said for the edification of the communicants. Yet he was found guilty and condemned to a year's imprisonment in the Gatehouse at Westminster—though he died before he had completed the sentence. Clearly the opinions of his judges, some of them dignitaries of the church, were very different from those of the men who in 1552 had caused the alterations in the Prayer Book and made it what it was. The views of the revisers were not considered as necessarily binding on the church in 1573, nor as conclusive with regard to the interpretation of the Book.

To make quite plain what was the intention of the church in the matter of a second consecration, an order

---

[1] See p 191
[2] *A Parte of a Register,* pp. 105–9.

was included among the canons of 1604. In Canon 21 we read:

> No bread or wine newly brought shall be used; but first the words of institution shall be rehearsed, when the said bread and wine be present upon the communion table[1].

This direction was considered of such importance as to be repeated in numerous episcopal injunctions for many years, making it quite plain that the doctrine of the extreme reformers had been definitely rejected.

[1] *Canons and Constitutions*, S.P.C.K. p. 13.

CHAPTER XII

THE SCOTTISH PRAYER BOOK AND THE PRAYER BOOK OF 1661

FOR the next stage in the development of the rubric of the English Prayer Book dealing with the disposal of the remains at holy communion we must go to Scotland. In a Lasco's liturgy for the Strangers' Church in Austin Friars we noticed the provision:

And the deacons at the doors of the temple collect the alms for the poor; and the remnants of the bread and wine, which were left over from the use of the supper, they bestow on the poor of the church as each one has need, especially if there are any who are infirm or aged[1].

What is intended is clearly that the remnants should be taken out of the church for use at home.

In the sixth of the reforming canons of 1636 for the church of Scotland we read:

In the ministration he (the priest) shall have care that the elements are circumspectly handled; and what is reserved thereof be distributed to the poorer sort, which receive that day; to be eaten and drunken by them before they go out of the church[2].

What is forbidden here is the practice which was prescribed in a Lasco's service, and which was probably the common practice among the Calvinists in Scotland, the carrying away of the remains for consumption at home. There can be no doubt about the time and place where the remains of the sacrament not required for communion are o be consumed, and that it is to be neither immediately

---

[1] See p 196 *Forma ac Ratio*, p 269.
[2] *Prayer Book Dictionary*, p. 611

after the communion nor at home, but at the end of the service in church. The rule is akin to that of the synod of Constantinople which we have quoted[1], and as this was known to and cited as authoritative by English divines, such as Anthony Sparrow[2], a little later, it probably suggested the wording. The decree reads:

The fragments of the consecrated oblation they ought not to eat save only in the church, until they have consumed everything[3].

For the consumption of the remains by the laity there was some mediaeval precedent in Britain as we saw in the decree of the council of Durham in 1220[4], but the commoner practice, when not used for communion another day, was to limit it to the clergy, following the directions of the pseudo Clement.

In the ill-fated Scottish Prayer Book of 1637, authorised by the canons of 1636 before it was actually published and having the personal approval of Charles I, the rubric of the Second English Prayer Book with reference to the disposal of the remains is clearly, and of course correctly from a historical point of view, interpreted as applying to the consecrated elements, though the priest is no longer to have them to his own use, for the rubric is combined with the canon. We read:

And if any of the bread and wine remain, which is consecrated, it shall be reverently eaten and drunk by such of the communicants only as the presbyter which celebrates shall take unto him, but it shall not be carried out of the church. And to the end there may be little left, he that officiates is required to consecrate with the least, and then if there be want the words of consecration may be repeated again over more either bread or wine[5].

---

[1] See p. 10. [2] See p. 211.
[3] *P G* cxxxviii col 944 [4] See pp 114–5.
[5] Dowden, *Annotated Scottish Communion Office*, pp 256–7 Hall, *Reliquiae Liturgicae*, vol II p 157

As the canon and prayer book were connected documents, and parts of the same reforming effort, one may plainly be taken as explanatory of the other. That it was only the communicants who were invited who were to consume the remains, and that they were to do it in church is clear from both, but a comparison shows also that "it shall not be carried out of the church" refers, not to anything which the priest might do, but to a possible carrying of the consecrated elements home by those to whom they were given in accordance with the Calvinistic custom. We may notice also that the phrase is almost identical with the similar order about unconsecrated hosts at the council of Clermont in 1268—"let them...not carry them out of the church[1]."

The Prayer Book contains also a rubric quite in accordance with traditional usage both in East and West with regard to the treatment of the sacrament while on the altar:

When all have communicated, he that celebrates shall go to the Lord's table, and cover with a fair linen cloth, or corporal, that which remaineth of the consecrated elements[2].

To speak strictly of course in the case of the chalice it could never happen that none would remain, a point made clear for example in a manuscript of the Hereford missal, where after the priest has communicated and consumed the remains but before he makes the ablution, we yet read "let him sign himself with the blood[3]." The rubric, however, seems to refer to something much more definite than this, and if we are to interpret it strictly it requires that there should always be some of the consecrated elements left, thus agreeing with the primitive practice which found expression in the ancient Roman rule which ordered a portion of the eucharist to remain

[1] See p 35.
[2] Dowden, p 253 Hall, vol II p 152
[3] See p 162. Henderson, p 134. Perhaps in origin a displacement

on the altar until the end of mass, so that, to quote the Gallican explanation of the custom, while the celebration was in progress the altar should never be without the sacrament[1], though in accordance with the other Scottish rubric it should be little.

We may notice how closely the rubric agrees both with the direction of the letter of the pseudo Clement, according to the usual translation, and also with the words of the synod of Constantinople:

But if any (hosts) remain, let them not be reserved until the morrow, but be carefully consumed by the clerks with fear and trembling[2].

The fragments of the consecrated oblation they ought not to eat save only in the church, until they have consumed everything[3].

The similarity is hardly accidental.

The later official interpretation of the rubric "If any remain" of the Second Prayer Book, which in England was left unaltered until the last revision in 1661, was that it referred to the unconsecrated elements. Though this was as we have seen historically incorrect, the original reference being to any remains whether consecrated or unconsecrated, those responsible for the Second Prayer Book recognising no real difference between them, yet in view of the fact that the extreme ideas of the revisers had been officially repudiated and expression of the change has been inserted in the Book of Common Prayer in the words of administration, it was perhaps a legitimate interpretation, and was necessary unless the doctrine of the book was to be self-contradictory. It is not surprising, however, that ultimately, to take away all excuse for profanity, the wording should be altered.

Cosin in his First Series of Notes on the Book of Common Prayer, contained in a Prayer Book printed in 1619, says:

[1] See p 63   Mabillon, II p 14   [2] P G. I col 484. See p 12
[3] P G cxxxviii col 944   See p 10

And if any of the bread and wine remain, etc. Which is not to be understood of the bread and wine already consecrated, but of that which remains without consecration; for else it were but a profanation of the holy sacrament to let the curate have it home to his own use. How unworthily they act who misuse this rubric to excuse so great a crime they themselves should see. It was Nestorianism once to think that the consecrated bread, if it were kept "till the morrow" became common bread again, if St Thomas...quoteth St Cyril of Alexandria right (*Ep. ad Calos.*)...There was order taken for it of old in the church, which were well to be observed still, that no more should be brought, at least consecrated upon the altar, than would suffice to communicate the people, and if any remained, that the priests should reverently receive it. "Let so many hosts be offered on the altar as ought to suffice for the people. Let not that which remains (of course from the hosts and consecrated elements) be kept until the morrow, but with fear and trembling be consumed with carefulness by the clerks" (Clem. P.P. *Ep.* II.)[1].

We notice that he founds his suggestion on the letter of the pseudo Clement according to the usual translation. Though he makes the quotation in Latin he gives it very freely. In the same series of notes we read again:

To his own use. We read in Clemens that after the communion was done the deacon took up that which was left and carried it into the *Pastophorium,* the room where the priests were lodged. In Origen that it was not kept till the next day. In St Jerome that after the communion they that had eaten it in the church spent all that remained of the oblations. In Hesychius that after the example of the old law, all that was left was cast into the fire. In Evagrius that it was an ancient custom at Constantinople, that if any of the sacrament remained, young children were called from the school to eat it up: which was retained in France as in the councils of Mâcon and Tours, held under Charlemagne[2].

[1] Parts of this and the following extract which are given by Cosin in Latin, are here translated *Works,* vol v pp 130-1 See pp 6, 7, 11-13.
[2] *Works,* vol v. p. 132 For references see pp. 6, 7, 9, 35

We notice that he falls into the same mistake as Becon and Jewel, and interprets what the pseudo Jerome says, not of the unconsecrated elements, as it should be, but of the consecrated.

In Cosin's Second Series of Notes to be found in a Prayer Book printed in 1638 we read:

And if any of the bread and wine remain, etc. Which is to be understood of that bread and wine, that the churchwardens provided, and carried into the vestry, not of that which the priest consecrated for the sacrament: for of this, if he be careful, as he ought to be, to consecrate no more than will suffice to be distributed unto the communicants none will remain[1].

This was written we may note before the present rubric was added, which like its Scottish parent assumes that some of the sacrament will always remain, and in accordance with ancient custom be on the altar until the end of the service.

A note written at some later time in the margin records a possible criticism:

Yet if for lack of care they consecrate more than they distribute, why may not the curates have it to their own use, as well as be given to children (Concil. Matisc. II), or be burnt in the fire (Isych. *In Levitic.*), for though the bread and the wine remain, yet the consecration, the sacrament of the body and blood of Christ, do not remain longer than the holy action itself remains for which the bread and wine were hallowed; and which being ended, return to their former use again[2].

This question can hardly be Cosin's own, for it directly contradicts his usual teaching and particularly what we find in the First Series of Notes, and agrees with the doctrine of the more extreme reformers which had inspired the alterations to be found in the Second Prayer Book, including the rubric which Cosin is so careful to explain

---

[1] *Works*, vol. v. p. 356.
[2] *Works*, vol v. pp 356–7. For references see p. 9 as above.

XII] AND THE PRAYER BOOK OF 1661 209

in accordance with the changed views upon the sacrament which had been adopted under the Elizabethan settlement, and in a sense other than the original.

Another note of the Second Series is a comment upon the rubric as referring to the unconsecrated, not the consecrated elements. We read:

The curate shall have it to his own use. It was the ancient manner of the church to offer a good quantity of bread and wine (every one of the people some) for use as well of the minister and priest, as for the poor, and the preparation of the sacrament[1].

In his Third Series of Notes arguing for his usual explanation of the rubric Cosin again confuses the unconsecrated with the consecrated elements. He says:

And if any of the bread and wine remain the curate, etc. Which needeth not be understood of that bread and wine which was blessed and consecrated, but of that which was brought to the church, and not used for the sacrament. And yet we read of some such thing in the Constitutions of the Apostles, Lib. VIII. c. 31. "Let the deacons distribute the remains of the blessings at the mysteries to the clergy according to the mind of the bishop or presbyters. To the bishop, four parts; to a presbyter, three; to a deacon, two; to the rest, subdeacons, readers, singers, or deaconesses, one part[2]"

In another collection of Cosin's entitled "Particulars to be considered, explained and corrected in the Book of Common Prayer," written in all probability as early as the days of Charles I for the most part, and now bound up with the 1619 Prayer Book which contains the First Series of Notes, we get further observations on the matter. We read:

It is likewise here ordered, that if any of the bread and wine remain, the curate shall have it to his own use. Which words some curates have abused and extended so far, that they

[1] *Works*, vol. v. p 357.   [2] *Works*, vol v p 481.

L E

suppose they may take all that remains of the consecrated bread and wine itself, home to their houses, and there eat and drink the same with their other common meats; at least the Roman Catholics take occasion hereby to lay this negligence and calumny upon the Church of England; whereas the rubric only intends it of such bread and wine as remains unconsecrate of that which was provided for the parish (as appeareth by the articles of enquiry hereabouts in the visitations of divers bishops). And therefore for the better clearing of this particular, some words are needful here to be added, whereby the priest may be enjoined to consider the number of them which are to receive the sacrament, and to consecrate the bread and wine in such a near proportion as shall be sufficient for them; but if any of the consecrated elements be left, that he and some others with him shall decently eat and drink them in the church before all the people depart from it[1].

This consideration evidently suggested the restoration of the rubric at the offertory requiring the priest then to place upon the table "so much bread and wine as he shall think sufficient," likewise influencing the alteration of the rubric about the consumption of the remains. Though at first sight it might seem to be the meaning intended, as a matter of fact there appear to be no episcopal articles before this date which deal with the rubric concerning what remains of the bread and wine, and the reference is only to their provision by the churchwardens, as mentioned also in the Second Series of Notes. Many bishops had put out enquiries of this kind in words based on Canon 20 of 1604[2]. As a specimen we may give the earliest, that of Bancroft, Archbishop of Canterbury, in 1605:

Whether the churchwardens do provide against every communion with the advice of the minister a sufficient quantity of fine white bread, and of good and wholesome wine for the number of the communicants that shall receive, and that to

---

[1] *Works*, vol v p 519.
[2] *Canons and Constitutions*, S.P C K p. 12

be brought in a clean and sweet standing pot of pewter, or of other pure metal[1]?

Anthony Sparrow, who was concerned with the revision of 1661, takes the same line as Cosin with regard to the interpretation of the rubric, and in his *Rationale upon the Book of Common Prayer*, published in 1657, we read:

If any of the bread and wine remain the curate shall have it to his own use. That is if it were not consecrated; for if it be consecrated, it is all to be spent with fear and reverence by the communicants, in the church[2].

He adds references to the letter of the pseudo Clement as given by Gratian[3], to the fifth answer of the synod of Constantinople to the questions of the monks, as given by Balsamon[4], and also to the seventh canon of Theophilus of Alexandria, though this as we saw is concerned really with the unconsecrated elements[5].

Among the criticisms and suggestions with regard to the Book of Common Prayer compiled by Bishop Wren, who was one of the revisers of 1661, evidently with a view to this work, being drawn up just before, apparently in 1660, we find one very similar to those of Cosin:

What remaineth of the bread of any loaf or wafer that was broken for the use of the communion, or of the wine that was poured out or had benediction, the curate shall after the service is ended take some of the communicants to him there to eat and drink the same. But all the rest in both kinds the curate shall have to his own use. As this was set down before much outcry was made against it[6].

Public opinion in the church being opposed to the original intention of the rubric, and the authorities being unanimous in explaining it otherwise and in accordance

---

[1] See App to *Second Report of Ritual Commission*, 1868, p 450 etc
[2] Sparrow, *Rationale* Ed Downes, 1722, p 180
[3] Pars III *De Consec* Dist II c 23 *P L*. CLXXXVII col 1740.
[4] *P G* CXXXVIII col 944   [5] See pp 10, 11. Cf p. 209.
[6] Wren, *Fragmentary Illustrations*, pp. 84–5.

with the traditional confession of faith in the sacrament added to the words of administration under the Elizabethan settlement, it was clear that there would be some modification or explanation which would make the intention beyond dispute, and that henceforth at any rate only the remains of what had not been consecrated should be taken out of church for consumption at home. In what is called the "Durham Book," which is a Prayer Book of date 1619, into which the bishops had entered such alterations of the Book of Common Prayer as they decided upon at their meetings after the adjournment of convocation on July 31, 1661, we read the following first authoritative draft of the new rubric dealing with the matter:

If any of the bread (and) or wine remain unconsecrated the curate shall have it to his own use. And if any remain that was consecrate it shall not be carried out of the church, but the priest and such other of the communicants as he shall then call unto him before the Lord's table shall there immediately after the blessing reverently eat and drink the same[1].

The rule is clearly based on the rubric of the Scottish Prayer Book, as that is on the Second Prayer Book and the canon of 1636. The word "there" brings out the point that it is the historical interpretation of the words "it shall not be carried out of the church," which is still intended, and what is forbidden is the carrying away of the remains by those to whom they have been given for consumption at home. It is "before the Lord's table" that the remains are to be distributed and it is "there" likewise that they are to be consumed.

In Sancroft's Fair Copy of the Durham Book, which was made in a Prayer Book of 1634, there is no change save that the original reading of the Second Prayer Book, "bread or wine," is the one adopted. It was the other

[1] Parker, *An Introduction to the History of the Successive Revisions of the Book of Common Prayer*, p ccxxxiii.

reading, however, "bread and wine," which finally passed the Houses of Convocation and received Parliamentary sanction, and is authoritative to-day. The rubric now reads·

And if any of the bread and wine remain unconsecrated, the curate shall have it to his own use: but if any remain of that which was consecrated, it shall not be carried out of the church, but the priest and such other of the communicants as he shall then call unto him, shall, immediately after the blessing, reverently eat and drink the same.

We notice that there have been several alterations from the Durham Book, and both the words "before the Lord's table" and "there" have disappeared, and with the latter the last specific link with the historical interpretation, and the reason for the preceding prohibition. The rubric, however, is still concerned only with the disposal of the remains, whether unconsecrated or consecrated, and the change from "and" to "but" at the beginning of the direction with regard to the latter makes the idea of contrast stronger, so that still the carrying out of the church which is forbidden is one comparable with that which is included in the notion of the curate having the unconsecrated elements to his own use, and its aim, as we see from the intentions of the revisers Cosin, Sparrow, and Wren, and the whole previous discussion which led up to the change, was to prevent a similar treatment of the consecrated elements. The alteration has, however, opened the way for the common interpretation according to which not only the carrying away of the remains for consumption at home, but also any taking of the sacrament out of church for purposes of communion is forbidden. If this be so it is only an unforeseen result of the new wording, for the point was never alluded to in all the discussion which resulted in the order so far as it has come down to us.

From the Scottish liturgy another rubric, agreeing as we noticed with the traditional practice of both East and West, when the blessed sacrament is on the altar, took its origin in 1661.

When all have communicated, the minister shall return to the Lord's table, and reverently place upon it what remaineth of the consecrated elements, covering the same with a fair linen cloth.

As in the Scottish Prayer Book the rubric is not conditional, but it assumes that something will always remain, and so it is not sufficient to regard it as providing for the treatment of a chance surplus. It is a definite order intended to apply to all occasions, and so is comparable with the ancient rule of the First Roman *Ordo* which required the sacrament to remain on the altar until the end of mass[1].

We may note that we have met with no evidence in any post-Reformation English authority for the consumption of the remains of the sacrament not required for communion before the close of the service, and that according to all rubrics or suggested rubrics dealing with the matter this is to be done after the benediction. It is probable that this was intended, as we saw, under the First Prayer Book, but in all editions of the Prayer Book since it has been quite plainly ordered, even if in such a way as to allow scope for irreverence, and the sacrament has remained on the altar according to ancient custom until the end of the liturgy. There was thus a deliberate break with the later mediaeval practice and a return to the primitive usage of both East and West, still retained to some extent in the East, but gradually modified as we saw in the West, so that the present custom apart from the occasions when the sacrament to be reserved remains on the altar until the end of mass is entirely different.

[1] See p. 63. Mabillon, II p. 14.

No idea of any ceremonial ablution of the chalice seems to have entered the minds of the Anglican divines of the seventeenth century, though they adopted various ceremonial practices unknown to the rubrics of the Book of Common Prayer. Under the First Prayer Book the ablutions were made more or less in accordance with traditional practice though probably, as we saw, at any rate on some occasions, at a different time, and it was the same also in the days of Elizabeth, if we may judge by the numerous complaints of bishops and others about the imitation of the Popish mass, but the practice seems to have died out until it was revived in the nineteenth century. As the universal custom from the seventeenth to the nineteenth century was for the remains of the sacrament to be consumed after the benediction, it is clear that there could have been no cleansing of the vessels before, and therefore there was a return to the earliest practice in England as in the rest of the West and elsewhere, such as we find in the Admonition of the pseudo Leo, by which they were washed in the vestry after the service.

Before concluding this part of our discussion it may be well to quote the judgment of the Archbishop of Canterbury in the Bishop of Lincoln's case in 1890 on the question of the ablutions, though its authority is not everywhere recognised and not unchallenged on canonical grounds. We read:

The cleansing of the vessels appears to be not an improper completion of this act which is ordered to follow the close of the service without any break or interval....The rubric gives a general direction as to what is to be done in the way of consuming what remains after the service, and is not so minute as to go beyond this, our book having abandoned many overniceties of regulation. If a conscientious scruple is felt as to not "carrying out of the church" slight remnants even into the vestry, it is not the duty of this court to over-rule it, and the credence is a suitable place for completing the consumption.

In ancient liturgies, which cannot be held to fail in punctilious reverence, after the words of dismissal the minister goes into the prothesis (the wide apse where the credence is) and there consumes the last remnants (see Goar, *Euch.*, p. 86[1]). In neither of those liturgies [copies of the liturgy of St Chrysostom] which were in Cranmer's hands and used by him (as we have seen) are any directions given. If it were the duty of this court to point out where and when, if not at the Holy Table, the minister would most properly complete the consumption of the consecrated elements in such a way as he might think to be necessary in compliance with the rubric, the court would unhesitatingly say "at the credence, or in the place where they had been prepared." Nevertheless the court cannot hold that the minister, who, after the service was ended and the benediction given, in order that no part of the consecrated elements should be carried out of the church, cleansed the vessels of all remnants in a reverent way without ceremony or prayers before finally leaving the Holy Table, would have subjected himself to penal consequences by so doing[2].

[1] This should be p 68. The error seems to be due to copying without verification a reference given in Scudamore's *Notitia Eucharistica*, p 895

[2] *Read and others v. the Lord Bishop of Lincoln Judgment* Nov. 21, 1890, pp 15-17.

CHAPTER XIII

THE WORSHIP OF THE LAMB

THAT the intention of the Prayer Book since the last revision is that the remains of the blessed sacrament after communion should remain on the altar reverently covered with a fair linen cloth until the end of the service admits of no doubt, and thus agreement with ancient usage, and particularly with what was the rule of the church of Rome on the subject, was effected. There was a still further return to ancient ideas with regard to the eucharist characterising the whole revision. In particular we may note the change in the Black Rubric which said that "no adoration is intended or ought to be done... unto any real and essential presence there being of Christ's natural flesh and blood," so as to read "any corporal presence of Christ's natural flesh and blood." The order requiring on every occasion "what remaineth of the consecrated elements" to be placed on the altar immediately after the administration brought it about that, as St Gregory the Great had said in his letter to John of Syracuse, the prayer which our Redeemer had composed is always recited over His body and blood[1], though not before the communion as originally. It may be well to enquire what other influence the new rubric had on the devotion of the worshippers during the latter part of the service.

We have noticed that according to Zwingli's ideas, as shown in the liturgy of Zurich, though he would not connect our Lord's presence directly with the elements, the concluding portion of the service was performed with a

[1] *P.L.* LXXVII. col 956–7.

deep sense of the reality of that presence as He is exhibited outwardly in symbolic actions and inwardly to the eye of faith in the act of communion, "the Lamb of God which taketh away the sin of the world," and that He is thus worshipped in the sacrament "present by the contemplation of faith." In later days the ceremonial commemoration of the sacrifice of Christ became one of the chief features of a celebration of the Lord's Supper among the followers of Zwingli and Calvin, and in the broken bread and the wine poured out the sacrifice is dramatically set forth for the edification of the worshippers. In the Puritan Prayer Book published by Waldegrave (*c.* 1585) we read:

During the which time [of the communion] some place of the Scriptures is read, which doth lively set forth the death of Christ, to the intent that our eyes and senses may not only be occupied in these outward signs of bread and wine, which are called the visible word; but that our hearts and minds also may be fully fixed in the contemplation of the Lord's death, which is by this holy sacrament represented[1].

The same words are found in the editions published at Middleburgh in 1586, 1587 and 1602[2]. In *The New Book of Common Prayer, according to the form of the Kirk of Scotland* issued in 1644 after the troubles which arose over the Prayer Book of 1637 we find an almost identical order, but the importance attached to the idea of the exhibition of our Lord and His death in the sacrament is shown by *"the Visible Word"* being printed in italics with capital letters[3].

It was as bringing out the idea of our Lord's sacrificial death that so much emphasis was laid on the breaking of the bread. In the Parliamentary Directory of 1644 we read·

According to the holy institution, command, and example of our blessed Saviour Jesus Christ, I take this bread, and

---
[1] Hall, *Fragmenta Liturgica*, vol 1 p 66
[2] Hall, *Reliquiae Liturgicae*, vol 1 p. 59
[3] Hall, *F L* vol 1 p 94.

XIII]   THE WORSHIP OF THE LAMB   219

having given thanks, I break it, and give it unto you (There the minister, who is also himself to communicate, is to break the bread and give it to the communicants). Take ye, eat ye, This is the body of Christ, which is broken for you, Do this in remembrance of Him[1].

We note the implication that not all those present would necessarily communicate, and the same point is brought out in the preliminary exhortation, though there it is only the "ignorant, scandalous, profane or (those) that live in any sin or offence against their knowledge or conscience" who are warned "that they presume not to come to that holy table"; but no interval is allowed in which they may withdraw.

Important evidence about the ideas of the Puritan party with regard to the sacrament is to be found in the liturgy prepared by Richard Baxter and submitted by him and the other Puritan divines to the Savoy Conference in 1661. As Baxter stated that he had no quarrel with the doctrines of the Book of Common Prayer, the proposed liturgy is to be regarded as much as an interpretation of that book according to his theological ideas as a substitute for it. According to the Puritan divines, the three chief elements in the ordinance were the consecration, the commemoration of the sacrifice, and the communion. Consequently in their exceptions to the Book of Common Prayer their complaint had been:

We conceive that the manner of the consecrating of the elements is not here explicit and distinct enough, and the minister's breaking of the bread is not so much as mentioned[2].

In Baxter's liturgy we see how the Puritans would bring out these ideas. From their point of view a description of the sacrament is as follows

The Lord's Supper, then, is an holy sacrament, instituted by

[1] Hall, *Reliquiae Liturgicae*, vol III p 57
[2] Cardwell, *Conferences*, 3rd Ed. p 321.

Christ: wherein bread and wine, being first by consecration made sacramentally, or representatively, the body and blood of Christ, are used by breaking and pouring out to represent and commemorate the sacrifice of Christ's body and blood upon the cross once offered up to God for sin; and are given in the name of Christ unto the Church, to signify and solemnize the renewal of His holy covenant with them, and the giving of Himself unto them, to expiate their sins by His sacrifice, and sanctify them further by His Spirit, and confirm their right to everlasting life[1].

With regard to the consecration we read:

Sanctify these thy creatures of bread and wine, which, according to thy institution and command, we set apart to this holy use, that they may be sacramentally the body and blood of thy Son Jesus Christ[2].

After the words of institution which are not part of a prayer but addressed to the people the minister says:

This bread and wine, being set apart, and consecrated to this holy use by God's appointment, are now no common bread and wine, but sacramentally the body and blood of Christ[3].

The commemoration of the sacrifice, which follows, is a very dramatic feature of the liturgy:

Then let the minister take the bread, and break it in the sight of the people, saying·

The body of Christ was broken for us, and offered once for all to sanctify us: behold the sacrificed Lamb of God, that taketh away the sins of the world.

In like manner let him take the cup, and pour out the wine in the sight of the congregation, saying:

We were redeemed with the precious blood of Christ, as of a Lamb without blemish and without spot[4].

We note how the words agree with the forms already quoted from a Lasco's liturgy, and the First Prayer Book,

---

[1] Hall, *Reliquiae Liturgicae*, vol IV p 57
[2] *R L.* vol IV. p 68.
[3] *R L.* vol. IV. p 69.   [4] *R.L.* vol. IV. p. 70.

though with regard to the latter, the draft Articles of 1549, Ridley's Injunctions of 1550, and Hooper's similar Injunctions of 1551, forbade "showing the sacrament openly before the distribution[1]." They are also very similar to the words of the Roman missal when the priest turns towards the people for the communion. Lifting up a particle of the holy sacrament he says:

Behold the Lamb of God, behold him that taketh away the sins of the world.

That non-communicants might remain throughout the service is plain, though they are not encouraged; yet they too take part in the commemoration of the sacrifice. We read.

See here Christ dying in this holy representation! Behold the sacrificed Lamb of God, that taketh away the sins of the world! It is his will to be thus frequently crucified before our eyes....See here his broken body and his blood, the testimonies of his willingness....Deny not your consent but heartily give up yourselves to Christ....Receive now a crucified Christ here represented, and be contented to take up your cross and follow him[2].

A striking feature of the liturgy is the adoration of Jesus exhibited to the faithful in the sacrament as the sacrificed and glorified Lamb of God. The idea behind it is the same as that of Zwingli in the Zurich liturgy, but its special interest is to be found in the light it throws upon the interpretation put upon the *Gloria in excelsis* as used in the Book of Common Prayer by such as Baxter. Immediately after the participation the minister prays:

Most glorious God, how wonderful is thy power and wisdom, thy holiness and justice, thy love and mercy, in this work of our redemption, by the incarnation, life, death, resurrection, intercession and dominion of thy Son! No power or wisdom in

---

[1] Frere, *Visitation Articles*, vol II. pp 192-3, 242, 276.
[2] Hall, *R.L.* vol. IV. pp. 61-4

heaven or earth could have delivered us, but thine. The angels desire to pry into this mystery: the heavenly host do celebrate it with praises saying, Glory be to God in the highest; on earth peace, goodwill towards men. The whole creation shall proclaim thy praises: Blessing, honour, glory and power, be unto him that sitteth upon the throne, and unto the Lamb for ever and ever. Worthy is the Lamb that was slain, to receive power, and honour, and glory. for he hath redeemed us to God by his blood, and made us kings and priests unto our God....With the blood of thy Son, with the sacrament, and with thy Spirit, thou hast sealed up to us these precious promises[1].

We must now examine the ideas of the church party at the Savoy Conference. In Cosin's First Series of Notes upon the Book of Common Prayer we read:

O Lord and heavenly Father. In King Edward's first service book, this prayer was set before the delivery of the sacrament to the people, and followed immediately after the consecration; and certainly it was the better and the more natural order of the two; neither do I know whether it were the printer's negligence, or no, thus to displace it. For the consecration of the sacrament being ever the first, it was always the use in all liturgies to have the oblation follow (which is this), and then the participation, which goes before, and after all, the thanksgiving, which is here set next before the *Gloria in excelsis*; in regard whereof I have always observed my lord and master Dr Overall to use this oblation in its right place, when he had consecrated the sacrament to make an offering of it (as being the true public sacrifice of the church) unto God, that by the merits of Christ's death, which was now commemorated, all the Church of God might receive mercy, etc. as in this prayer; and when that was done he did communicate the people, and so end with the thanksgiving following hereafter[2].

Cosin clearly misunderstood the rationale of the eucharistic prayer in the Eastern liturgies, for as in them the consecration is deemed to be effected by the Epiclesis and

---

[1] *R.L* vol. IV pp. 74–5. [2] Parker, *Introduction*, pp ccxxiii, ccxxiv.

not by the recitation of the words of institution, it follows and does not precede what he calls "the oblation." To Cosin, as to the Puritan divines, the three chief elements in the ordinance are the consecration, the commemoration of the sacrifice and the communion. The difference was that to the Puritans the commemoration of the sacrifice was an exhibition of the sacrifice to men, but to Cosin and his friends a presentation of the sacrifice to God. Consequently on one side the emphasis was on making an offering to the Father while on the other it was on the manifestation and the consequent adoration of the Son. As the order of the liturgy was finally settled neither side gained what they desired.

In his work on the *Catholic Religion of the Realm of England* of the year 1652 Cosin gave a description of the ceremonial at the consecration in the Lord's Supper. We read·

Then standing up by solemn prayers which contain the institution of the sacrament and the very words of Christ when instituting it, breaking the bread which he has taken into his hands and pouring out the wine into the chalice, he blesses each symbol, and consecrates them to be the sacrament of Christ's body and blood[1].

In the *Particulars to be considered* (No. 57) the breaking of the bread is still regarded as important, but nothing is said about the pouring out of the wine. We read:

No direction is given to the priest (as in King Edward's service-book there was, and as in most places it is still in use) to "take the bread and cup into his hands" nor to "break the bread" before the people, which is a needful circumstance belonging to this sacrament; and therefore, for his better warrant therein, such a direction ought here to be set in the margin of the book[2].

[1] Cosin, *Works*, vol IV. p. 359.
[2] Cosin, *Works*, vol. v. pp. 516–7   Cf Brightman, *English Rite*, vol. I p ccxix.

The possibility of the pouring out of the wine at the time of consecration is allowed according to Wren's suggestions for revising the Book of Common Prayer. His proposed rubric runs:

> Then the priest standing before the table shall so order and set the bread and the wine that, while he is pronouncing the following collect, he may readily take the bread and break it, and also take the cup, to pour into it (if he pour it not before), and then he shall say...[1].

The final rubrics on the point are clearly due to Cosin:

> When the priest, standing before the table, hath so ordered the bread and wine, that he may with the more readiness and decency break the bread before the people, and take the cup into his hands, he shall say the prayer of consecration, as followeth....*Who in the same night that he was betrayed* (Here the priest is to take the paten into his hands) *took bread; and when he had given thanks* (And here to break the bread), *he brake it.*

The Puritan idea of the commemoration of the sacrifice of Christ is thus entirely disallowed. Baxter had written:

> Bread and wine, being first by consecration made sacramentally, or representatively the body and blood of Christ, are used by breaking and pouring out to represent and commemorate the sacrifice of Christ's body and blood upon the cross once offered up to God.

Now the breaking of the bread is directed to take place before consecration, and there is no mention of the pouring out of the wine at all.

The rubrics finally adopted are found in the Durham Book and in this Cosin's suggestions for the sequence of the eucharistic prayer are also set out, for as in the First Prayer Book "Wherefore, O Lord and heavenly Father" follows the prayer of consecration immediately. A note

---

[1] Parker, *Introduction*, p. ccccxxv.

in Sancroft's hand shows, however, that this also was afterwards disallowed, and the old arrangement of the prayers restored. We read:

My lords the bishops at Ely House ordered all in the old method, thus—First the prayer of address, *We do not presume*; with the rubric, *When the priest standing*, etc., the prayer of consecration unaltered (only *one* for *own* and *Amen* at last) with the marginal rubrics. Then (the memorial or prayer of oblation omitted and the Lord's prayer) follow the rubrics and forms of participation....And then the Lord's prayer, the collect, *O Lord and heavenly Father*, etc., etc., to the end[1].

The bishops thus plainly refused to accept Cosin's suggestion and with it his idea of the eucharistic sacrifice. Consequently neither Baxter's nor Cosin's notion of the commemoration of the sacrifice of Christ was officially recognised, and churchmen were left free to hold the doctrine to be gathered from antiquity and the ancient liturgies on the subject, and to accept from each of the opposing parties the ideas which are most in accordance with these. Yet the fact of the commemoration of the sacrifice is deliberately recognised, for the second exhortation is altered to read: "so it is your duty to receive the communion in remembrance *of the sacrifice* of his death," the words in italics being an addition; while there is still of course the statement in the Catechism that the sacrament of the Lord's Supper was ordained "for the continual remembrance of the sacrifice of the death of Christ."

As is usual in all such cases the interpretation according to which the new version of the Prayer Book was accepted is of no less importance than the conflicting ideas which had made it what it was. Even the more Protestant recognised the reverence due to our Lord manifest in the sacrament as the sacrificed Lamb of God. Daniel Brevint, Canon of Durham, and afterwards Dean of Lincoln, in

---

[1] Parker, *Introduction*, p. ccxxii

The Christian Sacrament and Sacrifice, published in 1673, thus writes of the eucharist:

Therefore whensoever Christians approach to this dreadful mystery, and to the Lamb of God *lying and sacrificed* (as some say that the holy Nicene Council speaks) *upon the holy table*: it concerns their main interest in point of salvation, as well as in other duties, to take a special care, not to lame and deprive the grand sacrifice of its own due attendance[1].

Archbishop Laud in his defence of adoration towards the altar in his speech in the Star Chamber on June 14th, 1637, said

It is *versus altare*, towards his altar, as the greatest place of God's residence on earth[2].

And again:

Where Harding names divers ceremonies, and particularly *bowing themselves and adoring at the sacrament*—I say adoring at the sacrament, not adoring the sacrament: there Bishop Jewel approves all, both the kneeling and the bowing[3].

Adoration of Christ at the sacrament was also approved by Cosin. In his defence of the practice of receiving the communion kneeling in his Second Series of Notes on the Book of Common Prayer, we read:

True it is, that the body and blood of Christ are sacramentally and really (not feignedly) present, when the blessed bread and wine are taken by the faithful communicants.... Therefore whosoever so receiveth them, at that time when he receiveth them, rightly doth he adore and reverence his Saviour there together with the sacramental bread and cup, exhibiting His own body and blood unto them. But our kneeling, and the outward gesture of humility and reverence in our bodies, is ordained only to testify and express the inward reverence and devotion of our souls towards our blessed Saviour, Who vouchsafed to sacrifice Himself for us upon the cross, and now

---

[1] Brevint, *The Christian Sacrament and Sacrifice*, p 94
[2] Staley, *Hierurgia Anglicana*, Pt II 1903, p 88   [3] Pt II p. 89

XIII] THE WORSHIP OF THE LAMB

presenteth Himself to be united sacramentally to us, that we may enjoy all the benefits of His mystical passion, and be nourished with the spiritual food of His blessed body and blood unto life eternal[1].

"The inward reverence and devotion of our souls towards our blessed Saviour" was commonly expressed in the period immediately following the last revision of the Prayer Book by the use of the *Agnus Dei*, and it appears quite frequently in books of devotion for private use at communion[2]. This act of worship of our Lord in the sacrament is found not only before communion but afterwards in accordance with the ideas which seem to have caused the removal of the *Gloria in excelsis* to its new position in 1552. Thomas Burnet in *The Nature, Use and Efficacy of the Sacrament of the Lord's Supper*, published in 1731, and dedicated to members of the Royal Family, gives it thus for use immediately after communion·

O Lamb of God, who takest away the sins of the world, have mercy upon me. By thine agony and bloody sweat, thy cross and passion, good Lord deliver me[3].

The worship of our Lord exhibited as the Lamb of God in the sacrament, officially recognised in the *Gloria in excelsis*, was thus at the end of the seventeenth and the beginning of the eighteenth century a common element of private eucharistic devotion after as well as before reception. If the faithful coming to communion could be said to "approach to the dreadful mystery and to the Lamb of God lying and sacrificed upon the holy table" it was not unlikely that afterwards when what remained of the consecrated elements was reverently placed upon the holy table and covered with a fair linen cloth the same idea should be continued, the negations of the revisers

[1] Parker, *Introduction*, p ccxx.
[2] Legg, *English Church Life*, pp 57-60
[3] Burnet, *The Sacrament of the Lord's Supper*, p. 30

being forgotten but their positive ideas accepted, and that men should still "behold the sacrificed Lamb of God, that taketh away the sins of the world," and worship Him in "these holy mysteries" in the traditional phraseology of the *Agnus*, which is included in the *Gloria in excelsis*. The rubric requiring the sacrament to remain on the altar until the end of the service according to ancient custom made it impossible that it should be otherwise, when the negations of the sixteenth century were abandoned, and much of the earlier faith restored. The association of the *Gloria in excelsis* with the sacramental presence of our Lord was not a new thing. Thomas Becon in his *Displaying of the Popish Mass* says:

After these things ye go unto the midst of the altar, and looking up to the pyx, where ye think your God to be, and making solemn courtesy, like womanly Joan, ye say the *Gloria in excelsis*[1].

Nor could this worship of our Lord very well be limited to those who communicated on that particular occasion. Both the Parliamentary Directory and Baxter's liturgy recognised that non-communicants might be present during the celebration of the Lord's Supper, though it was not encouraged or regarded as fulfilling our Lord's command, and the same thing is the historical explanation of the form taken by some of the rubrics of the Book of Common Prayer, when under the First Prayer Book it was the ordinary custom. The strong condemnation of those who were present at the sacrament without communicating, inserted in the Second Prayer Book at Bucer's suggestion and based perhaps on words of St Chrysostom[2], was omitted in 1662 so that freedom in the matter was restored. According to Bishop Wren at this date there was no need for the words of the exhortation any longer, and

---

[1] Becon, *Displaying of the Popish Mass*. *Works* (Parker Society), vol. III p 263
[2] *In Epis ad Ephes* Cap 1 Hom iii, *P G* LXII. col. 29.

among his proposals for altering the Book of Common Prayer we read:

To stand by, as gazers and lookers on, is now wholly out of use in all parishes. And the Not-Communicants generally do use to depart, without bidding[1].

If these words were intended to refer to all non-communicating attendance, to the presence of those who were regular communicants on other occasions as well as of those who never communicated at all, it certainly was not the truth a little later. We read of John Evelyn in 1684, after communicating at an early celebration at Whitehall being present again at a later celebration, and there is nothing to show that it was anything exceptional, or confined to the court. He writes:

30 [March] Easter Day. The bishop of Rochester [Dr Turner] preached before the king, after which his majesty, accompanied with three of his natural sons...went up to the altar; the three boys entering before the king within the rails, at the right hand, and three bishops on the left, viz. London (who officiated), Durham, and Rochester with the Sub Dean Dr Holder. The king kneeling before the altar, making his offering, the bishops first received, and then his majesty; after which he retired to a canopied seat on the right hand Note there was perfume burnt before the office began. I had received the sacrament at Whitehall early with the Lords and Household, the Bishop of London officiating. Then went to St Martin's, where Dr Tenison preached,...then went again to Whitehall as above. In the afternoon went to St Martin's again[2].

The Bishop of London evidently duplicated, but Evelyn was present the second time without communicating. In a day so crowded with religious observance it is unlikely that Evelyn was there simply for sight-seeing,

[1] Parker, *Introduction*, p ccccxxv.
[2] Bray, *The Diary of John Evelyn, Esquire*, F R S. (The Chandos Classics), pp 456–7

and it appears not to have been the custom for non-communicants to depart. If the words of Baxter's exhortation were true even for those who refused the invitation to communion they could hardly be untrue for those who had communicated at an earlier service or on another occasion·

See here Christ dying in this holy representation! Behold the sacrificed Lamb of God, that taketh away the sins of the world! It is his will to be thus frequently crucified before our eyes[1].

The adoration of Christ, exhibited in His sacrament as the sacrificed and glorified Lamb of God, which is provided in the *Gloria in excelsis*, whatever its original purpose and scope, is put into the mouths of all, and is an act of worship for all. The private opinions of the revisers of the Book of Common Prayer at one period were never regarded as binding by the revisers of another, nor have they been regarded as necessarily binding on anyone except in so far as they have been incorporated in the text; and indeed as they have been so contradictory it would have been impossible. The Prayer Book must be interpreted not as expressing the views of one party or another, either in the sixteenth or seventeenth century, but in accordance with its own appeal to antiquity, in the light of that knowledge which is the privilege of the particular age.

In the liturgy of St James after the fraction at the consignation the priest says:

Behold the Lamb of God that taketh away the sin of the world, slain for the life and salvation of the world[2].

After the people's thanksgiving for communion at the last entrance when the priest returns to the sanctuary with the sacred elements the archdeacon says:

Glory to thee, glory to thee, glory to thee, O Christ the King,

---

[1] See p. 221. Hall, *Reliquiae Liturgicae*, vol. IV. p. 61
[2] Brightman, *Eastern Liturgies*, p. 62

XIII]   THE WORSHIP OF THE LAMB   231

the only begotten Word of the Father, for thou didst vouchsafe that we thy sinful and unworthy servants should enjoy thy spotless mysteries for the remission of our sins and eternal life. Glory to thee[1].

Similarly in the Syrian liturgy in a prayer of the fraction we read:

Thou art the Lamb of God that taketh away the sin of the world[2].

Returning with the mysteries at the last entrance the priest says:

Glory to thee, glory to thee, glory to thee, O our Lord and our God for ever. Our Lord Jesus Christ, let not thy holy body which we have eaten and thy propitiatory blood which we have drunk be unto us for judgment and for vengeance but for the life and salvation of us all: and have mercy upon us[3].

Thus in both the liturgies of the Syrian rite our Lord in the sacrament is recognised as the sacrificed Lamb of God, and He is worshipped after the communion in words very similar to the beginning of the *Gloria in excelsis*—"Glory to thee."

In the Nestorian liturgy we are told that "when the people have received the holy thing the priest takes back the vessels, with the mysteries to their place (and the veil is closed)"[4]; and there they remain until they are consumed when the celebrant makes his communion at the end of the service. At the end of the thanksgiving after the people's communion "one of the deacons binds up the veil," and the mysteries are again exposed to view. Those that are in the nave then say this psalm:

O praise the Lord of heaven : the Son who gave us his body and blood.

Praise him in the height · the Son who gave us his body and blood (*and the rest of Ps. cxlviii.* 1–6 *in like manner*).

[1] Brightman, p 65.   [2] Brightman, p 99.
[3] Brightman, p 104. [4] Brightman, p. 301.

And they proceed
O praise the Lord, all ye heathen: For his gift to us.
Praise him, all ye nations: For his gift to us
(*and the rest of Ps. cxvii*).
Glory be to the Father and to the Son and to the Holy Ghost:
To the Son who gave us his body and blood.
From everlasting to everlasting world without end, Amen
To the Son who gave us his body and blood.
Let all the people say Amen and Amen:
To the Son who gave us his body and blood.
Let us confess and worship and glorify:
The Son who gave us his body and blood.
And they proceed
Our Father which art in heaven,
three times (without farcings)[1].

Again we have adoration of the Son and thanksgiving to Him for the blessings of communion, while there is a further point of contact with the English liturgy in the use of the Lord's prayer after the communion, all in the presence of the blessed sacrament.

In the liturgy of St Chrysostom at the fraction the priest says:

Broken and distributed is the Lamb of God, who was broken and not divided[2].

The holy sacrament is twice exposed to the people to kindle their adoration after the communion of the ministers. On the first occasion which is after the communion of the people when any receive we have a benediction with the blessed sacrament. We read.

And thus they open the door of the sanctuary, and the deacon bowing once takes the holy chalice from the priest with reverence and goes to the door, and elevating it shows it to the people, saying, *In the fear of God, and faith and love draw near.* The choir, *Blessed is he that cometh in the name of*

[1] Brightman, pp. 302–3.   [2] Brightman, p. 393.

XIII]   THE WORSHIP OF THE LAMB   233

the Lord. God is the Lord and hath showed us light. And the priest blesses the people saying over them aloud, *O God save thy people and bless thine inheritance.* The choir the apolutikon of the day[1]. And both the deacon and priest return to the holy table, and the deacon puts down the holy cup upon it and says to the priest, *Exalt, sir.* And the priest censes it thrice saying to himself, *Be thou exalted, O God, above the heavens, and thy glory above all the earth.* Then taking the holy paten he puts it upon the head of the deacon, and the deacon takes it with reverence, looks outside towards the door, and saying nothing, departs to the prothesis and puts it down. And the priest bows and takes the holy chalice [containing the remains of the holy sacrament], and turns towards the door, and looks at the people saying, *Blessed be our God.* Then he says aloud, *At all times, now and always and for ever and ever*[2].

This attitude towards the holy sacrament is by no means simply modern, even if it does not belong to the earliest days. The blessing of the faithful by the priest after the communion while he, or the deacon by his side, holds the sacrament in his hands is as old as the beginning of the ninth century at any rate in the liturgy of the presanctified. St Theodore of the Studium (*c.* 800) in his work, *De Praesanctificatis,* says:

After the reception by the brethren there is said, *O God, save thy people and bless thine inheritance,* and he marks them with the divine sign of the precious cross. The divine gifts he on no account puts down on the divine table, but immediately puts them away in the prothesis[3].

The second act of reverence towards the blessed sacrament we find already in the eleventh century codex of the liturgy of St Chrysostom. We read:

And when he is about to return the holy gifts where they were set forth, on taking them from the holy table the deacon censes them thrice. The priest says to himself, *Be thou exalted,*

[1] A hymn of dismissal   [2] Brightman, pp 395-7.
[3] *P.G.* xcix. col. 1689

O God, above the heavens, and thy glory above all the earth, and taking them up he says aloud, *At all times, now and always, and for ever and ever*[1].

This taking up of the sacrament for removal to the prothesis is thus likened in the priest's prayer to our Lord's ascension, and allusions to this interpretation we find in various writers of different periods. An exposition of the liturgy written by Germanus, patriarch of Constantinople (†c. 740), but interpolated (c. 1100), says:

The taking up of the holy remnants which are left suggests the ascension of our Lord and God[2].

Similarly we read in the commentary of Simeon of Thessalonica († 1429) on the liturgy:

Censing the gifts the chief priest departs saying also those things which manifest the ascension of the Saviour[3].

In the Longer Catechism of the Russian Church, in accordance with such traditional expositions, a mystical interpretation is given to each of the two special acts of reverence towards our Lord in His sacramental presence after the communion. We read·

Q. What is set forth after this [the communion of the clergy] by the drawing back of the veil, the opening of the royal doors, and the appearance of the holy gifts?
A. The appearance of Jesus Christ Himself after His resurrection.
Q. What is figured by the last showing of the holy gifts to the people after which they are hid from view?
A. The ascension of Jesus Christ into heaven[4].

Almost the same symbolical interpretation is found in the Liturgical Homilies of Narsai († c. 502) which explain

---

[1] Swainson, p 141
[2] Goar, *Euchologion,* p 131, n 182
[3] Goar, pp. 131, 192
[4] Blackmore, *Doctrine of the Russian Church,* p. 94.

an early form of the Nestorian rite. After the priest's thanksgiving for communion we read:

Then all in the altar and without in the congregation pray the prayer which that lifegiving mouth taught. With it do men begin every prayer, morning and evening: and with it do they complete all the rites (or mysteries) of holy church. This it is said is that which includes all prayer, and without it no prayer is concluded. Then the priest goes forth and stands at the door of the altar; and he stretches forth his hands and blesses the people, and says—the whole people the priest blesses in that hour, symbolizing the blessing which our Lord Jesus gave to His twelve. On the day of His ascension He the High Pontiff, lifted up His hands and blessed and made priests of His twelve; and then He was taken up. A symbol of His resurrection has the priest typified by the completion of the mysteries, and a symbol of His revelation before His disciples by distributing Him. By the stretching out of the hands of the bright-robed priest towards the light he confers a blessing upon the whole congregation; and thus he says, *He that hath blessed us with every blessing of the Spirit in heaven, may He also now bless us all with the power of His mysteries...*and with his right hand he signs the congregation with the living sign[1].

We note the use of the Lord's prayer after the communion as in the Book of Common Prayer, and the blessing "with the power of His mysteries," not unlike the blessing "in the knowledge and love of...his Son Jesus Christ" after communion which has characterised the English rite since the publication of the *Order of Communion* in 1548.

The liturgy of the Armenians has also the benediction with the blessed sacrament after the communion as in the liturgy of St Chrysostom, though according to some texts there is no allusion to it in the rubrics[2]. We read.

[1] Connolly, *The Liturgical Homilies of Narsai*, pp 30–31.
[2] Issaverdenz, *The Armenian Liturgy*, p 81 *Translations of Christian Liturgies*, 1 *The Armenian Liturgy*, p 104 Fortescue, *The Armenian Church*, p. 107. Daniel, *Codex Liturgicus*, vol IV. p. 477

Then all who are worthy communicate. *The clerks sing...
This is the same Christ the divine Word who sitteth at the right
hand of the Father, and who sacrificed here amongst us taketh
away the sin of the world. He is blessed for ever with the Father
and the Spirit, now and ever for the time to come and world
without end.* When all have communicated the clerks sing in a
loud voice, *Our God and our Lord hath appeared to us. Blessed
is he that cometh in the name of the Lord.* Then the priest makes
over them the sign of the cross with the sacred gifts, and says,
*Save thy people, O Lord, and bless thine inheritance · govern them
and lift them up for ever.* The clerks sing, *We have been filled,
O Lord, from thy good things, tasting of thy body and blood: Glory
be on high to thee who hast fed us. Thou who continually feedest
us, send down upon us thy spiritual blessing: Glory be on high to
thee who hast fed us*[1].

We notice how the ideas of the *Agnus* are incorporated
in the communion hymn which is really a paraphrase of
part of the *Gloria in excelsis.* The hymn of thanksgiving
after the benediction with the sacrament also has affinity
with the *Gloria.*

Our examination of the ancient liturgies has shown that
the thought of our Lord as the sacrificed Lamb of God
manifest in the eucharist is found in almost all. The
worship of Him after the communion in His special sacramental presence is also very widespread, and in words
not very dissimilar from those provided in the *Gloria in
excelsis.* The Church of England in the original preface of
the Prayer Book now entitled, "Concerning the service of
the Church," appealed "to the mind and purpose of the old
fathers" of liturgy. Likewise at the last revision in 1661
the appeal was to "the most ancient liturgies," and to
these the revisers were referred by Charles II in his
Letters Patent of March 25th of that year[2]. Of the liturgy

---

[1] Brightman, pp 452–4 Cf Malan, *The Divine Liturgy of the Armenian Church,* p 50

[2] Cardwell, *Conferences,* 3rd Ed p 300

which bears the name of one of the "ancient fathers" St Chrysostom, the faithful have been reminded twice every day for centuries. It is in accordance with the consensus of the liturgies, not by the contradictory opinions of different sets of revisers, that "all sober, peaceable, and truly conscientious sons of the Church of England" have tried to interpret the Book of Common Prayer, as the book itself recommends. Thus all such have been able when "what remaineth of the consecrated elements" has been reverently placed upon the Lord's table, to recognise still "the Lamb of God lying and sacrificed upon the holy table," as Daniel Brevint said[1], and whether in thanksgiving for communion or in simple adoration to join with the angelic hosts in worshipping the "Lamb as it had been slain," "Who hath appeared unto us"—

O Lord God, Lamb of God. Son of the Father, that takest away the sins of the world, have mercy upon us, receive our prayer. Thou that sittest at the right hand of God the Father, have mercy upon us. For thou only art holy; thou only art the Lord, thou only, O Christ, with the Holy Ghost art most high in the glory of God the Father. Amen.

[1] See p. 226.

CHAPTER XIV

CONCLUSIONS

WE are now in a position to summarise our chief results. The primitive custom appears to have been that what was left of the consecrated elements after the communion at the eucharist should not be consumed at once immediately after the administration, but be reserved at any rate until the end of the service either in the sacristy or on the altar and generally, in accordance with the Mosaic rules for the disposal of the remains of the sacrifices, until the next day. This practice seems to have existed everywhere in the early days so far as we know, and lasted with slight modifications for many centuries. The remains were disposed of finally in a variety of ways, some of them very extraordinary to our modern notions, being burnt, a practice derived from the Jewish law, buried, or given to children. The more common usage was that any residue which was left, presumably of both kinds, should be carried into the sacristy, and in so far as it had not been intended for reservation should be consumed by the clergy or used for communion the next day. In the Greek church the remains are still carried into the prothesis, and, when there is no deacon or he has not communicated, consumed by the priest after the service, so that what was a very early custom has continued with little change until modern times. In the West the history was more or less identical for centuries, but as a rule it would seem the residue of the sacrament, commonly called the Sancta, was kept on the altar until the end of the liturgy, special provision being made at Rome that this should always be the case by the rule that the third part of the celebrant's host should be put down on the altar at the fraction, and remain there till the conclusion of mass. The remnants were disposed of finally in ways very similar to those which prevailed in the East as the letter of the pseudo Clement and its derivatives bear witness, being consumed generally by the clergy in the sacristy, originally not till next day, or according to the decrees of the Gallican councils consumed by children and others, in the later days apparently at the end of the liturgy and in the church.

In the earliest period all cleansing of the sacred vessels must have been performed in the sacristy after the consumption of the remains, and obviously not before the end of the service. According to the letter of the pseudo Clement it appears to have been the function of the minister. Modification of the practice seems to have been due to the change of custom by which the holy vessels, which formerly had been kept and cleansed in the sacristy, were kept and cleansed near the altar. The alteration took place originally it would appear in Gallican circles, and the Admonition ascribed to Leo IV (*c.* 847) seems to mark the beginning of the transition. The cleansing was now properly the function of the priest, a point on which the Admonition is emphatic, but in spite of discouragement the custom, which was perhaps really the more primitive, grew by which it was performed by the deacon or subdeacon, and consequently to bring it into agreement with current practice, various modifications were introduced into the original text of the Admonition of the pseudo Leo.

The washing of the priest's hands after the communion during the service is heard of first in the ninth century in the *Ordo* of St Amand, though curiously it does not mention the celebrant in this connection, and the washing of his hands first appears in the tenth century in the *Codex*

Ratoldi of Corbie, and in the Sixth Roman *Ordo*. The ceremonial ablution of the chalice with the consumption of the liquid used, apparently wine, is not found before the middle of the eleventh century, but then according to Peter Damien it is a well established and traditional usage. It is really of course only a preliminary to the older and more thorough cleansing of the chalice, and paten also, at the conclusion of the service. About the same time in the description of the ceremonies of mass as celebrated at Rouen, given by John of Avranches, we first read of the sprinkling of the priest's fingers, which took place in some churches on some occasions in a second chalice, but in others in the chalice of the mass. This ablution also as well as that of the chalice itself was consumed by the priest, in contradistinction to the more ancient usage at the washing of the priest's hands in bowls or at the piscina, when the water was always poured away. As time went on the ablutions became more and more elaborate, and frequently the final cleansing of the chalice as well as the ceremonial ablution took place in church and during the service. of this practice also John of Avranches is our earliest informant. As the whole action had come to be performed in church and was now the duty of the ministers of the altar, not of the celebrant, there was clearly no longer any reason why it should be postponed until the end of the liturgy, and convenience suggested that the consumption of the remains, both of chalice and paten, should take place as soon as possible after the communion, so that the cleansing of them could be completed while the priest was finishing the prayers, and the vessels, cleansed and ready for use another day, could be put away in the chest near the altar before the close of the mass, or carried away when the deacon and other ministers left the altar. Various relics of the older usage still survived for a long time in the details we find prescribed in the different orders regulating ceremonial, as in the Cistercian statutes of the twelfth century, and the rule of St Victor of the thirteenth, and the vessels are cleansed after mass and the minute remnants consumed. The customs of high mass, in which we find the proper norm of a rite, would naturally be followed with the necessary modifications at low mass, and so though there were numerous minor variations in different localities and survivals from older usage, as at Rouen, there was evolved what has been the general custom for centuries in most parts of the West.

With regard to the remains of the consecrated bread the history was somewhat different from what it was with regard to the wine, and at quite an early date at any rate at Rome the remnants were added to what was to be reserved. Until the end of the sixteenth century it was the general custom throughout most of the West and certainly at Rome, as witness Patricius, Marcellus, Burchard and de Grassis, that the consecrated hosts which were left over from the communion, if whole, should remain on the altar until the end of the mass so that every time communion was given in its proper place immediately after the consecration, the latter part of the service was said in the presence of the blessed sacrament, and it became almost a mass of exposition. The earliest to change this custom appear to have been the Dominicans and the Carmelites, whose ceremonial on so many points was similar and almost certainly derived from a common source, and another practice had been adopted by the thirteenth century. The change seems to have been adopted first on Maundy Thursday when in Carmelite churches, in imitation apparently of the custom which at one time obtained at Rome from about the tenth century until after the return from Avignon, being a development as we saw from the earlier ceremonial removal of the Fermentum, there was a procession soon after the communion of the consecrated host to the altar or other place of repose, as well as the procession of the consecrated oils at much the same point, the latter a function possible only in cathedral churches in the presence of the bishop. In other and particularly in monastic churches in which it was adopted the procession of the sacrament seems practically to have taken the place of the earlier procession of the oils in cathedrals, but where the two processions were necessary that of the sacrament in most places, except for some time in Rome, continued to be held immediately after the conclusion of mass. It was natural that the more elaborate custom of Maundy Thursday should tend to be imitated on ordinary days, and so we find that in the Dominican and Carmelite books the consecrated hosts to be reserved for another day were solemnly carried away by the deacon immediately the communion of the faithful was over without waiting for the final prayers. At York on Maundy Thursday the sacrament appears to have been put away by the bishop in the place of repose, or sepulchre, immediately after the communion, but nothing is said about a procession. We find this also, however, adopted at Holyrood in the fifteenth century. There appears to be no evidence that any such custom obtained in England on ordinary days according to any of the mediaeval uses; the traditional manner of reservation in a hanging pyx would hardly lend itself to such a practice.

At Rome the custom of removing the sacrament from the altar after the communion seems to have been adopted first in the sixteenth century at a pontifical mass because as Paris de Grassis explained it was difficult, if not impossible, to carry out the full ceremonial in the presence of the sacrament. In the *Caeremoniale Episcoporum* of 1600 the new practice is allowed as an alternative to the earlier custom of its remaining on the altar until mass was finished. In the edition of 1651 by the change of "vel etiam" into "et" the later alternative becomes the only

XIV] CONCLUSIONS 243

authoritative practice when a bishop celebrates, and so nowadays the consecrated hosts are no longer allowed to remain on the altar until the end of mass except on special occasions.

The customs of low mass being an adaptation of those of high mass, and those of an episcopal mass, it was inevitable that sooner or later at that type of service the priest should imitate the more elaborate order. The rule of the *Ordo Missae* of 1502 requiring the sacrament to be put away after mass disappeared in the revised *Ritus Celebrandi Missam* of 1570, and since that date there has been no definite order on the point, though a rubric added in 1604 provides for the possibility. In practice it has come to pass that on almost every occasion the hosts to be reserved are removed from the altar immediately after the communion and placed in the tabernacle Consequently the ancient usage survives only when communion is to be given after mass, or when mass is said at an altar where there is no tabernacle, and so many hosts are left over that the priest cannot conveniently consume them himself before the ablutions.

As the *Order of Communion* of 1548 was to be used "without the varying of any other rite or ceremony in the mass" the consumption of the remains of the sacrament according to Sarum use would take place before the thanksgiving *Gratias tibi* and immediately after the English Pax which was the concluding act in the communion of the people, and the ablutions would follow. Any hosts to be reserved, including probably any surplus from the communion which could not conveniently be consumed, would remain on the altar until the end of mass, when they would be placed in the hanging pyx and reserved over the altar.

Under the First Prayer Book some change in current practice seems to have been intended, and a reversion to more primitive use. Certainly when the sacrament was reserved for the communion of the sick at home the consecrated elements in both kinds must have remained on the altar until the service was over, and there are a number of points such as the wording of the thanksgiving and the use of the English communion Pax, which suggest that the compilers of the book intended this to be the ordinary custom, and that the latter part of the service should be said in the presence of the sacrament.

In the Second Prayer Book the rule is clear, when we consider the history, that the remains of both bread and wine are to remain on the holy table until after the blessing, when the priest is to have them, as well as anything which remained unconsecrated, to his own use, the revisers, whatever their private views, thus making possible for those who wished a return to the earliest usage of the church, by which the remains were consumed by the ministers in the sacristy after the service or another day.

In the revised Prayer Book of 1661 the new rubric quite plainly orders that "what remaineth of the consecrated elements," whether much or little, shall be placed upon the Lord's table and be reserved there until after the benediction and as the rule is not conditional it would seem that definite provision is to be made so that some of the sacrament may always remain on the altar until after the blessing, the rubric being thus in general agreement with the rule of the First Roman *Ordo* that the altar should never be without the sacrifice while mass is being performed, and the practice by which a piece of the Sancta remained on the altar until the end of mass. There is now no possible ambiguity on the point whether the final rubric refers to the consecrated or unconsecrated elements, and there is a plain direction, based on the letter of the pseudo Clement, and the words of the synod of Constantinople, that what is not required for communion should be consumed by the priest and other of the communicants immediately after the blessing. The sources of this rubric being concerned with any chance superfluity of the sacrament, not with what might be intended for reservation, it can hardly have a wider application, and that this was the sole purpose of the rubric comes out plainly from the known intentions of the revisers, and by a consideration of the discussion which led to its adoption. Sparrow makes it clear that it was in this sense that it was accepted by some at any rate in the church, and, we may add, Thorndike expressed a similar opinion.

The latter part of the communion service being necessarily said in the presence of the holy sacrament, the Lord's prayer, though said after instead of before the communion to which it has always been an adjunct, fulfils the requirement of Gregory the Great, and is recited over Christ's body and blood, in completion of the mysteries of the church, as Narsai says, and as an act of thanksgiving on the part of the sons of God for renewed sonship in Christ in the communion and worship of Him to Whom we are thus joined in fellowship and life, as the Nestorian liturgy suggests. The *Gloria in excelsis* said in the presence of the sacrament becomes an act of devotion to "the Lamb as it had been slain," comparable with similar forms found in various liturgies, when He is recognised still as "the Lamb of God lying and sacrificed upon the holy table," as well as an act of thanksgiving. In the saying of the English communion Pax while the elements are still on the altar we have agreement not only with one of the most important features of the *Order of Communion* of 1548, but also with the practice of the Western church ever since the Pax, removed to a place after the consecration, has become a benediction "with the power of His mysteries," not merely a sign of goodwill but an effectual token of "the peace and communion of our Lord Jesus Christ" bestowed in the sacrament, in the immediate presence of which the blessing is given.

The question of the ablutions, ceremonial or otherwise, so far as our information goes, does not seem to have been considered by the revisers of 1661, nor have we any evidence that the practice was introduced by any of the Caroline divines. Their appeal was not so much to old English practice as to more ancient authorities, and to the East, and to canonical rather than liturgical rules. They quote not mediaeval service books but the works of such authorities as Gratian and Balsamon for the disposal of the remains after the communion, and in accordance with their interpretation of the letter of the pseudo Clement they are ordered to be consumed at the end of the liturgy by the priest and others in church. There was thus an intentional break with mediaeval practice, or rather it was not considered, and any ablutions or cleansing of the vessels would of necessity be such as would be in agreement with the precedent found for the consumption of the remains, and must have taken place after the service, probably in the vestry. If the mediaeval ablutions are revived, as is desired by many, since they cannot precede the consumption of the remains of the sacrament, they too must follow the blessing. The time of a ceremony definitely ordered in the Prayer Book cannot be changed in order that the ablutions may still be performed at what superficially seems to correspond to the later mediaeval position; and in view of the great difference both in substance and importance between the conclusion of the Latin mass and the post-communion part of the communion service in the Book of Common Prayer, such a position does not really exist. The ceremonial ablutions have always been a preliminary to a more thorough cleansing of the chalice and paten later, and with few exceptions this has always taken place, as convenience dictates, after the service, though sometimes for greater reverence as at Citeaux and St Victor in church. The requirements of the Book of Common Prayer are quite in accordance with what must have been the Roman custom for over a thousand years, and with the practice which must have obtained in England after the coming of Augustine for nearly five hundred. They are in agreement too with the common usage in the East to-day, so that nothing can be more Catholic than what the rubrics prescribe.

APPENDIX

RESERVATION AND THE BOOK OF COMMON PRAYER

I.

THE question of reservation of the holy sacrament under the Book of Common Prayer in its various editions is of considerable importance, and as in the later versions of the book it is closely connected with the interpretation of the rubrics for the disposal of the remains of the consecrated elements not required for communion it may not be inappropriate to give a separate treatment of the whole subject, though there will necessarily be some repetition.

The full text of the rubric of the First Prayer Book dealing with the matter is as follows:

> And if the same day there be a celebration of the holy communion in the church, then shall the priest reserve at the open communion so much of the sacrament of the body and blood, as shall serve the sick person, and so many as shall communicate with him, if there be any And so soon as he conveniently may, after the open communion ended in the church, shall go and minister the same, first to those that are appointed to communicate with the sick, if there be any, and last of all to the sick person himself. But before the curate distribute the holy communion the appointed general confession must be made in the name of the communicants, the curate adding the absolution with the comfortable sentences of scripture following in the open communion, and after the communion ended the collect, *Almighty and everliving God, we most heartily thank thee*, etc.

The version of this as given in Aless's Latin Prayer Book of 1551 is somewhat different. We read:

> But if it happen that on the same day the Lord's supper is celebrated in church, then the priest in the supper shall reserve so much of the sacrament as suffices for the sick man, and soon after the mass is ended, together with some of those who are present, shall go to the sick man, and he shall first communicate those who attend on the sick man and were present at the supper,

BOOK OF COMMON PRAYER 249

and last of all the sick man. But first let the general confession be made and the absolution with the collect as is prescribed above[1].

We notice that the first direction in the order for the communion of the sick is that the priest shall reserve as much of the sacrament in both kinds as will suffice for the sick man and those who are intending to communicate with him, and this is evidently the normal method of providing for the communion of the sick, a consecration in the sick man's house being only for special cases. "The communion" we note is the act of administration and the reception together with others, emphasis being laid on the point that there should always be a "communion," if possible, and not a mere private participation. Yet when such a "communion" is clearly impossible, that the sick man may at least "receive the sacrament of Christ's body and blood," the priest may minister the reserved sacrament to him alone. No form of service however for use in such a case is provided, the thanksgiving, in accordance with the principles on which the First Prayer Book was drawn up, laying special stress on the fellowship with other communicants which in this case would be absent. Presumably also it was intended that the use of the reserved species would be the usual method of ministering the sacrament to permanent invalids, the aged and others who could not come to church and yet were desirous of the communion. In such cases there would be no particular urgency and they could wait for a celebration in church. There is indeed no provision of a celebration in a house for such as these—the collect, epistle and gospel, as also the service for the visitation of the sick, like the similar forms in the old manuals, are suitable only for those in danger of death—and the administration of the reserved sacrament is the only thing possible.

In the rubrics of Aless's Latin version of the First Prayer Book there are considerable changes from the original, and the procedure prescribed is indeed quite different. We have the new idea that some of those who were at the celebration in church should accompany the priest to the sick man's house,

[1] *Scripta Anglicana*, p 448.

instead of a company, of whose numbers notice had been given, awaiting his arrival from the church, and these who accompany the priest are to receive the sacrament with the sick, apparently for the second time. Union with the communicants in church is thus secured as well as a real "communion," and some of the objections to a private administration of the sacrament, felt in certain quarters at the period, are done away. The order prescribed however is more akin to that found, as we saw, in Pullain's Glastonbury service for the communion of the sick with the reserved sacrament[1] than to that given in the First Prayer Book, which it professes to be. A comparison of the phraseology of the two orders makes it not improbable that there is a literary connection between the two, and that Aless used Pullain's service, published earlier in the same year, in a manner similar to that in which he used the Latin of the ancient services and of Hermann's *Consultation*. Perhaps it was the practice to which in his long residence abroad he had become accustomed.

Though there were thus two different forms of procedure put forth for use when the sick were communicated from the church, that of the Prayer Book itself and that of Aless, it seems probable that very frequently it was neither of these but the traditional method of administering the reserved sacrament which was adopted, and that in some places, though not in others, there was continuous reservation in one kind as before; and this does not appear to have been always prevented by the civil authorities as we might have expected. Pyxes occur very frequently in the inventories of church goods made by the commissioners on their visitation in 1552, and not seldom they were allowed to be retained. In some cases they are spoken of as actually containing the blessed sacrament, as at Edlesborough, Bucks. and Flintham, Notts.[2] A noteworthy example is that of Saffron Walden where in connection with the visitation on Oct. 5, 1552 we read:

[1] See p 195
[2] Public Record Office, Ex Q R *Miscel. Ch Goods*, 1/37 and 7/82. See *Hierurgia Anglicana*, Pt II. p. 160

Goods delivered for the ministration of the divine service. To James Cowle and Thomas Marten, churchwardens, a chalice of silver and gilt, of xv ounces, a cope of red velvet, a carpet of blue velvet for the communion table, and vii linen cloths for the same, a little round box to carry the sacrament in, with a purse to put it in, and all the surplices[1].

We notice that this was within a month of the time, Nov. 1, when the Second Prayer Book would be obligatory.

The use of a pyx in the form of "a little round box" would hardly be necessary, or even particularly useful, if the sacrament in both kinds was to be taken from the church immediately after the service, and it seems evident that the rubrics of the First Prayer Book, which clearly as we have noted did not provide for every possibility, were not interpreted as forbidding continuous reservation. The Saffron Walden case indeed suggests that it was expected that it would continue even under the Second Book.

II.

In the Second Prayer Book, as we noticed, all reference to the practice of reservation was omitted. It is remarkable however in view of the strong opinions of Bucer, Peter Martyr, and others whose judgment had great weight in the revision, that there was no rubric actually forbidding reservation, and it would not have been surprising if it had been stringently condemned as in Hermann's *Consultation*[2], which also had been drawn up under the auspices of Bucer. Some other influence apparently was also at work, and just as in the case of the direction for the disposal of the remains after communion, the most extreme line was not taken. The only authoritative references to the custom of reservation are those which appeared a little later in 1553 in the Articles of Religion.

The sacraments were not ordained of Christ to be gazed upon, or to be carried about, but that we should rightly (duly) use them.

The sacrament of the Lord's Supper was not by Christ's ordinance kept (reserved), carried about, lifted up, or worshipped[3].

[1] *Proceedings of Essex Archaeological Society*, N S III p 62
[2] See pp 194-5 Hermann, f 97
[3] Articles xxv. and xxviii , formerly xxvi and xxix

Both articles however express only a truism to which the strongest advocates of reservation could assent, and the same statement, that there is no express ordinance of Christ on the subject could be made with equal truth with regard to infant baptism, which yet "is in any wise to be retained in the church, as most agreeable with the institution of Christ[1]." Both in the exhortations and rubrics the distinction still survived between receiving "the holy communion of the body and blood of our Saviour Christ," and receiving "the sacrament of Christ's body and blood." The latter might be possible for a sick man when a "communion" was out of the question, and it was to cover the case when the sick man would receive the sacrament alone, as we saw, that the words were put into the rubric of the First Prayer Book. It is only when for various reasons even the delivery of the sacrament to him alone is impossible that the priest is to give instruction, not with regard to spiritual communion, for "communion" would be considered in such a case impossible, but about the spiritual eating and drinking of the body and blood of our Saviour Christ. No provision is made for the reception of the sacrament apart from a "communion"; but this was true even in the First Prayer Book, for though the possibility is mentioned there, as we saw, the form of service given for the administration of the reserved sacrament provides only for a "communion," and would be unsuitable if no one communicated with the sick. Also, as in the First Book, there is no provision at all for invalids or for any but those in danger of death. Whatever the intention, the rubric of the First Prayer Book which reads "where the curate may reverently celebrate" has been carefully altered so as to admit the possibility of reservation, "celebrate" being changed to "minister." It will be well to give the rubrics at some length.

And having a convenient place in the sick man's house, where the curate may reverently minister, and a good number to receive the communion with the sick person, with all things necessary for the same, he shall there minister the holy communion ...At the

[1] Art. XXVII.

time of the distribution of the holy sacrament, the priest shall first receive the communion himself, and after minister unto them that be appointed to communicate with the sick ...When the sick person is visited and receiveth the holy communion all at one time, then the priest for more expedition shall cut off the form of the visitation at the psalm, *In thee, O Lord, have I put my trust*, and go straight to the communion.

The word "celebrate" in the Second Prayer Book is almost synonymous with "minister," as we can see from the exhortations and the preceding rubrics, and that it does not necessarily include a reference to the consecration we shall see later, but probably the fuller meaning is usually intended. The word "minister" however quite obviously need not include any reference to the consecration, and may refer only to the act of administration as in the rubric following the collect, epistle and gospel, and the rubric of the First Prayer Book about the delivery of the reserved sacrament. The title of the order is still "The communion of the sick," but that this refers strictly not to the whole service but to the administration of and common participation in the sacrament, which may be ministered with the reserved elements, is plain from its original use in the First Prayer Book, for there a further title was prefixed to the order requiring a consecration in the sick man's house—"The celebration of the holy communion for the sick." "The communion" is still used in this its proper sense very frequently in the Second Prayer Book, and means simply the double act of administration and reception in common. The use of the reserved sacrament, though no longer plainly ordered, is thus in no way precluded by the rubrics. In particular it would seem, the direction that when the sick person is visited and receives the holy communion all at one time the priest shall cut off the form of the visitation and "go straight to the communion" could be interpreted of the administration of the reserved sacrament.

We notice also the words "a good number to receive the communion with the sick person." Even in time of plague or sweat the insistence on the idea of a "communion" is so great that if no neighbours may be obtained the minister alone may communicate with the sick so as to realise the "communion," though the mere receiving of the sacrament of Christ's body and blood is recognised. Apparently the priest is to communicate at every "communion" of the sick though not necessarily at every administration of the sacrament, and so the chief advantage of using the reserved sacrament on such an occasion would be a saving of time.

If the whole service was ever intended to be used for the sick, the rubrics were not so interpreted later; and certainly nothing is said about the amount to be used: if there was no consecration it would be a minimum. In the First Prayer Book there was a distinct order to say the prayer of consecration, as there was also to reserve. In the Second Book both were omitted. In view of the opinions of many of the reformers which repudiated all idea of consecration as well as reservation it is as possible to argue that the prayer of consecration was to be omitted at the communion of the sick, as that the remains of the bread and wine which the curate is to have to his own use were not to be reserved. Perhaps both customs obtained in different circles, one party treating the service as practically a mass of the presanctified similar to what was usual at one time on Good Friday, an interpretation certainly adopted later, and the other omitting the preface, *Sanctus*, and prayer of consecration, and reading only the account of the institution for the edification of the assembled company. This last is exactly what is ordered in Hermann's *Consultation*, which like the Second English Prayer Book is to some extent a product of Bucer's labours. Hermann's order for the communion of the sick is as follows—exhortation, part of John vi (with explanation), confession and absolution, creed, prayer for the sick person, and the Lord's prayer. Then we read:

This being said, let him pray for peace for the sick man and all present. Then clearly and devoutly let him recite the words of the supper, *The Lord in that night in which he was betrayed*, etc. And after that recital let him deliver to the sick man and those of the company present who have offered themselves, as is meet, as guests at the table of the Lord, the whole sacrament with the words which are written above After the communion let him

BOOK OF COMMON PRAYER 255

conclude the Lord's Supper with thanksgiving and the benediction as described above[1].

We note that many elements of the public service, including the preface and *Sanctus*, have disappeared, so that there is nothing which can be regarded as a *prayer* of consecration. We are told also that the above order may be curtailed.

III.

Under the Elizabethan settlement it was the Second Prayer Book which with some alterations was adopted. In the Latin version, however, published by Haddon in 1560 with royal authority, in the order for the communion of the sick there is a rubric definitely providing for the reservation of the sacrament. We read.

But if it happen that on the same day the Lord's supper is celebrated in church, then the priest in the supper shall reserve so much of the sacrament as suffices for the sick man, and soon after the supper is ended, together with some of those who are present, shall go to the sick man, and he shall first communicate (with) those who attend on the sick man and were present at the supper, and last of all (with) the sick man. But first let the general confession be made, and the absolution with the collect as is prescribed above[2].

We note that the rubric is practically a reproduction of that of Aless's Latin Prayer Book, which, as we saw, is a modification of that of the First Prayer Book, chiefly by the addition of the direction, perhaps from Pullain's Glastonbury service, requiring some of the congregation in church to accompany the priest to the sick man's house, the only alterations being the substitution of "supper" for "mass," and "communicate with" for "communicate." The former shows that the reintroduction of the rubric in 1560 was not altogether unintentional. Whether the latter means that the priest is to receive the sacrament a second time or not is perhaps doubtful, for "he shall communicate with" ("communicabit cum illis") may only be

---

[1] Hermann, f. 98 b
[2] *Liturgical Services of Queen Elizabeth* (Parker Society), p. 404.

intended as better Latin for "he shall communicate" ("communicabit eos"), but in view of the fact that the members of the congregation who accompany him apparently receive the sacrament a second time and the rubric of the Second Prayer Book requiring the priest always to communicate first, it is not improbable. Though the directions are practically those of the First Prayer Book, as the Second Book says nothing about what parts of the service were to be used at a private communion, the order does not seem to be impossible as an exposition of what might be done under the rubrics of that book broadly interpreted, if the communion were given with the reserved sacrament. It seems indeed not unlikely that this was a common, perhaps the official, gloss on the directions of the Second Prayer Book under the new conditions, and was perhaps a record of what was already the practice in certain quarters.

That reservation for the sick was common at the beginning of Elizabeth's reign seems to be the only possible interpretation of a letter of Calvin, preserved in substance by Strype, who thus explains the occasion.

The mention of Calvin must bring in a very remarkable letter which he wrote in the month of August this year (1561) concerning ecclesiastical rites used in our office of private prayer newly established, which were scrupled by some of the English exiles upon their return, chiefly because not used by the reformed church in Geneva, concerning which they had sent to Calvin for his resolution and judgment.

The first three of the questions put to him were, whether it was expedient after the public confession to have any absolution, concerning the using of certain proper words to every communicant singly, and how often the Lord's supper should be administered. The fourth with the answer must be given in full:

The fourth query was, Whether it were convenient to communicate the sick? And if so with what number and company? And whether in this private communion the public office should be used, or no office, but the consecrated bread only brought from the church unto the party home to his house? To which Calvin gave in substance this answer, That the sick should not be denied the sacrament, many and weighty causes moved him: for should they not be communicated, it would be a very blameworthy neglect of Christ's institution. But that when the sick party was to partake, there should be some assembly of the kindred, friends, and neighbours, that so there might be a distribution, according to Christ's commandment. And that the holy action should be joined with an explication of the mystery, and that nothing should be done differently from the common form and way of the church. He liked not carrying the sacrament up and down promiscuously; for the avoiding of superstition in some, and ambition and vain ostentation in others, many for such ends being apt in those days to come to these private sacraments. Which he esteemed a very difficult thing to prevent. And that therefore the greater judgment and care should be used to whom they gave it. And lastly, he looked upon it as a preposterous thing to bring bread as holy from the church; but to carry it in pomp, by no means tolerable[1]

Though communicating the sick with the reserved sacrament was thus not one of the "rites used in the English liturgy" of which Calvin approved, yet it is clear that it must have been regarded as in no way incompatible with the Book of Common Prayer, and indeed a common practice, or there would have been no occasion to put the question at all. In neither question nor answer is there mention of anything but the bread, suggesting the continued use of the pyx, as perhaps at Saffron Walden and other places, which apparently was carried "in pomp." We note too the question about what service should be used, and in Calvin's reply the insistence on the "communion," and his emphasis not on the consecration but on "an explication of the mystery" for the benefit of the sick.

Anthony Sparrow, afterwards successively bishop of Exeter and Norwich, in his *Rationale*, first published in 1657, when the rubrics were still those of the Second Prayer Book, explaining the order for the communion of the sick, likewise gives it as his judgment that reservation is still allowable:

The rubric at the communion of the sick, directs the priest to deliver the communion to the sick; but does not there set down how much of the communion service shall be used at the delivering

[1] Strype, *Annals of the Reformation*, vol I. Pt I Ch. xxi. Oxford, 1824, p. 387

of the communion to the sick; and therefore seems to me to refer us to former directions in times past. Now the direction formerly was this, "If the same day..."[1].

We note how this appeal to the practice under the First Prayer Book agrees with what we concluded was a possible interpretation of the rubrics of the Second Book, and with what was apparently the official view of the matter in the days of Elizabeth as set out in the rubric of the Latin Prayer Book, and also the common practice at that time as disclosed in the letter of Calvin.

IV.

The question of the lawfulness of reservation under the Prayer Book of 1661 depends upon the interpretation in its revised form of the rubric which orders the consumption of the remains of the sacrament. This runs, as we noted:

> But if any remain of that which was consecrated, it shall not be carried out of the church, but the priest and such other of the communicants as he shall then call unto him, shall immediately after the blessing, reverently eat and drink the same.

From a literary point of view the rubric is connected with the Scottish canon of 1636 and the corresponding rubric in the Scottish Prayer Book of 1637. In the canon, already quoted, we read:

> In the ministration he (the priest) shall have care that the elements are circumspectly handled; and what is reserved thereof be distributed to the poorer sort which receive that day; to be eaten and drunken by them before they go out of church[2].

From the phraseology alone it is clear that reservation of the sacrament in the technical sense does not come within the original scope of the canon, and that it has to do with reverence in the administration of the sacrament and reverence in the disposal of the surplus, and the intention was to prevent the remnants of the consecrated bread and wine being taken away by the communicants for consumption at home.

---

[1] Sparrow, *Rationale*, Ed Downes, pp 223-4
[2] See p 203   *Prayer Book Dictionary*, p 611

BOOK OF COMMON PRAYER 259

In the Scottish Prayer Book of 1637 which was authorised before publication by the canons of 1636 the substance of the canon was incorporated, as we saw, in the rubric of the Second Prayer Book which deals with the disposal of the remains of the elements, and we read:

And if any of the bread and wine remain, which is consecrated, it shall be reverently eaten and drunk by such of the communicants only as the presbyter which celebrates shall take unto him, but it shall not be carried out of the church.

The directions of the rubric, as we noticed, are in no wise unprecedented and they may be traced back in part to the letter of the pseudo Clement[1] through the Second Prayer Book, and in part to the words of the synod of Constantinople[2] under Nicholas Grammaticus (c. 1085) through the canon of 1636.

(a) The question about what it was which remained, whether the consecrated or unconsecrated elements which according to the rubric of the Second Prayer Book the priest was to have to his own use, which had been so much discussed by Cosin and other Anglican divines of the seventeenth century, was clearly determined in the 1661 revision. The addition then made however with the intention of settling this point, has itself proved to be ambiguous, and upon its interpretation depends the whole question of the reservation of the sacrament for the sick. Does it refer to that portion of the sacrament which is not needed for the communion in church, thus precluding anything in the way of reservation, or does it refer only to that which is in excess of what is sufficient for those who are to receive the sacrament, whether in church or at home, which the priest had in mind, when taking the bread and wine at the offertory? Historically it is plain that the intention of the rubric had nothing whatever to do with reservation, for the point was never alluded to in all the discussion which finally resulted in the new order, so far as it has come down to us, and the literary antecedents of both the Scottish and

[1] See pp 11-3   P.G I col. 484
[2] See p 10   P G cxxxviii col 944

English rubrics were concerned only with the disposal of the surplus elements not required for communion. If all reservation is now precluded it must be by inadvertence. Is the rubric to be interpreted in this sense? What was the contemporary interpretation? In view of the importance of the matter it may be well to enquire somewhat fully into these points in the light of history and by comparison with similar forms found elsewhere.

At the offertory in the First Prayer Book there was the rubric:

> Then shall the minister take so much bread and wine as shall suffice for the persons appointed to receive the holy communion.

Here the question of sufficiency, as we saw, is certainly not limited by the number of those who are to receive the communion in church, but the priest takes into consideration the number of those for whom he wishes to reserve, just as in the direction from the letter of the pseudo Clement which is the ultimate basis of the order—"Let so many hosts be offered on the altar as ought to suffice for the people[1],"—and also in the allocution to the subdeacon in *Missale Francorum*[2], in the pontificals of Egbert and Dunstan, and various other English and continental service books[3]—"Only so much as is able to suffice for the people ought to be placed on the altar." In the Second Prayer Book, as we noticed, this rubric at the offertory together with any definite provision for reservation was taken away, apparently because it was no longer believed by the revisers that consecration made any real difference to the elements, and because of Bucer's criticism of it:

> From the fourth paragraph of this order, in which it is prescribed that the minister ought to take only so much bread and wine as will suffice for those about to communicate, some make for themselves the superstition that they consider it unlawful if anything of the bread and wine of the communion remain over when it is finished to allow it to come to common use ...Conse-

[1] *P G* I col 484
[2] Thomasius, *Opera*, vol VI p 343
[3] Martene, vol II lib I. cap. VIII Art XI Ord II III. IV XIV XVII. pp 34, 38, 42, 70, 84

BOOK OF COMMON PRAYER 261

quently however much bread and wine remain from the communion there are yet some who consider that the whole of it must be consumed by themselves[1]

The opinion of the revisers in 1661 and also of the church at large at that date was the exact opposite of this. The words of the pseudo Clement were frequently quoted as supplying a rule to be followed. In particular we remember the suggestion of Cosin:

> Some words are needful here to be added, whereby the priest may be enjoined to consider the number of them which are to receive the sacrament and to consecrate the bread and wine in such near proportion as shall be sufficient for them: but if any of the consecrated elements be left that he and some others with him shall decently eat and drink them in the church before all the people depart from it[2].

We have here the substance with but slightly different wording of the rubrics of the present Book of Common Prayer dealing with the same points·

> The priest shall then place upon the table so much bread and wine as he shall think sufficient....But if any remain of that which was consecrated it shall not be carried out of the church, but the priest and such other of the communicants as he shall then call unto him shall immediately after the blessing, reverently eat and drink the same

Both Cosin and Sparrow quoted the letter of the pseudo Clement as supplying a rule it would be well to adopt[3]. It is remarkable how closely the rubrics adopted agree with the directions of this letter, where, following the usual translation, we read·

> Let so many hosts be offered on the altar as ought to suffice for the people. But if any remain let them not be reserved until the morrow, but be carefully consumed by the clerks with fear and trembling[4].

As the letter of the pseudo Clement included those who would be communicated with the reserved sacrament among those for whom the elements were to suffice, there seems no

---

[1] See p 188   *Scripta Anglicana*, p. 464
[2] See p 210   *Works*, vol v p 519
[3] See pp. 207, 211.   [4] *P G* I. col. 484   Cf p 12 above.

reason why the present rubric, from a literary point of view its direct descendant, should not do the like, as in the First Prayer Book, and in the old English and other pontificals which were based upon *Missale Francorum* and contained a similar order. If this be so that which is referred to in the rubric "If any remain" would be what was not required to suffice for those who were to receive the sacrament whether in church or at home. The direction would then correspond exactly with the answer of the synod of Constantinople to the monks, which cannot be considered as hostile to reservation, though we find it saying, in words referred to by Sparrow as suggesting an English rubric to the same effect:

The fragments of the consecrated oblation they ought not to eat save only in the church, until they have consumed everything[1].

Such an interpretation of the rubric "If any remain," has the advantage as we saw in the case of the similar Scottish directions, of doing full justice to the difference in the wording of the two separate rubrics which refer to what remains, that after the administration of the sacrament being positive—"what remaineth of the consecrated elements"—while after the blessing it is the conditional form which is retained—"if any remain of that which is consecrated." The suggestion is that though something must always remain after the communion of the people in church there is a chance that nothing may remain which requires consumption after the blessing. If so there must be a possibility that some portion of the sacrament, perhaps the whole of what has not been consumed, is required for some other purpose, having indeed been consecrated with this intent, and so would not come under the rubric for dealing with what is superfluous. This purpose could hardly be anything else but the communion of the sick or others not able to attend the celebrations in church.

(*b*) The rubric "If any remain" is not one of those which give instructions for the performance of the service, and it is not concerned with the administration of the sacrament. It is a direction dealing with the disposal of the remains of the

[1] *P G.* cxxxviii col. 944.

BOOK OF COMMON PRAYER 263

elements, consecrated and unconsecrated, after the liturgy is over, being comparable with the other rubric which has to do with the disposal of the money collected at the offertory; and the conjunction "but" makes it plain that the carrying out of church of the consecrated elements intended is something similar to that involved in the curate having the unconsecrated to his own use. The whole rubric is conditional, and has to do only with occasions on which there is an accidental superfluity of bread or wine, whether consecrated or unconsecrated. If this state of things does not exist the rubric does not apply, and this would be the case both if some of the bread and wine provided by the churchwardens were reserved for use another day, and if it were arranged for someone to be communicated from part of the sacrament consecrated in church, whether it was reserved for a longer or shorter period after the service was over. In such a case as definite provision would have to be made as for the communion in church, and it would in no way depend upon the existence after the administration in church of a merely chance surplus, even if this were allowed under the rubric which precedes the Lord's Prayer, yet it is only for the disposal of such an accidental surplus after the service to prevent abuse that the rubric provides. In some cases as we saw the portion of the host which according to the ancient Roman rule remained on the altar until the end of mass was used for the communion of the sick[1]: only the possibility of a similar use of "what remaineth of the consecrated elements," which are required to be reverently placed upon the Lord's Table after the communion in church, would reasonably account for the element of uncertainty about the existence of any remains to be consumed after the service, which is shown in the conditional form of the rubric "If any remain."

(c) Yet in accordance with the rubrics of the present Prayer Book as of the First Book the use of the reserved sacrament is only possible on certain occasions. Under the First Prayer Book there were three methods of giving the sacrament to the

[1] See Chap v. above.

sick. (1) The whole celebration of the Lord's supper, including the consecration, might take place in the sick man's house, and he would thus receive the "communion" with as many of his friends as were present. (2) The sick man and his friends might receive the reserved sacrament together, and thus it would still be a "communion." (3) The sick man might receive the reserved sacrament alone. If even this last is impossible, and for various reasons the sick man cannot "receive the sacrament of Christ's body and blood" at all, the curate is to give instruction, as we noticed, not about spiritual "communion," for in the sense in which this word is used in the Prayer Book it would be impossible, but about the spiritual eating and drinking of the body and blood of our Saviour Christ. Spiritual reception is thus not looked upon as in any way taking the place of the "communion," but only of receiving the reserved sacrament alone. Under the present Prayer Book, unlike the First Book, the provision of the order for the communion of the sick clearly makes the actual celebration in the sick man's house the normal method when he desires a "communion," and it is possible, but such a celebration of the Lord's Supper, (1), is definitely forbidden unless there are "three or two at the least" to communicate with the sick person, save when the sick desires a "communion" in time of plague. At all times indeed the possibility of (1) depends upon the fulfilment of various conditions. The sick man may not desire a "communion" or be able to bear it, or any but the shortest service. At certain times of the year no amount of timely notice will be sufficient in large parishes for the curate to arrange a separate consecration for each chronic sick person who will rightly desire to receive the sacrament. In many cases it would be impossible to arrange that there should be "three or two at the least" to communicate with the sick. Still in many places there is no "convenient place" where "the curate may reverently minister," and the whole service would be impossible. For many cases therefore, to which (2) and (3) would apply, the Prayer Book makes no definite provision at all, and unless many of the faithful are to be permanently deprived of the sacrament recourse must be had to the ancient traditional method of supplying the need. Historically the rubric requiring the priest to give instruction in spiritual reception when the sick man cannot "receive the sacrament of Christ's body and blood" refers to the administration of the reserved sacrament, though in the case of (3), when no one could communicate with him, even the First Prayer Book provided no form of service, and consequently it suggests the same thing today. The instruction about spiritual reception is still ordered only when on a particular occasion (3) is impossible, and not as an alternative to his never receiving the sacrament at all. The use of the reserved sacrament is the only method of supplying the need, which the phraseology of the Prayer Book itself suggests.

(d) Both reservation of the sacrament and a second communion on the same day were contrary to the ideas of those responsible for the Second Prayer Book, and the provision for both found in the First Book disappeared. The reasons for their objections, that there is no such thing as a consecration of the elements themselves, and that every communion must be more or less of a general communion, have long been abandoned, and the Prayer Book modified in consequence, the traditional confession of faith in the sacrament being added to the words of administration, and the words "except there be a good number to communicate with the priest" altered; yet no rubric definitely ordering either reservation or a second celebration on the same day has been added. Since the provision for two communions on Christmas Day and Easter Day was omitted from the Second Prayer Book, the Prayer Book has arranged for only one celebration on any day even at the great festivals, and the rubrics provide for no other. Yet before the close of 1662, the year in which the revised Prayer Book came into use, the holding of two celebrations of the communion on the same day in the same church was well known, and by the end of the seventeenth century they were widespread[1]. At the present time indeed the great majority of the communions made in the English Church take place at

[1] Legg, *English Church Life*, pp. 48–50

an early eucharist, frequently one of several on the same day, a practice as abhorrent to the reformers of the sixteenth century as reservation, and equally unprovided for in the Book of Common Prayer. The rise of this custom involved a new method of interpretation being applied to some of the rubrics, and in particular to that arranging for the disposal of the remains of the unconsecrated elements which had been provided "for the communion":

> And if any of the bread and wine remain unconsecrated, the curate shall have it to his own use.

For any second celebration of the holy communion on the same day in the same church to be possible at all it really demands the addition of some such gloss as "when provision has been made for every administration of the sacrament required," and unfortunately this has led to the rubric becoming entirely a dead letter, and so one of the most primitive practices enjoined by the Prayer Book has been lost. The same gloss applied to the second part of the rubric dealing with the consecrated elements would serve rather to make the historical meaning clearer, that it refers only to what is not required for purposes of communion, and has nothing to do with the primitive practice of the reservation of the sacrament. Yet though the traditional method of providing for the communion of the whole by a second celebration of the Lord's Supper on the same day has been generally adopted, the traditional method of providing for the communion of the sick has not been so widespread, yet neither can be said to be contrary to the present doctrinal standard of the Book of Common Prayer, and what is lacking is only a definite provision which was omitted because of opinions which the church has long since repudiated, if ever committed to them.

(*e*) For the correct understanding of a rubric contemporary practice or interpretation is of value as illustrating the meaning according to which it was accepted. We have already noticed the opinion of Sparrow on the interpretation of the rubrics of the Prayer Book before its revision in 1661:

> The rubric at the communion of the sick directs the priest to deliver the communion to the sick; but does not there set down how

much of the communion service shall be used at the delivering of the communion to the sick· and therefore seems to me to refer us to former directions in times past[1].

Cosin had also criticised the inadequacy of the unrevised rubrics assuming likewise that it could not be intended that the whole service should be used, parts being unsuitable. In his *Particulars to be considered* we read:

What part of the public order at the communion is to be used, and what omitted (as some part of it seems needful to be), is not here said[2].

The new rubrics are undoubtedly much more definite than they were before the revision, for now when certain conditions are satisfied the priest is directed to "celebrate the holy communion beginning with the collect." Yet it is impossible to build much upon the alteration from "minister" to "celebrate," a change the exact opposite of what was made in the Second Prayer Book, though not at quite the same point, and to argue that the consecration is now definitely ordered. Cosin clearly employs the word "celebrate" of the reception of the sacrament, and without any direct reference to the act of consecration, using it indeed of the action of the people. In his First Series of Notes on the Prayer Book we read:

And there shall be no celebration, etc. except there be a great number. This was made against the *Solitariae Missae* that the papists are nowadays content withal. It was an abuse springing up about Charlemagne's time (it seems), to have the priest communicate and say mass, though there were none to celebrate with him. Therefore the council of Mentz then made a canon against it[3].

If such a meaning could be attached to the word "celebrate" by the revisers it is plain that we have still no clear direction for a consecration, even though the word does seem on occasions to include it. This plainly seems to have been Sparrow's opinion—and as one of the chief revisers it has special weight —for in the various editions of his *Rationale* published after the revision he made no alteration in his recommendation of reservation, suggesting that he still considered it allowable and

---
[1] See pp. 257-8 *Rationale*, p 223.
[2] *Works*, vol. v. p. 524. Parker, *Introduction*, p. ccxci.
[3] Parker, p. ccxxx

his reasons not obsolete. This conclusion is confirmed by the fact that no alteration was made in the rubric dealing with the occasions on which the sick man was visited and received the Holy Communion at the same time, for then the priest is still required to cut off the form of visitation at the psalm and "go straight to the communion," a phrase of considerable ambiguity, as we have noticed, being used frequently and more correctly of the acts of distribution and reception, and including in the First Prayer Book a reference to the distribution of the communion with the reserved sacrament. It is unlikely that Sparrow, successively bishop of Exeter and Norwich, and therefore responsible for the administration of the revised Prayer Book, would continue to recommend in the various editions of his *Rationale* a practice which was generally and officially regarded as forbidden under the new rubrics. His attitude indeed he had already made clear in his book, and from the historical point of view it is the only one possible. After all the addition to the rubric "If any remain" is only a carrying out of his suggestion, based he says upon the directions of the pseudo Clement and the synod of Constantinople, for the disposal of the remains of the sacrament[1], and it is plain that he saw nothing in it contradictory to his advocacy of reservation in the same book, agreeing thus exactly with the only interpretation historically considered of which his authorities, the letter of the pseudo Clement and the answer of the synod of Constantinople to the monks, are capable. Samuel Downes in his edition of the *Rationale* published in 1722 took occasion to explain in a footnote the altered conditions under the revised rubrics[2], but it is not improbable that Sparrow himself, who had assisted in the revision, is a more competent authority on what was their intention, and the proper interpretation.

Another of the revisers who expressed an opinion on the matter was Herbert Thorndike, a Prebendary of Westminster. In his *Reformation of the Church of England better than that of the Council of Trent*, written about 1670, though not then published, he advocates even continuous reservation. We read:

[1] See p 211.   [2] *Rationale*, p 223 n.

BOOK OF COMMON PRAYER 269

And thus far I will particularize, as concerning the eucharist that the church is to endeavour the celebrating of it so frequently that it may be reserved to the next communion For in the meantime it ought to be so ready for them that pass into the other world that they need not stay for the consecrating of it on purpose for every one. The reason of the necessity of it for all, which hath been delivered, aggravates it very much in danger of death. And the practice of the church attests it to the utmost Neither will there be any necessity of giving it in one kind only, as by some passages of antiquity may be collected if common reason could deceive in a subject of this nature[1].

Thorndike in this work is comparing Roman and Anglican practices, and is by no means unfriendly towards the Church of Rome, but however much he was inclined to bring forward the ideal of the Church of England rather than the actual, there could be no point in arguing from that which was generally regarded as forbidden. It would be an extraordinary method of showing that the reformation of the Church of England was better than that of the Council of Trent to put forward as evidence of its superiority a practice which was common in the Roman Church, but was not allowed by the Book of Common Prayer.

There appear to be no opinions of the revisers in existence which take the opposite view of reservation. The fact however that the new rubric could be interpreted as making reservation impossible by those who were unaccustomed to the practice, or even opposed to it, and who cared nothing for the traditional application of the words of the pseudo Clement and of the synod of Constantinople, was realised on both sides as early as the beginning of the eighteenth century. We have already noticed the explanation of Samuel Downes in his edition of Sparrow's *Rationale* in 1722. In the Communion Office of the Non Jurors published in 1718 it was evidently thought well that the direction should be altered so as to avoid the possibility of any such wresting of its meaning, and a modification of part of the rubric of the First Prayer Book from the order for the communion of the sick dealing with the matter is prefixed to the rubric ordering the consumption of the remains

[1] Ch. xxxix § 4. *Works*, vol. v p. 578.

immediately after the blessing, with the result that the scope of the rubric is entirely changed. We read.

If there be any persons who through sickness, or any other urgent cause, are under a necessity of communicating at their houses; then the priest shall reserve at the open communion so much of the sacrament of the body and blood, as shall serve those who are to receive at home. And if after that, or if, when none are to communicate at their houses, any of the consecrated elements remain, then it shall not be carried out of the church; but the priest and such other of the communicants as he shall then call unto him, shall immediately after the Blessing reverently eat and drink the same[1]

V.

We may now gather up the results of our enquiry. The practice of the reservation of the sacrament, together with that of holding a second celebration of the holy communion in the same church on the same day, both of which were prescribed in the First Prayer Book, was omitted from the Second Book out of deference to the opinions of certain of the extreme reformers, yet not condemned. No rubric altering the lack of prescription of the use of the reserved species has since been inserted in the Book of Common Prayer, yet the omission was not regarded as forbidding it, and in the days of Elizabeth according to Calvin reservation was a well-known practice and the officially authorized Latin Prayer Book recommends reservation for the sick in a rubric slightly modified from that of Aless's Latin version of the First Prayer Book, and the practice was continued it would seem up to the time of the Rebellion and later in certain circles, for we find Sparrow in his *Rationale* published in 1657 interpreting the absence of definite directions about the amount of the service to be used for the communion of the sick as referring back to the rubrics of the First Prayer Book, and allowing reservation. In 1661 on the recommendation of Cosin, Sparrow and Wren, an addition, based on the rubric of the Scottish Prayer Book, and also directly on the words of the pseudo Clement and the synod of Constantinople for dealing with the residue of the sacrament

[1] Dowden, *The Annotated Scottish Communion Office*, p 321. Hall, *F.L.* vol. v. pp. 51–2.

not required for communion, by consumption in church, was made to the rubric "If any remain," and this forbade, "if any remain," the carrying of these remains out of church. Such a reverent disposal of the remains according to the traditional interpretation of the pseudo Clement and the answer of the synod of Constantinople to the monks, whence the wording of the rubric was drawn, in no way touched the question of what was in their days the universal custom of reserving the sacrament for the sick, and Sparrow was clearly of the same opinion, for in his *Rationale*, after the insertion of the new rubric as well as before, he advocated both the practices which are supposed to be contradictory. The same view was evidently taken also by Thorndike another of the revisers who advocated reservation, while there appears to be no opinion of any reviser to the contrary. The order for the communion of the sick, like that for the visitation of the sick, is only possible on occasions, being intended as is plain for the dying and those in danger of death, and not for chronic invalids or the like, and the conditions for its use are such as can seldom be satisfied. The recommendations that when the sick man is visited and receives the communion at the same time the priest should, instead of saying the psalm, "go straight to the communion," and that when the sick man does "not receive the sacrament of Christ's body and blood," not when he cannot receive the "communion," the priest should instruct him about spiritual reception, both originally referring to the possible use of the reserved sacrament and worded accordingly, suggest a return to this ancient practice of the church to supply the many cases for which the Prayer Book makes no provision; and such a practice alone gives point to the difference of wording of the two rubrics before the Lord's Prayer, and at the end of the service with respect to what remains at the two points. That reservation has not been so widely adopted for the sick as a second celebration the same day has been for the communion of the whole seems to depend ultimately on other considerations than the wording of the rubric "If any remain," the first portion of which, if interpreted in the same way, would forbid two celebrations in a church on any day; and the explanation of the rubric would appear to be rather a consequence of the general disuse of reservation in days when a low view was taken of the necessity of the communion of the sick, and not the disuse of reservation a consequence of the rubric Had the practice been general it is difficult to see how any one reading the rubric would have imagined it was forbidden, any more than that a second celebration is forbidden by the same and other rubrics. Few writers seem to have approached the matter from the purely historical point of view, and the tradition of centuries in the interpretation of the directions of the pseudo Clement and of the synod of Constantinople, the basis of the rubric, has been generally ignored, though a similar interpretation of the words referring to the unconsecrated remains, which can boast no such precedent, has passed without question, and the holding of two celebrations on the same day has been common since the end of the seventeenth century. A communion of the sick in which all the conditions laid down by the rubrics were fulfilled must have been at any period comparatively rare, but it is a curiosity of interpretation that while private celebrations of the holy communion, held at the suggestion of the curate and not after timely notice given to him, for invalids and others not in danger of death, with nothing whatever prepared by the sick man or his friends, without the required number of communicants, and with a different collect, epistle, and gospel, on each of which points the Prayer Book directions are very precise, should have been considered as quite legitimate, while a communion with the reserved sacrament against which the Prayer Book says nothing should have been so often regarded as entirely forbidden. It might have been thought that, even on the interpretation of "If any remain" which ignores the long history and traditional interpretation of the source of the rubric, and the intentions of some at any rate of the revisers to the same effect, apart from controversy there would have been at least as much freedom in one case as in the other.

INDEX

Abingdon, Edmund of, Abp of Canterbury, 138, 153
Abu'l Bircat, 23
Adai and Mari, SS, Liturgy of, 26, 197
Adalbert, St, Bp of Prague, 37, 67
Admonition of the pseudo Leo IV, Synodical, 56, 98–9, 119–23, 127, 139, 149, 169, 215, 239
Agnus Dei, 66, 82, 129, 187–8, 227–8, 236
Alcuin, Pseudo, 37, 53, 66–7
Aless, Alexander, Latin Prayer Book of, 195, 199, 248–50, 255, 258, 270
Alexander of Hales, Glos, 131, 150
Alexius Comnenus I, 10
Alfred's Trans of Bede's *Eccles Hist*, 40
Alnwick Castle, 162
Amalarius, *Ecloga* of See *Ecloga* of Amalarius
Amalarius of Metz, 52–3, 65–6, 87
Amand, St, *Ordo* of Abbey of, 50–1, 53, 55, 68, 76, 82, 125, 239
Ambrosian Rite, 96, 146, 175
Andrews, St, Diocese of, 166, 170
Angers Missal, 46
Anianus, Bp of Bangor, Pontifical of, 154, 170
Antidoron, 30–2
Antoninus Pius, 1
Apostolic Constitutions, 7, 16, 209
Aquinas, St Thomas, 18, 41, 72–3, 131, 207
Arabic Canons of Nicaea, 8, 14
Arbuthnott Missal, 166
Aridius, St, 48
Arles, Pontifical of, 61
Armariolum, 81, 84–5, 135–6
Armenian Rite, 33, 235–6
Arsenal Library, Paris, 80, 155
Articles of Religion, 251–2
Articles to be followed, etc (1549), 176–7, 221
Athanasius, St, Canons of, 15–6
Augustine, St, Abp of Canterbury, 247

Augustine, St, Bp of Hippo, 5
Augustinian *Ordinale* of Holyrood, 79, 97
Austin Friars, 196, 203. See Strangers' Church
Austria, 33
Avignon, 84, 97, 241
Avranches, John of See John of Avranches

Bacon, Nicholas, Lord Keeper, 199
Balsamon, Theodore, 10–11, 211, 246
Bancroft, Richard, Abp of Canterbury, 210
Bangor, Use of, 154, 158
Baptistery, 118, 121, 123
Barberini MS, 28
Barsalibi, Dionysius See Dionysius Barsalibi
Basil, St, Coptic Liturgy of, 23
Basil, St, Liturgy of, 28, 29
Baxter, Richard, 219, 221, 225
Baxter's Liturgy, 219–22, 228, 230
Bayeux, 106. See Councils and Synods
Bayswater, Greek Church in, 30
Beauvais, *Ordo* of, 61
Bec, Customs of, 78, 86
Becon, Thomas, 197, 208, 228
Bede, *Ecclesiastical History* of, 40
Bede, Penitential of, 43
Benet, St, Church of, Paris, 48
Benignus, St, of Dijon, Customs of, 36, 60, 77–8, 101–2, 135
Bernold of Constance, *Micrologus* of, 69, 82
Beroldus, *Ordo* of (Ambrosian), 96
Besançon, *Ordo* of, 61
Birkbeck, the late Mr W. J, 31–2
Black Rubric, 217
Blasien, St, MS of, 125
Bobbio Missal, 174–5
Bobbio, Penitential of, 43
Bodleian Library, Oxford, 159–60, 168–9
Bologna, Customs of, 108
Bologna, Library of University of, 80, 155, 160, 162, 169

L E   18

274 INDEX

Bonner, Edmund, Bp of London, 182
Bourges Cathedral, 48
Boys consume remains of eucharist, 9, 15, 26-7, 35-6, 43, 238-9
Brandenburg Order, 178
Brescia *Rituale*, 112
Brevint, Daniel, Dean of Lincoln, 225, 237
Brixen *Sacerdotale*, 113
Bucer, Martin, 177, 183-4, 187-9, 191-4, 196, 201, 228, 251, 254, 260
Bullinger, Heinrich, 196, 199
Burchard, Bp of Worms, 38
Burchard, John, Papal Master of Ceremonies, 109, 113, 116, 141-2, 241
Burnet, Thomas, Prebendary of Salisbury, 227
Bute, Marquess of, 25
Byzantine Rite, 33 See Chrysostom, St, Liturgy of, etc

Caeremoniale Episcoporum, 93, 95, 111-2, 116, 242
Caesarius, St, Bp of Arles, 5
Cajetan, James, 83, 85
Calosyrius, Bp of Arsinoe, 6, 14, 17, 189, 207
Calvinists, Customs of, 203, 205
Calvin, John, 199, 218, 256-8, 270
Cambridge University Library, 156
Canons of 1604, 202, 210
Canons of 1636, Scottish, 203-4, 212
Canterbury, Abp of (Edward White Benson), 215
Carmelite Rite, 85, 97, 105-6, 111, 145-6, 241-2
Caroline divines, 246. See names of individuals
Carthusian Rite, 77, 106, 129, 145-6
Catalani, Joseph, 112
Catalogue of Bishops of Rome, 48-9
Catechism of Russian Church, Longer, 234
Cautelae Missae, 115
Censura of Bucer, 177, 183, 188, 191-2, 194, 260
Chaldaean Uniats, Rite of, 33
Charles I, 204, 209
Charles II, 229, 236
Charles the Great, 35, 207, 267

Chartres, Use of, 145-6
Chrysostom, St, Abp of Constantinople, 228, 237
Chrysostom, St, Liturgy of, 22, 28-32, 216, 232-3, 235-7
Cistercian Rite, 103-4, 122, 134, 241, 246
Clement, Letter of the pseudo, 11-18, 37, 40-3, 98, 118-22, 139, 182, 189-91, 193, 204, 206-7, 211, 239, 244, 246, 259-61, 268-72
Clement, St, Liturgy of, 7
Cluny, Constitutions of, 36, 76-8, 101-2, 116, 122, 135, 149
Codex Ratoldi, 125-6, 239-40
Codex Tilianus, 173
Colbertine MS. Penitential, Bibliothèque Nationale, Paris, 43
Colbertine MSS , Bibliothèque Nationale, Paris, 43, 45, 47, 63
Colewich, or Colwich, Staffs, 158
Columban, St, Rule of, 42
Commemoration of Sacrifice of Christ, 218-25
Common Prayer, Book of See Prayer Book
Communion of sick. See Viaticum
Communion Pax, 173, 175-6, 179, 181, 243-5
Conditorium, 45
Consecration of elements, 67, 99, 180, 188-9, 191, 199-202, 204, 207-13, 219-20, 222-4
Constantinople, 9, 26-7 See Councils and Synods
Constitutions, Apostolic, 7, 16, 209
Constitutions (English), Anon ,138, 154
Consuetudinary (or *Ordinale*), 79, 80, 116, 151, 156-7, 166, 170, 242
Consuetudinary of Exeter, 151
Consuetudinary of Salisbury, 151, 156-7, 166, 170
Consuetudinary of Wells, 151
Coptic Constitutions, 8, 15
Coptic Liturgy, 23
Coptic Liturgy of St Basil, 23
Coptic Rite, 8, 15, 19, 23, 25
Coptic Uniats, Liturgy of, 25
Corbie, Ordinary of, 36
Corbie, *Ordo* of Monastery of, 60, 67, 76
Corinthians, First Epistle to, 9
Corpus Christi College, Oxford, 156, 158, 166, 169

INDEX

Corpus Juris Canonici, 38, 130
Cosin, John, Bp of Durham, 208, 211, 213, 222–6, 259, 261, 270
Cosin's First Series of Notes, 206–9, 222, 261, 267
Cosin's Second Series of Notes, 208–10, 226
Cosin's Third Series of Notes, 209
Cosin's *Particulars to be considered*, 209, 223, 267
Cotton MS, Tiberius C I, 149, 169
Councils and Synods
 Aberdeen, 138, 153
 Aix-la-Chapelle, 41
 Bayeux, 35
 Bordeaux, 36
 Clermont, 35–6, 205
 Cologne, 138
 Constantinople, 10–11, 204, 206, 211, 244, 259, 262, 268–72
 Durham, 138, 152–4, 204
 Mâcon II, 9, 15, 207–8
 Mentz, 267
 Nicaea, 8, 14, 226
 Nîmes, 138
 Oxford, 138, 153
 Paris, 35
 Quiercy, 65–6
 Rodomum, 36, 44
 Toledo XVI, 36
 Tours III, 35, 44, 207
 Trent, 110, 143, 145, 268–9
 Westminster, 138, 151, 153, 156
 Worms, 41
Cranmer, Thomas, Abp of Canterbury, 110, 179, 189, 191–3, 196, 199, 201, 216
Crawford Sarum Missal, 80, 154–5, 158, 169, 174
Cyprian, St, Bp of Carthage, 6, 46
Cyril, St, Abp of Alexandria, 6, 14, 17, 189, 207
Cyril, St, Bp of Jerusalem, 4

Damien, Peter, 128, 240
Decentius, Bp of Gubbio, 49, 82
Decretum of Gratian, 38, 41, 64–5, 180, 211, 246
Despoticon, 23–4
Didache, 46
Didier, St, of Cahors, 48
Dionysius Barsalibi, 20, 22
Dionysius, St, 191
Directory, Parliamentary, 218, 228
Dominican Rite, 104, 106, 111, 115, 145, 241–2
Downes, Samuel, 268–9

Dunstan, St, Pontifical of, 39, 260
Durandus, William, Bp of Mende, *Rationale* of, 58, 73, 100, 132
Durham, Bp of (Nathaniel Crewe), 229
Durham Book, 212–3, 224
Durham Cathedral, 117

Eastern Liturgies, Chapter II, 216, 222, 230–7
Ecloga of Amalarius, 56–7
Edgar, Canons under, 43
Edlesborough, Bucks, 250
Egbert, Penitential of, 43
Egbert, Pontifical of, 39, 59, 260
Egyptian Church Order, 2, 3, 6, 13
Einsiedeln *Ordo*, 51–3, 82–3
Elizabethan Settlement, 195, 198–202, 209, 212, 215, 255–6, 258, 270
Elizabeth, Prayer Book of See Prayer Book of Elizabeth, or James I
Ely, Bp of (Thomas Goodrich), 177
Ely House, 225
Emmeram, St, at Ratisbon, Library of, 49
English divines, 11, 215, 246, 259
Ephesus, Eucharist at, 1
Epiclesis, 222
Etienne, St, Rouen, Church of, 146
Eucharist buried, 8, 19, 42–3, 238
Eucharist burnt, 8, 9, 15, 19, 42–3, 238
Eulogiae, 99, 209
Eutychiani Papae Exhortatio, 119
Evagrius, 9, 26, 207
Evelyn, John, 229
Exeter *Ordinale* (or Consuetudinary), 80, 151
Exodus, 13, 14, 183
Ezekiel xl, Jerome on, 7

Fermentum, 48–51, 54, 57, 82–3, 97, 241
Fidei ratio of Zwingli, 185
First Prayer Book See Prayer Book, First
Flacius Illyricus, Mass of, 58
Flintham, Notts, 250
Fortunatus, Venantius, Bp of Poitiers, 48
Franciscan Use, 141
Fulco, St, of Angers, 61

Galicia, 33
Gallican Councils, 9, 35–7, 239

Gallican influence, 50, 54, 56, 63–4, 69, 75, 81, 83–4, 100, 115, 124–5, 206, 239
Gallican *Ordines*, 69, 100, 125
Gallican Rite, 47, 66
Gallican Sacramentary, 47
Gall, St, MSS, 59, 63, 174–5
Garrard, Master, 200
Gattico, J B, 100
Gaul, 9
Gelasian Sacramentary, 39, 40, 54, 75
Gemma Animae of Honorius of Autun, 71–2
Gemma Ecclesiastica of Giraldus Cambrensis, 40
Geneva, Reformed Church in, 256
German form of clinical communion, 173
Germanus, Patriarch of Constantinople, 234
Germanus, St, Bp of Paris, 47
Germanus, St, Monastery of (St Germain des Prés), Paris, 61
Giraldus Cambrensis (de Barri), 40
Glastonbury, French Church at, 195–6, 250, 255
Gloria in excelsis, 50, 184, 186, 188, 221–2, 227–8, 230–1, 236, 245
Gloucester Cathedral, 117, 149
Gonville and Caius College, Cambridge, 150
Gorgonia, Sister of St Gregory Nazianzen, v
Grandisson, John de, Bp of Exeter, 80
Grassis, Paris de, Bp of Pesaro, Papal Master of Ceremonies, 91, 93, 107–8, 111–2, 143, 241–2
Gratian, Francis, *Decretum* of, 38, 41, 64–5, 180, 211, 246
Gratias tibi, 154–9, 161–6, 168–9, 174–6, 179
Greek Church, 30, 238
Gregorian Sacramentary, 172–3
Gregory, Cardinal, *Polycarpus* of, 38
Gregory, St, Bp of Tours, 47
Gregory, St, Monastery of, Basle, 58
Gregory III, Penitential of, 43

Haddon, Walter, 199, 255
Hales, Alexander of, 131, 150
Halitgar, Bp of Cambrai, Penitential of, 43
Hallel, 185–6

Harding, Thomas, Fellow of New College, Oxford, 226
Hereford Cathedral, 117
Hereford Missal, 80–1, 162, 167, 170, 205
Hereford, Use of, 150, 162
Hermann, Abp of Cologne, *Consultation* of, 76, 187, 194, 250–1, 254
Hesychius, 9, 15, 189, 207–8
Hincmar, Abp of Rheims, Capitular of, 119–21
Hippolytus, 2
Hippolytus, Canons of, 3
Hirshau, Constitutions of, 102
Holder, Dr, Subdean of Chapels Royal, 229
Holyrood *Ordinale*, 79, 242
Honorius of Autun, 71–2
Hooper, John, Bp of Gloucester, 177, 183, 221
Hugh of St Victor, 71
Humbert, Cardinal, 19

Imperial Library, Vienna, 61
Irish Rite, 59, 174–5
Isidore, Pseudo, 38
Ivo of Chartres, 38, 64, 126, 130, 132

James, St, Liturgy of, 19, 230
James, St, Lord's brother, 11, 37
James, St, Syriac Liturgy of, 22
Jerome, Pseudo, 11, 197, 207
Jerome, St, 7
Jerusalem, 19
Jesus College, Cambridge, 149
Jewel, John, Bp of Salisbury, 197, 208, 226
John, Bp of Syracuse, 217
John of Avranches, Abp of Rouen, 70, 99, 127, 145, 149, 240
Johnson, Robert, Preacher at Northampton, 199–201
Justice, Lord Chief, 199
Justin Martyr, St, 1, 2

King Edward VI, First Prayer Book of See Prayer Book, First, of Edward VI
King Edward VI, Second Prayer Book of See Prayer Book, Second, of Edward VI
King's Majesty's Injunctions and Proceedings, 176–7

Lacy, Edmund, Bp of Exeter, Pontifical of, 78–9

INDEX

Lando, Bp of Rheims, 48
Lanfranc, Constitutions of, 36, 77–8
Langton, Stephen, Abp of Canterbury, 138, 153, 166
Laon, Church at, 48
Lasco, John a, 183, 187, 196, 203, 220
Lateran, Church of the, St Saviour, 50, 52, 59
Laud, William, Abp of Canterbury, 226
Lawrence, St, Church of, Rouen, 48
Lay Folks Mass Book, 150, 170
Leofric Missal, 40, 75
Leonine Sacramentary, 174
Leviticus, 6, 9, 13–5, 126, 189, 208
Liber Familiaris Clericorum, 110
Liber Pontificalis, 48, 187
Liber Sacerdotalis, 110
Lincoln, Bp of (Edward King), 215
Lincoln Cathedral, 149
Llanthony, Abbey of, 150
Lombard, Peter, 71
London, Bp of (Edwin Sandys), 199–201
London, Bp of (Henry Compton), 229
Lord's prayer after communion, 184, 217, 225, 232, 235, 245
Lumley, Lord, purchaser of many of Cranmer's books, 110
Luther, Martin, 197
Lyndwood, William, *Provinciale* of, 41, 165–6
Lyons, Use of, 145–6
Lytlyngton, Nicholas, Abbot of Westminster, 161

Mabillon, John, Roman *Ordines* of, 45, 57. See Roman *Ordo I*, etc.
Magdalen College, Oxford, Pontifical of, 78–9
Maguelonne, Bp and Cathedral of, 130
Malabar Rite, 21
Mansionary, 50, 92–3
Manual, 113, 156, 169
Marcellus, Christopher, Bp of Corcyra, 88, 90, 96, 107–8, 110, 112, 143, 241
Marmoutier, Monastery of, Tours, 48
Maro, John, Patriarch of Antioch, 20
Maronites, 20, 22

Martial, St, Abbey of, Limoges, 40–1
Martin, St, Church of, in the Fields, 229
Martin, St, Church of, Leicester, 149
Martyr, Peter, 193, 199, 201, 251
Mary, Queen, 117
McClure (or Blew) MS. Manual, 156
Micrologus, 69, 82
Middleburgh Prayer Book, 218
Milan, Use of, 96
Missale Francorum, 39, 121, 260, 262
Missale Mixtum, 96
Moléon, Sieur de, 145–6
Mosaic law, 6, 13–5, 17, 42, 126, 238
Mozarabic Rite, 46, 96, 146
Musculus (Reginald Wolf), 199

Narsài, Liturgical Homilies of, 26, 234, 245
Nestorianism, 207
Nestorian Rite, 26, 33, 197–8, 231, 235, 245
Nicephorus Callistus, 26
Nicephorus, Patriarch of Constantinople, Typicon of, 27, 29
Nicholas Grammaticus, Patriarch of Constantinople, 10, 259
Nîmes, Use of, 138–9
Non-communicants, 228–30, 237
Non-jurors, 269

Odo of Paris (Eudes de Sully), 35
Orderic, Canon of Siena, 131
Order of Communion, 171–6, 179–80, 194, 235, 243, 245
Ordinale (or Consuetudinary), 79, 80, 116, 151, 156–7, 166, 170, 242
Ordinale of Exeter, 151
Ordinale of Holyrood, 79, 116, 242
Ordinale of Salisbury, 151, 156–7, 166, 170
Ordinale of Wells, 151
Ordo, First Roman, etc See Roman *Ordo I*, etc
Ordo Missae of Burchard, 109–10, 113, 116, 142, 243
Ordo of St Amand See Amand, St, *Ordo* of Abbey of
Origen, 4–6, 13, 207
Osmund, St, Bp of Sarum, 149
Oswestry, Missal of Church of, 158–61, 166

278 INDEX

Overall, John, Bp of Durham, 222

Pardoner's Churchyard, 110
Parliamentary Directory, 218, 228
Paschal Chronicle, 27
Pastophorium, 7, 207
Paten, Ablution of, 20–1, 24–5, 29, 31, 127, 133–4, 136–7, 152–3, 240
Patricius, Bp of Pienza, 88, 90, 96, 107–12, 121–2, 143, 241
Paul, St, 1, 9, 187
Paul, St, Cathedral of, London, 182
Pax, Communion. See Communion Pax
Pearl (fragment of sacrament), 30–1
Peru *Manuale*, 113
Peter Damien, 128, 240
Peter Lombard, 71
Peter Martyr, 193, 199, 201, 251
Petri, Laurence, Abp of Upsala, 197
Philotheus, Patriarch of Constantinople, 29
Piscina, 123, 129, 132, 134, 146–7, 149, 240. See Sacrarium and Place (for pouring ablutions)
Place (for pouring ablutions), 119–20, 122–3, 126, 128, 130, 132, 139, 147, 149, 151, 240
Polycarpus of Cardinal Gregory, 38
Poor, Richard le, Bp of Salisbury, 138, 153
Popes of Rome
 Benedict XII, 85
 Clement I. See Clement, Letter of the pseudo, and Clement, St, Liturgy of
 Clement VI, 85
 Clement VIII, 93, 95, 111–3, 144–5
 Eutychianus, 119
 Gregory the Great, 40, 184, 217, 245
 Gregory III, 43
 Gregory XI, 85
 Innocent I, 49, 82
 Innocent III, 71, 130–2, 150
 Innocent VI, 85
 Innocent VIII, 107
 Innocent X, 112
 John XXII, 85
 Leo IV See Admonition of the pseudo Leo IV, Synodical
 Leo X, 112
 Leo XIII, 33

Popes of Rome (*cont.*):
 Miltiades, 48
 Pius V, 92, 110, 116, 145
 Sergius I, 64–6, 71–3, 187
 Siricius, 49
 Sixtus IV, 90, 97
 Urban V, 85
 Urban VI, 85
 Urban VIII, 145
Prayer Book, 181, 196–7, 203, 214, 230, 232, 235, 248, 264–6, 270
Prayer Book, First, of Edward VI, 110, 175, 177–8, 180–3, 186–8, 191, 193–6, 198–9, 201, 214–5, 220, 222–4, 228, 236, 243, 248–56, 258, 260, 262–5, 268–70
Prayer Book, Second, of Edward VI, 183–4, 187–8, 191–2, 194–5, 198, 201, 204, 206, 208, 212, 228, 244, 251, 253–60, 265, 267, 270
Prayer Book of Elizabeth, or James I, 198–201, 206, 208–9, 211–2, 215, 219, 221–4, 226, 229, 257
Prayer Book of Charles II, 1, 196, 213, 217, 224–5, 227–8, 230, 232, 235–7, 244, 246, 258, 260–1, 263–6, 268–9, 271–2
Prayer Book of Kirk of Scotland, 218
Prayer Book, Puritan, 218
Prayer Book, Scottish, 204–6, 208, 212, 214, 218, 258–9, 262, 270
Prothesis, 28–32, 216, 233–4, 238
Provinciale of William Lyndwood, 41, 165–6
Pullain, Valerand, 195–6, 250, 255
Puritans, 218–9, 223–4
Pyx, 19, 45–8, 52, 56, 71, 83, 88, 102–7, 109–11, 113–4, 116–7, 145, 228, 242–3, 250–1, 257

Questions and Answers according to the Doctrine of the Fathers (Coptic), 24

Ratherius, Bp of Verona, 119
Regino of Prum, 38, 56, 98–9, 119–22
Remi, St, Codex of, 172, 175
Remigius, Bp of Coire, 38
Remigius of Auxerre, 66–7
Remigius, St, Abp of Rheims, 148
Renaudot, Eusebius, 3, 22–3, 25
Rhabanus Maurus, 66
Rheims Missal, 46

INDEX

Rheinau, Penitential of, 43
Ridley, Nicholas, Bp of London, 177, 221
Ritus Servandus in Celebratione Missarum, or Ritus Celebrandi Missam, 110, 112–3, 116, 144, 243
Riva, Missal of Bp of, 61
Robert of St Victor, Penitential of, 43
Rochester, Bp of (Francis Turner), 229
Rock MS Manual, 156
Roman Catholics, 210
Roman Missal, 43, 87, 92, 95–6, 110, 113, 116, 141, 143–6, 158, 197, 221
Roman Ordines, 46, 52–3, 58, 61, 65–7, 69, 82, 87, 99, 100, 102, 112, 125, 132, 165
Roman Ordo, Common, of Hittorp, 59–61, 67
Roman Ordo I, 45, 50, 52, 54, 56–8, 61, 65, 75, 82, 112, 118, 123–5, 205, 214, 217, 244, 263
Roman Ordo I, Appendix, 54, 75, 99, 124
Roman Ordo II, 52, 56–8, 61, 119, 124
Roman Ordo III, 58, 64, 119, 124–5
Roman Ordo IV, 57, 64
Roman Ordo V, 64
Roman Ordo VI, 100, 107, 115, 125–6, 240
Roman Ordo X, 82–5, 106, 128, 132, 140
Roman Ordo XIV, 81, 83–5, 139
Roman Ordo XV, 81, 84–5, 100, 140
Roman Pontifical, 88, 121–2
Roman Ritual, 107, 114
Romsey Abbey, Hants, 149
Rouen, Use of, 127, 145–6, 149–50, 170, 240–1
Russian Rite, 31–2, 234
Ruthenian Rite, 33
Ryarsh, Kent, 149
Rylands Library, Manchester, 80, 154

Sacrarium, 129, 155–62, 164–9 See Piscina and Place (for pouring ablutions)
Sacred Ceremonies and Ecclesiastical Rites of the Holy Roman Church, of Patricius, 107
Sacristy, or Vestry, 7, 9, 12–4, 16, 27–8, 34, 39, 40, 43–4, 54, 75, 82–3, 96, 119–20, 122, 127, 147, 190, 193, 208, 215, 238–9, 244, 246
Saffron Walden, Pyx at, 250, 257
Sahidic Ecclesiastical Canons, 7
St Gall MSS., 59, 63, 174–5
Salisbury Cathedral, 157
Salzburg, Pontifical of, 173
Sancroft, William, Chaplain to Cosin (Abp of Canterbury 1678), 212, 225
Sancroft's Fair Copy, 212
Sancta, Chapter IV, 83, 238, 244
Sanctum, 46
Sarum Consuetudinary (or Ordinale), 151, 156–7, 166, 170
Sarum Customary, 156, 158–9, 161, 163, 165–6, 168–9, 170
Sarum Manual, 156, 169
Sarum Missal, 43, 80–1, 115–6, 154–6, 158–9, 161–2, 166–70, 173–5, 243
Sarum Ordinale (or Consuetudinary), 151, 156–7, 166, 170
Saviour, Church of the, Lateran, 50, 52, 59
Savoy Conference, 219, 222
Scottish Canons of 1636, 203–4, 212, 258–9
Scottish Prayer Book. See Prayer Book, Scottish
Scutella, 101, 102–3, 135
Second Prayer Book. See Prayer Book, Second
Sens, Pontifical of, 61
Sherborne, Church of, 162
Sibbald, James, Vicar of Arbuthnott, 166
Sidney Sussex College, Cambridge, 163, 166
Siena, Order of Offices at, 131
Sigibert, Constitutions of, 76
Simeon of Thessalonica, 234
Soissons Cathedral, 106, 117, 132
Sparrow, Anthony, Bp of Exeter 1667, Norwich 1676, 204, 211, 213, 245, 257, 261–2, 266–71
Stowe Missal, 174–5
Strangers' Church, Austin Friars, 187, 196, 203
Strasburg, French Church at, 195
Strype, John, Historian, 256
Sweden, Church of, 197
Synods See Councils and Synods
Syriac Liturgy of St James, 19–21, 33, 231
Syrian Jacobites, Rite of, 21–2, 33

Syrian Jacobites, Uniats, Rite of, 33

Tenison, Thomas, Rector of St Martin's in the Fields (Bp of Lincoln 1692,Abp of Canterbury 1695), 229
Tertullian, 2, 6, 46
Testament of our Lord, 3
Thanksgiving after communion, 20–2, 26, 28–30, 32–3, 126, 174–6, 178–81, 184–6, 188, 195, 221–2, 230–2, 236–7, 243–5, 248–9, 255 See *Gratias tibi*
Theodore, Abp of Canterbury, Penitential of, 43
Theodore, St, of the Studium, 233
Theophilus, Bp of Alexandria, 10–1, 211
Third part of the host Chapter v, 104, 107, 115, 239
Thomas, St, Christians of, 21
Thorndike, Herbert, Prebendary of Westminster, 245, 268–9, 271
Tirpinus, Abp of Rheims, Pontifical of, 59
Tower (for sacrament), 47–8
Tuki, Ralph, Bp of Arsinoe, 25
Turner, Francis, Bp of Rochester, 229

Ubertus, 128
Ulrich, Abbot of Cluny, 36, 77, 101–3, 122, 135, 149
Ulrich, Bp of Augsburg, 119
Unconsecrated oblations, 10–2, 14, 16, 30–2, 35–6, 99, 197, 207, 209, 211
Uniats, 20, 25, 33
University College, Oxford, 162–3

Val des Choux, Abbey of, Burgundy, 104

Verdun, Church of, 58
Vernon MS, 151
Verona Fragments of Egyptian Church Order, 3
Vestry. See Sacristy
Viaticum, and Communion of sick, 37, 40–1, 56, 65, 67, 70–1, 73–4, 86–7, 95, 172–3, 178–9, 181, 194–6, 248–9, 250–72
Victor, St, Abbey of, Paris, 41, 122, 133–4, 241, 246
Victor, St, Robert of, Penitential of, 43
Vienna, 33, 61
Vienna, Imperial Library of, 61
Visible Word, 218
Vito, St, of Verdun, Penitential of, 43

Waldegrave, Robert, Printer, 218
Wells, Consuetudinary (or *Ordinale*), 151
Westminster Abbey, 161
Westminster, Dean of (Gabriel Goodman), 199–201
Whitehall, Chapel at, 229
William, Abbot of Hirshau, 102
Wolf, Reginald (Musculus), 199
Wren, Matthew, Bp of Ely, 211, 213, 224, 228, 270
Wylson, Doctor, 201

Ximenes, Francis, Cardinal, 96

York Breviary, 163, 166
York Minster Library, 163
York Missal, 43, 81, 115, 163, 166–7, 170, 242

Zurich Service, 183–7, 195, 217, 221
Zwingli, Huldreich, 185, 187, 189, 217–8, 221

www.ingramcontent.com/pod-product-compliance
Lightning Source LLC
Chambersburg PA
CBHW070238230426
43664CB00014B/2348